SCOTTISH JOURNAL OF THEOLOGY

Current Issues in Theology

Edited by
ALASDAIR HERON
IAIN TORRANCE

SCOTTISH JOURNAL OF THEOLOGY

Current Issues in Theology

Edited by
ALASDAIR HERON
IAIN TORRANCE

This is a series of short books specially commissioned by the editors of *Scottish Journal of Theology*. The aim is to commission books which stand between the static monograph genre and the more immediate statement of a journal article. Following the long tradition of the *Journal*, the editors will commission authors who are questioning existing paradigms or rethinking perspectives. It is hoped that the books will appeal to a wide range of readers.

Believing that living theology needs an audience and thrives on debate, the editors will invite the authors to present the themes of their topics in four public lectures at the University of Aberdeen (*The Scottish Journal of Theology Lectures*), and the books, which will be published subsequently, will be developed from these.

The *Scottish Journal of Theology* is an international refereed quarterly journal of systematic, historical and biblical theology published by T&T Clark Ltd, 59 George Street, Edinburgh EH2 2LQ, Scotland. Subscription details are available on request from the Publishers.

In the same series:

A. C. Thiselton, *Interpreting God and the Postmodern Self* (1995)

THE RISEN LORD

THE RISEN LORD

The Jesus of History as the Christ of Faith

MARGARET BARKER

T&T CLARK
EDINBURGH

T&T CLARK LTD
59 GEORGE STREET
EDINBURGH EH2 2LQ
SCOTLAND

First published 1996

ISBN 0 567 08537 6

British Library Cataloguing-in-Publication Data
A catalogue record for this book is available from the British Library

Typeset by Waverley Typesetters, Galashiels
Printed and bound in Great Britain by Bell & Bain Ltd, Glasgow

For Peter Dawson, OBE

Contents

Introduction

He who never made a mistake, never made a discovery.

SAMUEL SMILES

THE real Introduction to *The Risen Lord; The Jesus of History as the Christ of Faith* is my earlier book *The Great Angel; A Study of Israel's Second God*, which showed that the religion of the first temple had not been monotheism. Yahweh, the LORD, had been the second God, the guardian angel and patron deity of Israel, the Son of El Elyon. Once the Deuteronomists had introduced monotheism into the life, and more importantly, into the records, of the people of Judah, Yahweh and El Elyon were no longer distinct. The older beliefs, however, did not disappear and the evidence of Philo confirms that this second deity was still known in the period of Christian origins. Many of his titles were taken over by the early church to describe Jesus. The earliest Christian beliefs must have been rooted in those of the first temple (hence the title of my first book; *The Older Testament*), and when Jesus was proclaimed as the LORD, the Son of God, the original Palestinian church used imagery derived from the temple cult (as I showed in my book *On Earth as it is in Heaven*).

This theory broke away from many conventional assumptions about the nature of Israel's religion and I was pleased that it was so well received. Some readers, however, misunderstood me and my ideas were at times misrepresented. In order that such misconceptions do not cause further confusion, the conclusions of *The Great Angel*, which form the premise of *The Risen Lord*, are these: some, perhaps most, of the heirs to Israel's ancient religion continued to believe throughout the second temple period that Yahweh, the LORD, was the Great Angel, the Second God. These people identified Jesus as that second divinity and they did not become a small sect (another misrepresentation of my views) but were the original Palestinian church. When they proclaimed 'Jesus is LORD', they meant '*Jesus is Yahweh*, come to save his people'.

In *The Risen Lord* I argue that this belief originated with Jesus himself. Again, I am breaking away from many conventional assumptions about the nature of Christian origins and the arguments are complex and inter-related. I have therefore given an outline of the theory in the text and kept detail in the notes. As with *The Great Angel*, so here, I present no more than a sketch of vast possibilities consequent upon the basic paradigm shift which I propose: that Jesus' resurrection was his own mystical experience and that the ministry recorded in the gospels was the life and teaching of the Risen LORD.

Having lived with these ideas and developed them over many years, their very familiarity has made it difficult to reconstruct the stages by which I reached my conclusions. I hope there are not too many gaps. I console myself with the words of J. H. Charlesworth: 'I once stood in admiration of New Testament scholars who are cautiously reticent until they can defend virtually infallible positions. Now I have grown impatient with those who feign perfection, failing to perceive that all knowledge is conditioned by the observer . . . and missing the point that all data, including meaningful traditions, are categorically selected and interpreted phenomena. Moreover, such scholars have severely compromised the axiom that historians do not have the luxury of certainty; they work at best with relative probabilities' (*Jesus within Judaism*, p. 17).

The original Christian proclamation did not originate on the cluttered desk of a biblical scholar looking for a new way to read texts. One of the first things a preacher has to learn is to make the message relevant to the needs of the congregation. So too with any theory of Christian origins; it cannot assume that the Christian proclamation was just a great leap forward in the history of ideas. There must have been numbers of people in first-century Palestine who recognized that this proclamation was more than a creative re-reading of the text. It spoke to their situation and was presented in terms they could understand and recognize as fulfilment.

In *The Risen Lord* I have not attempted to find a place for all ideas and methods of reading scripture known to have existed in first-century Palestine; I have taken and developed one set of ideas which could reasonably have been known at that time and in that place. This one set of ideas is exemplified by the Qumran Melchizedek text. Some people were thinking and hoping in that way. They looked for a heavenly priest figure from the cult of the first temple who would bring salvation and atonement in the last days. As Psalm 110, the Melchizedek Psalm, is the most frequently used text in the New Testament, it seemed an obvious place to start. In *The Risen Lord* I show that this one set of ideas is compatible with the earliest Christian beliefs about Jesus and thus most likely to have been their matrix. The bones of the argument use only texts and ideas which could have been known in first-century Palestine although explanatory details have been drawn from other times and places.

The first four chapters of this book were originally delivered as the Scottish Journal of Theology Lectures, 1995, in the University of

Aberdeen. I should like to thank Dr Iain Torrance for inviting me to deliver them and for his hospitality and encouragement. The fifth chapter is an expanded version of 'The Servant in the Book of Revelation' which was published in the *Heythrop Journal* 36.4 (1995). Some related material has been published as 'The Secret Tradition' in the *Journal of Higher Criticism* 2.1 (1995) and some read as a paper to The Society for Old Testament Study in 1994, and published as 'Atonement. The Rite of Healing' in the *Scottish Journal of Theology*, 49.1 (1996).

I am, as always, indebted to friends who help in so many ways: Ernst Bammel, George Bebawi, Robert Murray, Gerard Norton and Nicholas Wyatt. I should like to dedicate this book to a fellow preacher who has supported me with wise counsel.

MARGARET BARKER
Epiphany 1996

Abbreviations

Books and articles generally appear in the text with author's name and short title. Fuller details are shown in the bibliography, which is in alphabetical order of author/editor.

Publications

AES	*Archives Européennes de Sociologie*
ANET	*Ancient Near Eastern Texts relating to the Old Testament*, J. B. Pritchard, 3rd edn
BASOR	*Bulletin of the American Schools of Oriental Research*
BDB	*Hebrew and English Lexicon of the Old Testament*, F. Brown, S. R. Driver and C. A. Briggs (Oxford 1907, 1962)
BHS	*Biblica Hebraica Stuttgartensia*
CB	Coniectanea Biblica
CG	*Coptic Gnostic Library*
DJD	*Discoveries in the Judean Desert* (Oxford 1955–)
ET	English Translation
ExpT	*Expository Times*
HSS	Harvard Semitic Studies
HTR	*Harvard Theological Review*
HUCA	*Hebrew Union College Annual*
ICC	International Critical Commentary
JBL	*Journal of Biblical Literature*
JHC	*Journal of Higher Criticism*
JJS	*Journal of Jewish Studies*
JQR	*Jewish Quarterly Review*
JSJ	*Journal for the Study of Judaism*
JSNT	*Journal for the Study of the New Testament*
JSP	*Journal for the Study of the Pseudepigrapha*
JSQ	*Jewish Studies Quarterly*
JSS	*Journal of Semitic Studies*
JTS	*Journal of Theological Studies*

LCL	Loeb Classical Library
LXX	The Septuagint; a Greek version of the Old Testament adopted by the early churches
MT	Masoretic Text; the standard text of the Hebrew Bible
NT	*Novum Testamentum*
NTS	*New Testament Studies*
OTP	*The Old Testament Pseudepigrapha*, ed. J. H. Charlesworth (New York & London)
PG	*Patrologia Graeca*, ed. J. P. Migne
SBT	Studies in Biblical Theology
SJT	*Scottish Journal of Theology*
SNT	Supplements to Novum Testamentum
SNTS	Studiorum Novi Testamenti Societas
TGUOS	*Transactions of the Glasgow University Oriental Society*
TU	Texte und Untersuchungen
TynB	*Tyndale Bulletin*
UF	*Ugarit-Forschungen*
VC	*Vigiliae Christianae*
VT	*Vetus Testamentum*
ZAW	*Zeitschrift für die Alttestamentliche Wissenschaft*

Dead Sea Scrolls

CD	Damascus Rule
1QH	Hymns
1QIs^a	Isaiah Scroll complete
1QIs^b	Isaiah Scroll incomplete
1QM	War Scroll
1QpHab	Commentary on Habakkuk
1QS	Community Rule
1QSb	Blessings
11QMelch	Melchizedek Text
11QT	Temple Scroll

Shorter texts and fragments are designated by number only.

Pseudepigrapha

1 En.	*1* (Ethiopic) *Enoch*
2 En.	*2* (Slavonic) *Enoch*, also known as *The Book of the Secrets of Enoch*
3 En.	*3* (Hebrew) *Enoch*, originally known as *Sepher Hekhalot*
Apoc.Abr.	*Apocalypse of Abraham*

Asc.Isa.	*Ascension of Isaiah*
Ass.Mos.	*The Assumption of Moses* also known as *The Testament of Moses*
Jub.	*Book of Jubilees*
T.Lev.	*The Testament of Levi* and
T.Naphtali	*The Testament of Naphtali* are both part of the *Testaments of the Twelve Patriarchs*

Other Texts

The Targums are translations of the Hebrew Scriptures into Aramaic, sometimes incorporating other legendary materials.

T.Ps.J (Targum Pseudo-Jonathan), *F.T. (The Fragment Targum) and T.N. (Targum Neofiti)* are all Targums to the Pentateuch in the Palestinian tradition. *T.O. (Targum Onkelos)* is the Targum to the Pentateuch in the Babylonian tradition.

The *Mishnah* is a compilation of Jewish common law of Palestine early in the third century CE. It has sixty-three tractates. Commentaries on the Mishnah were collected both in Palestine and in Babylonia during the fifth and sixth centuries. They formed the Palestinian and Babylonian Talmuds. Thus m. indicates a tractate of the Mishnah, e.g. *m.Yoma*; b. of the Babylonian Talmud, e.g. *b.Yoma*.

The *Mekhilta of R. Ishmael* is a commentary on Exodus probably completed by the third century CE.

The *Midrash Rabbah*, the great midrash, is a collection of commentaries on scripture compiled in the middle ages but incorporating some material which originated in fifth-century Palestine.

Genesis R. (= Rabbah) and *Leviticus R.* are two of these commentaries.

I

The Resurrection

To question all things; – never to turn away from any difficulty; to accept no doctrine either from ourselves or from other people without a rigid scrutiny by negative criticism; letting no fallacy, or incoherence, or confusion of thought step by unperceived; above all to insist upon having the meaning of a word clearly understood before using it, and the meaning of a proposition before assenting to it; – these are the lessons we learn from the ancient dialecticians.

JOHN STUART MILL
Inaugural Address as Rector, University of St. Andrews
1 February 1867

RESURRECTION is central to any understanding of Jesus. The New Testament tells us that the resurrection happened on the first Easter Sunday when the tomb was found empty and Jesus was seen by several of his disciples. They soon realized that the death and resurrection had been for their sins and in accordance with the scriptures (1 Cor. 15:3). Peter declared in his Pentecost sermon that the crucified Jesus had been made Lord and Christ (Acts 2:36). Paul wrote to the Romans that Jesus had been designated son of God by the resurrection (Rom. 1:4). He had also been exalted, as the result of his obedient death, to receive the name which is above all names (Phil. 2:9). Everything that the first Christians proclaimed about Jesus – that he was Lord, Christ and Son of God, and that he had made atonement for their sins – everything depended on the death and resurrection. As Paul said: 'If Christ has not been raised then our preaching is in vain and your faith is in vain' (1 Cor. 15:14).

But what would the first Christians have understood by resurrection? There were several possibilities. Resurrection could mean the revival of the dead to live a renewed human life in the kingdom of the Messiah, enjoying great prosperity in a fertile and peaceful land. This is the picture in the earliest parts of *1 Enoch*, and was probably what the Sadducees had in mind when they asked Jesus about the woman who had been married seven times; whose wife would she be? It is also implied in the *Mishnah*: 'All Israelites have a share in the world to come, for it is written, "Thy people also shall all be righteous, they shall inherit the land for ever; the branch of my planting, the work of my hands that I may be glorified"' (Isa. 60:21; *m.Sanhedrin 10.1*). Resurrection could also mean being raised from the dust to face the judgement, some to punishment and some to everlasting life, envisaged as a transformed state when the righteous shone like stars. This is the picture in Daniel 12:2–3 and is implicit in Jesus' reply to the Sadducees: 'Those who are accounted worthy to attain to that age and to the resurrection from the dead neither marry nor are given in marriage for they cannot die any more, because they are equal to angels and are sons of God, being sons of the resurrection' (Luke 20:35–6). For others, influenced by Greek ideas, it had come to mean immortality, the survival of the soul set free from the body at death, perhaps to be reincarnated. Resurrection, as opposed to immortality, was something for the last days, a preliminary to the last judgement.

For Paul, the resurrection was the time when Jesus had been designated Son of God and he seems to be quoting an established formula when he says: '(Jesus) descended from David according to the flesh and designated son of God in power according to the Spirit of holiness by his resurrection from the dead' (Rom. 1:4).[1] If divine sonship was Jesus' post-resurrection state our initial question must become two: What would the first Christians have understood by resurrection? And what did they mean when they said Jesus was Son of God? Jesus' reply to the Sadducees suggests that he understood 'son of God' to mean an angel, a son of the resurrection. Luke's comment on the Sadducees, '(they) say that there is no resurrection, nor angel nor spirit . . .' (Acts 23:8) confirms this. The understanding of resurrection implicit in these passages is that all the righteous dead were raised as angels, sons of God.[2] When Paul says that Jesus was designated Son of God by his resurrection he must have meant something more than this.

I have already explored the topic of divine sonship in my book *The Great Angel*; I concluded that for some of the heirs to Israel's ancient religion, Yahweh was not the name of God the Father but of God the Son. Yahweh was the chief of the seventy sons of El Elyon and the guardian deity of Israel. The Yahweh of the Old Testament, the LORD, was Israel's second God. We have become accustomed to think of the LORD of the Old Testament as God the Father but this is not how the first Christians read their scriptures. Justin, one of the few writers from

---

[1] Presumably this 'established formula' originated in Palestine and not in Greece. Was the 'spirit of holiness' in fact the Holy Spirit, and had this been a reference to the time when Jesus was 'designated son of God', a reference to his baptism? His raising from the dead would then have meant something very different from the revival of his body after crucifixion.

[2] Viviano, 'Sadducees', p. 498, showed that the more natural way to read this was: 'The Sadducees say there is no resurrection either as an angel (i.e. in the form of an angel) or as a spirit (i.e. in the form of a spirit) but the Pharisees acknowledge them both.'

the sub-apostolic period whose works have survived in any quantity, wrote this:

> ... then neither Abraham nor Isaac nor Jacob nor any other man ever saw the Father and Ineffable Lord of all things whatever and of Christ himself; but (they saw) him who according to his will is both his Son and his angel from ministering to his will (*Trypho* 127, PG vi 773).

Irenaeus, Hippolytus and Novatian all read their Old Testament in the same way;[3] for them the LORD of the Old Testament became the LORD of the New Testament. Early in the fourth century Eusebius offered this explanation of Psalm 45:6–7: 'Your throne O God is for ever and ever ... therefore God, your God, has anointed you ...':

> ... the Anointer, being the Supreme God, is far above the Anointed, he being God in a different sense. And this would be clear to anyone who knew Hebrew. ... Therefore in these words you have it clearly stated that God was anointed and became the Christ. ... And this is he who was the beloved of the Father and his Offspring and the Eternal Priest and the Being called the Sharer of the Father's throne (*Proof* IV.15, PG xxii 305).

Eusebius explained that the LORD had been manifested in former times in his angel or messenger and also in the king and the high priest. Finally, he had come to his people in Jesus who had been declared Son of God by his resurrection.

To the question: How did Jesus become the LORD, the Son of God? the answer of the first Christians could well have been: 'In the same way as the kings and high priests had become the LORD', *and this was not after they had died*. The original meaning of resurrection must be sought in this context, amongst the ideas and beliefs available to those who demonstrated the truth of their case by reference to the Old Testament.[4] I shall establish my case by using only material which would

---

[3] For example, Irenaeus, *Demonstration* 44–5; Hippolytus, *Commentary on Daniel* iv, PG x 645; Novatian, *On the Trinity*, 18 CC Latina iv, p. 44; also my *The Great Angel*, pp. 190–212.

[4] (i) The temptation to explain the origin of resurrection beliefs in terms of dying and rising fertility gods of the mediterranean world must be resisted. It cannot be proved that there were such cults in first-century Palestine. G. Kittel in 'Deutsche Theologie', IV (1937), p. 159, found virtually no evidence of such cults in first-century Palestine (Pannenberg, *Jesus*, p. 91).

(ii) Eliade, *Birth*, pp. 117–18, observed:

> For the earliest Christian communities, the resurrection of Jesus could not be identified with the periodic death and resurrection of the God of the mysteries. Like Christ's life, suffering and death, his resurrection had occurred in history, 'in the days of Pontius Pilate'. The resurrection was an irreversible event; it was not repeated yearly, like the resurrection of Adonis, for example. It was not an allegory of the sanctity of cosmic life, as was the case with the so-called vegetation Gods, nor an initiatory scenario, as in the mysteries. It was a 'sign' that formed part of the Messianic expectation of the Jewish people, and as such it had its place in the religious history of Israel, for the resurrection of the dead was an accompaniment

have been known in first-century Palestine. Parallels from other times and places will be used to add detail, but they will not form the basis of my argument.

Resurrection, according to one way of reading the New Testament, was God's confirmation of Jesus' pre-Easter ministry, confirmation of his claim to authority.[5] But why should Jesus, by resurrection, have been recognized as the Messiah and a pre-existent divine being rather than just a revived body?[6] If resurrection was accepted as proof of

---

of the coming of the Time. The resurrection of Jesus proclaimed that the last age (the *eschaton*) had begun. As St. Paul says, Jesus was resurrected as 'the first-born from the dead' (Col. 1:18). This explains the belief which we find recorded in the Gospels, that many resurrections followed that of Jesus: 'The graves were opened; and many bodies of the saints which slept arose' (Matt. 27:52). For the earliest Christians, the resurrection established a new era of history – the validation of Jesus as Messiah, and hence the spiritual transmutation of man and the total renewal of the world.

Eliade is correct to distance the resurrection from the dying and rising gods, but see n. (iv) below.

(iii) Hengel, *Studies*, p. 72: 'His person and work charge us with the task of a "whole" biblical theology that above all fully realizes its Jewish heritage, a biblical theology that does not eradicate the lines between the Old and New, but properly defines them.' Yes!

(iv) Lapide, *Resurrection*, p. 45, makes the point that only Jews saw the risen Lord and therefore it must have been a 'Jewish' experience.

(v) Barr, *Garden of Eden*, p. 19, summarized the problem well:

It is striking how difficult it has been for scholars to give an adequate account of the history, within Israel, of beliefs in resurrection and immortality. One reason for this, I suggest, is that they have too often been influenced by the conception that what they are looking for is something after death. And life after death does certainly appear within the tradition. But the starting point seems to me to lie rather in the immortality that is normal for the gods, an immortality where there is no death anyhow, an eternal life that is normal for the gods but might, in very exceptional circumstances, have been granted to humans.

Such a definition would explain why the resurrected were called the sons of God, but 'immortality', no matter how carefully redefined, is perhaps not the best word to use. Resurrection in the oldest traditions was apotheosis and it is not hard to see why later 'orthodoxy' sought to veil this fact.

[5] Pannenberg, *Jesus*, pp. 53–66.

[6] (i) Cf. Lapide, *Resurrection*, p. 15, 'When the resurrection of Jesus is viewed from the standpoint of Jewish faith, there is no necessary link to the claim of Messiahship.'

(ii) The link between resurrection and Messiahship was central to Wrede's hypothesis of the messianic secret and all its consequences for twentieth-century scholarship, but Sanday's critical question, *Life*, p. 75, is valid: 'Supposing that the resurrection accounts for the rest of Christianity, what is left to account for the Resurrection?' He quoted Bousset, *Jesus*, p. 168: 'It is quite inconceivable that the first disciples of Jesus, who by his death and burial had seen all their hopes shattered and their belief in his messiahship destroyed, might have returned to that belief under the influence of the resurrection experiences, if they had not formerly possessed it on the ground of the utterances and general conduct of Jesus.'

(iii) Schweitzer, *Quest*, p. 343: 'How can the appearances of the risen Jesus have suggested to the disciples that Jesus, the crucified teacher, was the Messiah? ... In certain circles ... the resurrection of the Baptist was believed in; but that did

4

divinity, there must have been something in the disciples' pre-understanding of resurrection which associated it with becoming the Son of God, the LORD, and also something which distinguished Jesus' resurrection from that of Lazarus, Jairus' daughter, the young man of Nain or even those restored to life by Elisha.

Jesus' resurrection was closely associated with ascent to heaven, something not stated of other resurrection miracles. We are left to assume that Jairus' daughter, for example, resumed her normal life; she did not ascend to heaven nor was she seen in radiant form by her friends. Luke separates the resurrection and ascension by forty days, but elsewhere in the New Testament resurrection and ascension are not distinguished. For example, in Philippians 2:8 the obedient death of Jesus is followed by exaltation and enthronement: '. . . he became obedient unto death . . . therefore God has highly exalted him'. Outside the New Testament resurrection and ascension are separated by far more than forty days; according to *The Apocryphon of James*, Jesus spoke to his disciples for five hundred and fifty days after he had risen from the dead and the *Pistis Sophia* begins by stating that Jesus spent eleven years in discourse with his disciples after he had risen from the dead. The consensus outside the New Testament, however, is that the period from resurrection to the final departure was about eighteen months.[7] Even Paul's experience on the road to Damascus, which he regarded as an encounter with the risen LORD, took place long after the forty-day period. It would thus be unwise to treat Luke and his forty-day period between resurrection and ascension as a primary datum, even though he offers the most detail. If, on the other hand, the risen LORD had been experienced from the beginning as the ascended LORD, this would explain both the death-then-exaltation sequence implied in Philippians and the tradition of appearances over several months and even years as there would not have been any final departure from earth. The most detailed account of a resurrection appearance is in Revelation, apparently long after Luke's forty days or Paul's experience on the road to Damascus, which he claimed was the last appearance (1 Cor. 15:8). John on Patmos saw Jesus as a human figure in dazzling light, with eyes of fire and feet of glowing bronze. This is the language of an

---

not make John the Baptist the Messiah . . . How then did the appearance of the risen Jesus suddenly become for them proof of His Messiahship and the basis of their eschatology?'

(iv) Hengel, *Studies*, p. 10: 'The mere revivification of a person or, as the case may be, his translation into the heavenly realm, establishes neither messianic majesty nor eschatological mission, nor could it, of itself, supply the content of a message of salvation.' He is not entirely correct: revivification certainly did not establish anything, but translation did, as we shall see.

[7] In the *Ascension of Isaiah* (OTP 2) the period is 545 days. Irenaeus, *Against Heresies* I 3.2, PG vii 469; I 30.14, PG vii 703, says the Valentinians taught that Jesus had remained with his disciples for eighteen months.

Old Testament theophany.[8] If resurrection and ascension were not initially distinguished, post-resurrection would have meant post-ascension and all the resurrection appearances would have been theophanies.

But, it will be objected, the Old Testament theophanies were something from the remote past, the stuff of sagas and legends. Who, apart from the first Christians, were still claiming to see theophanies in the first century? The answer to this question may lie with the merkavah mystics of whose origin and practices all too little is known. Their traditions were, by their very nature, esoteric, but when they do break the surface, they are descriptions of heavenly ascents and visions of the throne, and we glimpse the intense religious experiences of those who believed they had stood in God's presence and been transformed into angels, sons of God. In this chapter *I shall show that the earliest understanding of resurrection may have been this experience of mystical ascent and the transformation it effected.*[9]

---

[8] (i) Many enquiries into the nature of resurrection have excluded the possibility of theophany, e.g. MacDonald, *The Resurrection*, p. 19, commenting on Revelation 1:13–16 as a resurrection appearance. 'One is bound to ask whether there is anything in common between this composite apocalyptic extravagance and the appearances of the man Jesus in the gospels.'

(ii) It is also implicit in the thought of Moltmann. Ricoeur, *Essays*, p. 159, summarized thus: 'Moltmann . . . removes (Resurrection) from the Hellenistic schemas of epiphanies of eternity'. The true meaning of resurrection has been '. . . disguised by the Greek Christologies, which have made the Incarnation the temporal manifestation of eternal being and the eternal present, thus hiding the principal meaning, namely that the God of the promise, the God of Abraham, Isaac and Jacob, has approached, has been revealed as He who is coming for all. Thus disguised by epiphanic religion, the Resurrection has become the pledge of all divine presence in the present world: cultic presence, mystic presence. The task of a hermeneutics of the Resurrection is to reinstitute the potential of hope, to tell the future of the Resurrection. The meaning of the Resurrection is in suspense insofar as it is not fulfilled in a new creation, in a new totality of being.'
One wonders how the God of the promise can have 'approached' without some element of epiphany. Stark contrasts such as these do not reflect the subtleties and complexities of the religious milieu in which the earliest Christian belief took shape. An 'epiphanic' view of resurrection was central in these beliefs, derived from temple rituals, as was a hope that the future would bring the renewal of the creation, also derived from temple tradition. But the renewal was not a part of the resurrection belief; *it was part of the closely related concept of atonement, as I shall show in Chapter 3.*

[9] *The ascent texts are the record of a real experience, and not just a literary fiction.* It is of limited value to study them as mere compilations from Old Testament sources. The work of, for example, Eliade, *Myths*, and *Shamanism*; or Halifax, *Shamanic Voices*; shows the wider context of this material, and there is now interesting medical evidence. Pinard, 'Spontaneous Imagery', pp. 150–3, was a pioneer, but there is now all the evidence of near-death experiences, see Fenwick, *The Truth*. The most remarkable example of a recent experience is in Harvey, *A Journey in Ladakh*, pp. 234–5, my emphases.

> And when you have imagined the Bodhisatva in all his splendour, seated on his lotus, in his jewels, in the many colours of his robes, with the sacred syllables of his crown radiating thousands of beams of light on which exalted and sacred beings are seated in meditation, when you have visualized all this so powerfully that you feel you could reach out your hand and touch the Bodhisatva himself who is looking

After the resurrection, we have been told, all manner of developments took place in the Christian community's understanding of Jesus, giving rise to the perennial questions of how to relate the Jesus they proclaimed to the pre-Easter, historical Jesus and his teachings. Jesus rose into the kerygma, according to Bultmann's famous dictum, but there are so many assumptions and difficulties in a statement like this. It may be true that we only know the post-resurrection, the proclaimed, Jesus and that the canonical gospels reflect to a large extent the established beliefs of those who wrote them. What cannot be demonstrated, however, is that the Jesus of the kerygma was radically different from the 'historical' Jesus.[10] Is it possible that the 'historical' Jesus was completely unaware of who he was and what he was doing? Just the briefest reflection on this possibility shows how enormous are the implications of saying that Jesus did not know who he was and what he was doing. The only reasonable answer to the questions about Jesus' self-

---

into your eyes with a look of immense love, then you are ready to begin the most exalted stage of all. In this, you offer yourself to the Bodisatva – you offer him your senses, your body, your heart, your spirit. You make a sacrifice to him of everything that you are and *then you merge with him, you melt into him. You become your highest self, which is He. And in this state you will see everything with his eyes, hear all sounds with his ears.* You will see the world as his body and you will hear all sounds singing his sacred mantra. Even the noise of a car will be singing his mantra; even the whirr of an aeroplane; even the singing of a farmer in the fields; even the barking of a dog. . . . You must understand that this merging with the God that you have projected out of yourself, that you have visualized from your own deepest energies, is not an ecstasy that the ego can claim for itself. *It is an experience of power, yes, of immense power, but of a power transformed and purified by love and dedicated to all beings to the salvation of all life.* And to save you from any possibility of vanity, there is a final stage in the meditation which you must also perform. You must dissolve the meditation; you must dissolve your own projection; you must unmake your own ecstasy; you must rest your mind in all emptiness that has no form, neither your own, nor that of the Bodhisatva that your mind has visualized. You must enter in this last stage into the Sunyata that is the mother of all projections, the Emptiness from which all forms are born, yours, mine, and all the imaginations of our minds and heart, there must be nothing left of yourself or of the experience of the Bodhisatva or your delight in his splendour, and in your own, nothing but Sunyata, and the clear radiance of the void.

[10] (i) The outcome of this type of presupposition is such works as B. L. Mack, *The Lost Gospel*, which suggests that the Jesus people took the simple teachings of a Galilean cynic philosopher, added several 'bits and pieces of diverse mythologies' (p. 161), and produced Christianity. He regards the Letter to the Hebrews as 'a preposterous elaboration of the Christ myth' (p. 221), and describes the fourth gospel as a 'novel account of Christian origins' (p. 223). I shall treat both as rich, primary sources!

(ii) Charlesworth, *Jesus*, p. 13, makes the important point that the very existence of the gospels proves that the pre-crucifixion life of Jesus was important for the early church; 'There must have been some historical interest in Jesus of Nazareth.' What we have, in fact, is a proclamation of the risen LORD but an emphasis on his pre-Easter life. Little is said of the post-Easter LORD. The obvious conclusion to draw would be that the 'earthly life' was the risen state.

consciousness must be: Jesus was aware of who he was and what he was doing and any study of Jesus must address this question of his self-consciousness.[11]

The remarkable early testimony in Romans 1:4 to Jesus having 'become' son of God, Lord and Christ after the resurrection must imply that if Jesus himself was aware of his being Son of God, Lord and Christ, *he must himself have experienced the event which was described as his resurrection*. I want to explore the possibility that his resurrection was originally a mystical experience and that Jesus was a mystic who ascended and experienced transformation into the angelic state. There is an extraordinary passage in the *Gospel of Philip* which suggests that Jesus' resurrection did occur before his death.

> Those who say that the Lord died first and then rose up are in error for he rose up first and then died (*Philip* 56).[12]

This could be a gnostic fantasy but I think not. This extraordinary statement is the key to a whole new way of reading the New Testament. The original raising of Jesus was at the start of the ministry.

Closely linked to the question of Jesus' self-consciousness must be the question of soteriology. Put in simple terms: If he knew who he was he must have known what he was doing. How, then, did Jesus' death, resurrection and ascension come to be seen by the early church

---

[11] (i) Dunn, *Christology*, p. 254, spoke for many when he wrote, 'We cannot claim that Jesus believed himself to be the Incarnate Son of God; but we can claim that the teaching to that effect as it came to expression in the later first century Christian thought was, in the light of the whole Christ event, an appropriate reflection on and elaboration of Jesus' own sense of sonship and eschatological mission.' Was it really just 'appropriate reflection and elaboration'? And what does that mean anyway?

(ii) Schweizer, *Jesus Christ*, p. 1. 'Whether Jesus thought himself to be the Messiah therefore, is not important. It may, after all, have belonged to the status of his humiliation that he did not know of his messiahship, even as, for instance, he did not know that the earth was round.' (!)

(iii) Hengel, *Studies*, p. 11, makes an important point: 'Does this mean then that in the eyes of the disciples Jesus became Messiah only after God's act of raising him from the dead, that is, that – in opposition to the clear verdict of all four gospels – the earthly Jesus had no messianic consciousness of his divine mission, or possessed no messianic authority?'

[12] (i) The *Gospel according to Philip* in Nag Hammadi Studies XX, ed. B. Layton, Leiden, 1989, pp. 152–3. The lines which follow this extract are unclear, 'no doubt because the manuscript he copied from was damaged or illegible at this point'. The lines I quote are quite clear.

(ii) Thiering, 'Gospel of Philip', questions the assumption that this is a second or third century collection of secondary material and argues for an early date. '... the *Gospel of Philip* is a work stemming from the first century which throws considerable light on the diversity of doctrine at the time of Christian origins' (p. 103). It reflects the earliest Christianity, before it had abandoned its Jewish identity (p. 104). She does not deal with the text I cite, but my suggestion for its origin and significance is compatible with her thesis.

as the great atonement?[13] And how did it come about that someone declared to be Son of God made this atonement? Where in the traditions available to the original disciples in Palestine do we find a belief or a hope that it was a divine being or even the LORD himself who was the atonement sacrifice? The priestly laws of the Old Testament are both complex and obscure on the matter of atonement; the details about lambs and goats are clear enough, but the theology which the rituals expressed is still largely unknown. This must be a major obstacle in any attempt to understand Christian origins because it is a very big step indeed from goats and lambs in the temple to the human sacrifice of one declared to be the LORD, the Son of God. *This step is un-acknowledged in any account I have read of atonement in the New Testament.* These, then, are the questions I shall attempt to answer in these chapters: what was resurrection, when was Jesus' resurrection and how did this relate to the great atonement?

Resurrection or Resuscitation?

The earliest description of the resurrected state in the New Testament is in 1 Corinthians 15 where Paul explains that the resurrection body will be a spiritual body, not a physical body (1 Cor. 15:44). This is not a description of Jesus, but he has already stated that the resurrection of Jesus was similar: 'For if the dead are not raised then Christ has not been raised' (1 Cor. 15:16). For Paul, the resurrection is a trans-formation into a spiritual existence, *and it is not necessary to die in order to attain that state.* 'We shall not all sleep', he wrote, 'but we shall all be changed, for this perishable nature must put on the imperishable' (1 Cor. 15:51, 53). These two ideas, that resurrection is a transformation of the earthly body, rather than a resuscitation, and that it is no different from what happened to Jesus, appear together in Philippians 3:21: 'the Lord Jesus Christ . . . will change our lowly body to be like his glorious body'. Further, Paul is emphatic that what he had passed on to the church at Corinth about the death and resurrection of Jesus was what he received, presumably from his mentors in Palestine and Damascus: everything was in accordance with the scriptures, the death had been 'for our sins' and Jesus had been raised on the third day (1 Cor. 15:3–4). Paul also describes the resurrection as ascension; those who sleep will rise and those who are still alive will be caught up with them 'in the clouds to meet the Lord in the air' (1 Thess. 4:17).

Paul lists those who have seen the risen LORD. Some of them are still alive, he says, and so presumably can be called upon to confirm what he is saying. If 1 Corinthians was written in 56/7 CE it is quite likely that several of those who received resurrection appearances were still alive. Paul is in touch here with the original tradition of the church

---

[13] See my 'Atonement'.

and he can count his own experience on the Damascus road as a resurrection appearance. He describes a 'revelation of Jesus Christ' and how God 'was pleased to reveal his Son' to (literally 'in') him. The revelation experience which Paul describes thus in Galatians 1:12 and 16ff., must have been what the churches of that time understood by a resurrection experience. In 1 Corinthians 9:1 he says he has seen 'Jesus our Lord'. The three accounts in Acts have to supply the details of what Paul experienced: a light from heaven, a voice, a heavenly vision, but Paul is clear in his words to Agrippa that he had seen a heavenly vision (Acts 26:19).[14] Paul listed this experience, along with those of the other disciples, as the resurrection appearances which were proof of his teaching that the resurrection of the body was a transformation to a spiritual state.

Jesus himself says very little about resurrection, but what he does say is revealing. The dead were those who did not follow him: Follow me, he said to a would-be disciple who hesitated, and leave the dead to bury their own dead (Matt. 8:22/Luke 9:60). It is also clear from his answer to the Sadducees that he did not envisage a physical resurrection. They had asked about the marital status of a women who had had seven husbands and Jesus replied that in heaven there would be no marriage: '. . . They are equal to angels and are sons of God because they are sons of the resurrection' (Luke 20:36). The God of Abraham, Isaac and Jacob was a God of the living and not of the dead; the patriarchs were alive in his presence. In the parable, the rich man and Lazarus do not have to wait for the Last Judgement in order to receive their rewards; Lazarus goes immediately to Abraham's bosom and the rich man to his punishment (Luke 16:22–3). To the righteous thief he said: 'Today you will be with me in Paradise.' Jesus did not envisage the resurrection as a physical resuscitation in the distant future; it was an angelic state, living in the presence of God.[15]

[14] In Acts 9:3ff. the experience is described as a light from heaven and a voice. The accounts in Acts 22 and 26 are broadly similar, there being discrepancies over whether the travelling companions saw the light or heard the voice.
[15] (i) McDannell and Lang, *Heaven*, pp. 24–32.
(ii) We should know a great deal more of what Jesus thought on this subject if we had the original of the saying which appears in Matthew 10:28 and Luke 12:5, but in different forms. The implication of both seems to be that the physical body can be killed by persecutors but God can destroy the whole person. What Matthew calls 'the soul' survives physical death but is not of itself immortal.
(iii) It is interesting to reflect that Cerinthus, depicted as a notorious heretic, was condemned for believing in a physical resurrection. Eusebius, quoting from Dionysius, bishop of Alexandria in the mid-third century, wrote:
> This, they say, is the doctrine he taught . . . that Christ's kingdom would be on earth. And the things (Cerinthus) lusted after on earth . . . filled the heaven of his dreams (*History* 7.25, PG xx 697).
(iv) LAB 64.6 (OTP 2) is ambiguous: the witch raises Samuel from the dead and she describes the "*elohim*" of the MT 1 Samuel 28:13 as the dead Samuel, not having the appearance of a man, but clothed in a white robe and led by two angels. Despite

The post-Easter accounts in the gospels give no clear account of Jesus' risen state. Their confusion is in itself significant. The original Mark describes only the empty tomb and there are no appearances of the risen LORD, but in the longer ending of the gospel Jesus appears 'in another form' to the two disciples as they walked into the country. Matthew says that the disciples worshipped the risen Jesus; what had they seen to cause that reaction? Luke says the risen Jesus invited them to touch his physical body because they had wrongly supposed he was a spirit. There is no doubt in the gospel accounts as to who had been seen but there is considerable doubt as to exactly what had been seen.

The problem with all the gospel accounts is their date and their accuracy. They are the latest evidence for the resurrection in the New Testament, and the physical resurrection appearances in Luke and John are at variance with the evidence in older accounts. What we read in the gospels reflects a situation well along what J. M. Robinson has called 'the trajectory' between Easter and later orthodoxy. The emphasis on the physical reality of the resurrection could well have been a reaction to gnostic teaching about the resurrection.

> For Jesus to rise in disembodied radiance, (and) for the initiate to re-enact this kind of resurrection in ecstacy . . . is as consistent a position as is the orthodox insistence upon the physical bodiliness of the resurrected Christ (and) the futurity of the believer's resurrection back into the same physical body. . . . Neither is the original position; both are serious efforts to interpret it (p. 37).[16]

I should prefer to say that both were serious *efforts to explain it to contemporaries in a different culture*. Our ideas about resurrection have been formed by the canonical gospels and only one possibility has been seriously considered. The picture of Jesus himself, however, is now being enriched and in many ways radically altered by a reappraisal of material outside the New Testament. A part of this process must be to set the whole question of resurrection in a wider context.

As more light is shed on the second temple period, so more is known about the belief in resurrection. It is no longer possible to say that the belief developed as a result of the persecutions under Antiochus and the need for post-mortem vindication. Hope for a final judgement on evil was an important factor in the development of ideas about life after death but it cannot explain why the resurrected were transformed into angels or stars.[17] Puech has recently shown that Josephus' account

---

Harrington's note *ad loc.*, the white robe would not have been his shroud! He had become an angel, but nevertheless thought he had been awakened for the judgement!

[16] J. M. Robinson, 'From Easter', p. 37.

[17] Puech, *La Croyance*, pp. 316–19. Daniel 12:2–3 shows the two aspects side by side; many who sleep in the dust will awake, some to life, some to punishment. The wise will shine and those who turn others to righteousness will become like the stars.

of Essene beliefs does not agree with what can be deduced from the Scrolls. He has shown that the writers of the scrolls, far from holding neopythagorean ideas about immortal souls being imprisoned in bodies destined for corruption,[18] believed in a resurrection of the body, which was envisaged as the whole person entering the presence of God.[19] Further, they had a vivid sense of realized eschatology; they had already been taken into the presence of God and learned the secrets of heaven.

> I walk on limitless level ground
> and I know there is hope for him
> whom thou hast shaped from dust
> for the everlasting council.
> Thou hast cleansed a perverse spirit of great sin
> that it may stand with the host of the holy ones
> and that it may enter into community
> with the congregation of the sons of heaven (1QH III, cf. VII, XI)

> *Or*

> May you be as an angel of the presence in the abode of holiness . . .
> May you decree destiny in the company of the angels of the
>   presence . . .
>
> (1Q Sb IV)

Thus it would seem that for some contemporaries of the first Christians, resurrection of the body meant being taken up into the presence of God, anticipating the life of the age to come. They believed that they had already become angels.[20]

Nickelsburg's study of resurrection in the inter-testamental period reached different but significant conclusions. Resurrection, he suggested,

---

[18] Josephus, *War* II, 154. 'For this opinion is strongly held among them, that bodies are corruptible and their material impermanent, but that souls will endure immortal for ever.'

[19] Puech, *La Croyance*, p. 786. Also Nickelsburg, *Resurrection*, pp. 166–7, 'The Qumran materials . . . make no reference to a persecution unto death which requires a post-mortem vindication. . . .' There are, however, ideas of present participation in eternal life. The source used by Josephus and Hippolytus 'attributed to the Essenes a belief in, or akin to, immortality of the soul, but not resurrection' (p. 169).

[20] (i) The Therapeuts, according to Philo, also believed that their mortal life had ended (*On the Contemplative Life* 13).

(ii) Alexander, 'The Historical Setting', p. 179: 'In Hekhaloth literature . . . the ascent is made during lifetime and followed by descent . . . There is no obvious "redeemer figure" in the Jewish texts.'

(iii) Chernus, *Mysticism*, p. 15, observed that ascent in Judaism was not associated with salvation and so differed from the ascent of the gnostics. 'The ascent in Judaism took place during life as a temporary event, rather than after death. Thus the ability to make such an ascent could never in itself be evidence that one had been in any sense "saved" . . .' These conclusions, however, could not apply to 2 *Enoch* 64 (OTP 1), where the re-ascending and departing Enoch is acknowledged as a saviour.

(iv) There can be no doubt that this ascent material was available in first-century Palestine. The Book of Revelation is the most outstanding example, but there are also the *Songs of the Sabbath Sacrifice* 4Q400–7, 11Q5–6 and texts such as 4Q286–7.

had originally been associated with a persecuted wise man as depicted in the Wisdom of Solomon. He was exalted to the heavenly court where he served as vice-regent to the heavenly king. His death had been the moment of his assumption to heaven. 'The precise mode and time of exaltation' in the underlying tradition, he said, could not be determined, but it had points of contact with the Servant theology of the Second Isaiah. As the tradition developed further, 'it de-emphasized, or even expunged, the motif of the righteous man's exaltation to authority, transforming it into the motifs of the vindication (or reward) of the righteous and/or the condemnation of the wicked'. In the *Similitudes of Enoch* the righteous man had been replaced by the Son of Man, the heavenly judge. In Daniel 12 the judge is Michael, the angel prince of Israel. Thus what had originally been the glorious state of the exalted one developed into the exalted state of all the righteous. 'Exaltation to a high function in the heavenly court becomes simply ascension to heaven. Concomitant with this is a democratization which makes such ascension the prerogative of all the righteous who are resurrected.'[21] *Resurrection, he concluded, had originally been the process by which a righteous human being was taken to heaven and installed there as a ruler.* The exalted one was wise, had a glorious appearance and had much in common with Isaiah's Suffering Servant. Resurrection as exaltation to serve as a heavenly ruler is an important observation.[22] The most important evidence of all is the link between the resurrection and the Servant figure in Isaiah, a link to which we shall return.

Let us return to Robinson's trajectories. He offered two alternatives: Jesus risen in disembodied radiance, the gnostic view, or the physical bodiliness of the resurrected Christ, the 'orthodox' view. Neither, he suggested, was the original position. If we retroject them to a point of convergence, however, they could both have originated in first-century Palestine among people who believed that their life with the angels had already begun, that they had already been raised into the presence of God. It was a bodily resurrection, and so the 'orthodox' had kept an important element, but it was not a physical resuscitation to resume earthly life because it did not follow upon a physical death. It was a transformation into the angelic existence, and so the resurrection radiance of the gnostics was also an important element. Each had transferred the resurrection belief from its original context and each had introduced distortion in the process. Paul was quite accurate when he wrote: 'It is sown a physical body; it is raised a spiritual body' (1 Cor. 15:44), but he had already begun to transfer the mystical experience to a post-mortem state.

[21] Nickelsburg, *Resurrection*, pp. 170–4.
[22] I suspect that the Son of Man figure in Enoch and the angel prince in Daniel are not a development but vestiges of the original tradition and that it was the persecuted wise man who was the innovation, a democratization of the older royal mythology.

The Experience of Ascent

The antecedents of those experiences described in merkavah ascent and transformation texts were the original context of the Christian belief in resurrection, and it is no coincidence that the only real description of the practice of ascent is to be found in a late first-century Christian text, the *Ascension of Isaiah*. Whether this is a pre-Christian account of the prophet's martyrdom which has been expanded by a Christian hand or an entirely Christian composition is irrelevant to this enquiry. It gives a thinly veiled description of the Christian community in first-century Palestine; they are persecuted prophets and 'the faithful who believed in the ascension into heaven' (*Asc.Isa.* 2:9). The text does not specify whose ascension was at issue but the fact that ascension into heaven was singled out as the characteristic of the persecuted group must be significant.[23] Contemporary Jewish (i.e. non-Christian, but it is difficult to draw lines of demarcation in this period) texts are plainly hostile to ascent claims as we shall see and there was apparently a major disruption within the merkavah tradition in the early third century;[24] Christian involvement could have been a factor. Later the *Ascension of Isaiah* describes how the prophet ascended and what he saw.

> They were all in the presence of Isaiah. And when Isaiah spoke with Hezekiah the words of righteousness and faith, they all heard a door being opened and the voice of the Spirit. And the king summoned all the prophets and all the people who were to be found there. And Micah and the aged Ananias and Joel and Josab were sitting on his right. And when they all heard the voice of the Holy Spirit they all worshipped on their knees and they praised the God of righteousness, the Most High, the One who (dwells) in the upper world and who sits on high, the Holy One, the One who rests among the holy ones, and they ascribed glory to the One who had thus graciously given a door in an alien world, had graciously given it to a man. And while he was speaking with the Holy Spirit in the hearing of them all, he became silent and his mind was taken up from him, and he did not see the men who were standing before him. His eyes indeed were open but his mouth was silent, and the mind in his body was taken up from him. But his breath was (still) in him for he was seeing a vision. And the angel who was sent to show him (the vision) was not of this firmament

---

[23] (i) Opinion is divided as to the origin of the *Ascension of Isaiah* (OTP 2): Knibb favours the traditional view of a pre-Christian text which the church adopted and expanded; others, e.g. Hall, 'Ascension', Bauckham, *Climax*, pp. 87–9, think it an wholly Christian composition. It depicts the Christians as the heirs to the ancient prophets.

(ii) Knibb comments on 2:9, which he renders '. . . the faithful who believed in the ascension into heaven . . .': 'So Eth; Gk "who believed that he had ascended into heaven". Gk refers to the ascension of Isaiah and makes no sense; Eth is much more vague, but apparently refers to the ascension of Jesus; neither version seems to preserve the original (Jewish) text . . .' According to Acts 4:2 the cause of the trouble was not belief in the ascent but preaching the resurrection, another indication that resurrection was ascent.

[24] See Chapter 2 n. 39.

nor was he from the angels of glory of this world, but he came from the seventh heaven. And the people who were standing by, apart from the circle of prophets, did [not] think that the holy Isaiah had been taken up. And the vision which he saw was not from this world but from the world which is hidden from the flesh (*Asc.Isa.* 6:5–15).

The prophet ascended through the heavens and in the sixth heaven he was told that he would receive a robe to transform him and make him like an angel, not on his first visit to heaven but when he returned and was able to remain there (*Asc.Isa.* 8:14–15).

There are also curious ascent traditions about James, the brother of Jesus who became the first bishop in Jerusalem. In the writings of Hegesippus, 'who belonged to the first generation after the apostles',[25] James was described as an ascetic who wore linen robes and entered the Holy of Holies to pray for the sins of the people. In any other context this would identify him as the high priest. James is not called a high priest, but he was clearly a man whose spoke with authority in the temple and was known as the Righteous One. The authorities in Jerusalem demanded that he should deny any belief in Christ but when he declared at Passover that Jesus was the Son of Man, seated in heaven at the right hand of the Great Power, he was thrown down from the sanctuary parapet and stoned to death. A book called *The Ascents of James*, of which nothing more is known, was used by the Ebionites. What might all this suggest? That James, the leader of the Jerusalem church, had been a high priest, practised ascents and had seen a vision of the throne and the Son of Man?

Jewish texts from this period have a very different view of ascent: in one of his visions, Uriel reminds Ezra that, as he cannot even understand this world, he cannot hope to understand the ways of the Most High. He has not gone down into the deeps nor yet ever ascended to heaven (2 *Esd.* 4:8). The *Mishnah* also forbade knowledge of what was above and what was below (*m.Hag* 2:1) but this was nothing new. The *Mekhilta of R. Ishmael*, an early commentary on Exodus, records what must be a polemical statement:

R. Jose says: Behold it says The heavens are the heavens of the LORD but the earth hath been given to the children of men (Ps. 115:16). Neither Moses nor Elijah ever went up to heaven, nor did the Glory ever come down to earth. Scripture merely teaches that God said to Moses:

[25] Eusebius, *History* 2.23, PG xx 201.

A Rechabite had tried to save James. According to *The History of the Rechabites* (OTP 2), a work of uncertain date, the Rechabites had abandoned the temple in Jerusalem at the time of the exile and had gone to live as a community of the Blessed Ones, as the angels of heaven, who dressed in garments of glory and offered prayer day and night. The sons of Rechab, I suggest, had been the earliest devotees of the divine chariot, which is what the name suggests. They practised ascent to the angelic state and one of their number went to the defence of James.

Behold, I am going to call you through the top of the mountain and you will come up. As it is said: And the LORD called Moses to the top of the mount.[26]

The denial that Moses and Elijah went to heaven or that the Glory ever came down to earth must be a comment on the Transfiguration, or a denial of the tradition on which that experience was based.[27]

The 'ascent and transformation' texts are vitally important to any discussion of resurrection, and it is to these I now turn. One of the characteristics of the Enoch books is their descriptions of the mystical ascent and the heavenly visions; Enoch sees the righteous in glory, risen from the earth and safe on the Day of Judgement. They are the resurrected. But the heavenly ascent also transforms Enoch himself so that he 'becomes' a heavenly being, *even though this is not a post-mortem experience*. He returns to this world with messages from heaven. All the texts in question are difficult to date, and all by their very nature are obscure. It may be that they only describe the process by which all the Therapeuts or the members of the Qumran

---

[26] *Mekhilta of R. Ishmael* on Exodus 19:20; there is a similar text in *b.Sukkah* 5a. 'Ascent' disappears from Jewish revelation texts at this time; 2 *Esdras* and *Syriac Baruch* have angelic revelations without ascent.

[27] (i) This belief in transformation was part of the Enochic tradition. Wherever an 'animal' is transformed into a 'man' it means that a human has become divine. Thus *1 Enoch* 89:1: Noah is taught a secret by an archangel and is then transformed from a 'bull' into a 'man', cf. 89:36, 52. The fallen angels had already been changed from 'stars' into 'bulls', *1 Enoch* 86:4. In *1 Enoch* 93:4, 5, 8, certain unnamed worthies of Israel's history are named as 'men' and one of them 'ascends' just before the temple is destroyed.

(ii) Himmelfarb, 'Revelation and Rapture', shows from Cologne Mani Codex that Adam, Seth, Shem, Enosh and Enoch all ascended and some were transformed into great angels. The Codex only gives extracts from otherwise unknown apocalypses and therefore a complete picture is impossible, but there is enough evidence to show that ascent and transformation of great leaders and patriarchs was a widespread belief. Also now Morray-Jones, 'Mysticism' and Quispel, 'Transformation'.

(iii) Compare 1QH IV.23ff.; 'Thou hast revealed Thyself and Thy power as perfect light and Thou hast not covered my face with shame.'

(iv) Smelik, 'Transformation' shows how 'mystical' Old Testament texts were interpreted metaphorically, p. 123: 'The rabbinic reluctance to articulate the concept of mystical transformation is inextricably bound up with the designation of the righteous as gods . . . It is no doubt not the transformation itself they feared but the impact of apotheosis.' He notes the importance of the sevenfold shining of the righteous as a description of 'likeness in supernatural being' p. 131, and suggests the sevenfold shining might have been associated with the light mysticism of the menorah, p. 144. Menorah symbolism was a sensitive issue at the end of the second temple period, as I show in *The Older Testament*, pp. 221–32, and that its sevenfold light was linked to a belief in apotheosis is entirely consistent with the older royal cult as I reconstruct it. I disagree with Smelik's conclusion, p. 144: 'The apotheosis of the faithful had to be suppressed to counter heretics who stuck to light mysticism which entailed the danger of veneration of angelic beings visibly represented by stars.' The heretics were not Jews attracted to 'popular magic and mysticism . . . in the age of the rabbis' but Christians.

(v) Philo says that Moses' body and soul were *both* transformed into 'mind pure as sunlight' (*Life* II.288).

community entered into the angelic life, but they seem to be describing the experience of one particular figure, a chosen leader; the name Enoch means one who has been dedicated or initiated.[28] In *Jubilees* Enoch seems to be a priest, burning incense in the holy place (*Jub.* 4:25), and in *1 Enoch* he enters the heavenly sanctuary, another priestly prerogative. The Enoch texts could well be a record of the mystical experiences of the high priesthood. The frequent duplications of ascent and judgement material suggest an anthology and the recurring theme, as we shall see, is the Day of Atonement.

2 Enoch is thought to be an Egyptian Jewish text from the first century AD, even though it has only survived in a variety of forms in Old Slavonic and was transmitted by Christian scribes. It describes how Enoch the wise man ascended to heaven into the presence of the LORD. Michael was told to robe him in a garment of Glory and he became like one of the glorious ones (*2 En.* 22). He was then told: 'Go down onto the earth and tell your sons what I have told you' (*2 En.* 33:6). After his allotted time on earth, Enoch returned to the highest heaven accompanied by angels (*2 En.* 55). At his departure, the people acknowledged his greatness; he had been chosen by the LORD as the revealer of heavenly things and he was the one who carried away the sins of his people (*2 En.* 64).[29] As he was talking to them, darkness came on the earth and he was taken by angels to heaven, to stand before the face of the LORD (*2 En.* 67). It is inconceivable that this originated with a Christian writer; Enoch, the initiated one who revealed secrets and made atonement, must have been a pre-Christian figure.

There are similar passages in *1 Enoch*, fragments of which have been found at Qumran. Like *2 Enoch*, this text has only survived elsewhere in Christian communities. There is no unambiguous account of transformation, but only a description of how Enoch was taken up to heaven to stand before the throne and then told to act as the messenger of the Great Holy One, to warn the fallen angels that their judgement was near (*1 En.* 14–16). This must have been the heavenly counterpart to the Day of Atonement, as I shall show in the third chapter; Enoch

[28] Reif, 'Dedicated'.

[29] (i) Andersen's translation (OTP 1) *ad loc.* is very interesting: 'This outstanding encomium ... could hardly please a Christian or a Jew. The turbulence of the manuscripts betrays the embarrassment of the scribes ... even so the key term survives ...'

(ii) *Two ascents.* With the first Enoch became an angel being; with the second he was acknowledged as the revealer and the one who atones. Philo knew Moses' two ascents: the first his initiation as god and king and the second his death (*Life* II.288–91). Jesus' two ascents survive in Acts 13: i) raised i.e. begotten as Son, v. 33; ii) raised after death, v. 34. Fusing the two ascents caused the confusion now apparent in the New Testament.

(iii) There was some sensitivity about Enoch as can be seen from the Targums to Genesis 5:24: *T.Ps.J* says he ascended to heaven and became Metatron the great scribe; *T.N.* says nobody knows where he is because God took him; and *T.O.* simply says he was no more because the Lord caused him to die. Some versions of *T.O.* however, say that the Lord did not cause him to die. See Ginzberg, *Legends* v, pp. 162–4.

entered the heavenly sanctuary and emerged bringing judgement. In the *Similitudes* Enoch gazed at the glory of the throne, his 'face was changed' and he could no longer look at it (*1 En.* 39:14). Such descriptions occur throughout the book. Enoch saw a great commotion in the heavens as the angels prepared for the day of judgement; he fell on his face in fear and was lifted up by Michael (*1 En.* 60:2–6). He was raised up in the chariot of the spirit (*1 En.* 70). His spirit was taken up into the heavens where he saw the sons of God and the fiery throne; he fell on his face in fear until an angel raised him up. The text at this point is far from clear, but it seems that Enoch was commissioned by the Ancient of Days as his envoy (*1 En.* 71).

There is no such ambiguity about the so-called *3 Enoch*, an Enoch book which has survived in the Jewish community and is more correctly called the *Sepher Hekhalot*, the Book of Palaces. Enoch's ascent and transformation are described in detail several times and it is quite clear that he became the greatest of the heavenly beings and was enthroned in heaven. This looks like a later elaboration of the pre-Christian tradition in *1 Enoch* but the similarities to certain Christian claims about Jesus must make it unlikely that these ideas originated in the Jewish community after the advent of Christianity.[30] Although there is no agreement on the date of *3 Enoch*, it has affinities with the Enoch traditions of Palestine and should be considered as the deposit of a school of mystics rather than the work of a single and possibly un-

[30] (i) Cf. Himmelfarb, 'Revelation and Rapture', p. 84, 'Now the transformations in 2 Enoch and Sefer Hekhalot are quite extraordinary. Enoch does not become merely an angel, but an exalted angel. If it were not for the Apocalypses of Adam and Seth (quoted in the Cologne Mani Codex) one might be inclined to treat this sort of transformation as the peculiarity of a couple of ill-understood texts about Enoch.'

(ii) There is a curious collection of merkavah material in Schäfer ##384–400 (MS New York, JTS 8128) described by Halperin, *The Faces*, pp. 491–5. In the heavenly court there is a 'youth' na'ar, who is also the 'prince' śar. The angels attend the youth who enters beneath the throne of glory. He possesses all wisdom and is sealed with the seal of the sacred name. The text is fairly opaque but the youth is associated with seven voices #396 and he was 'given' to Moses, quoting Exodus 23:21 and 33:15. His name was revealed to Moses. His six men stand by the throne of glory (as in Ezek. 9:2). Halperin deals with the material as it relates to Moses, but much of it is very significant for Christian origins; Moses receives the Great Name from the prince and 'More important, the prince himself seems to be given (*nittan*) to Moses. We cannot be sure exactly what this means. But the text gives the impression that Moses has received something of the prince's essence, binding him to the prince in a way that goes beyond anything the patriarchs before him had known', p. 426. One is reminded of Philo's account of Moses (*Life* 1.155–8) entering into the presence of God to be made 'God and King'. Philo does not give the details of how this was done but this undateable merkavah text does. The heavenly 'patron' is given, along with his name, to the human figure. If for 'Moses' we substitute 'Jesus' we have a picture very similar to that of Revelation 5 and Philippians 2. The heavenly 'youth' was the Servant figure, the Lamb, and Jesus became that figure at his ascent.

(iii) Eusebius, *Proof* 4.15, PG xxii 305, says that one of the names for the Christ was Sharer of the Father's throne, a possible meaning for the name Metatron, see Alexander, *3 Enoch*, p. 243; or fuller Gruenwald, *Apocalyptic*, pp. 234–41.

representative author. What it reveals about ascents and about Metatron, the greatest of the angel princes, is very interesting indeed. R. Ishmael, himself described in some versions as a high priest, questioned the great angel prince Metatron and asked him:

> Why are you called by the name of your Creator with seventy names? You are greater than all the princes, more exalted than all the angels, more beloved than all the ministers, more honoured than all the hosts . . .

> Metatron replied: Because I am Enoch the son of Jared. When the generation of the flood sinned and turned to evil deeds, and said to God 'Go away, we do not choose to learn your ways', the Holy One, Blessed be he, took me from their midst to be a witness against them in the heavenly height . . .

> Therefore the Holy One, Blessed be he, brought me up in their lifetime, before their very eyes, to the heavenly height, to be a witness against them to future generations. And the Holy One, blessed be he, appointed me in the height as a prince and ruler among the ministering angels. (3 *En.* 4, Schäfer #886)

Metatron had formerly been Enoch, a human figure exalted to heaven and transformed into the greatest of the angels, the one who bore the divine name. Another account describes how Enoch was taken up to the heights in a fiery chariot (3 *En.* 6, #890).[31] He was given all wisdom and knowledge and then enthroned at the door of the seventh palace:

> And the herald went out into every heaven and announced concerning me: I have appointed Metatron my servant (*'ebed*) as a prince and ruler over all the denizens of the heights, apart from the eight great honoured and terrible princes. . . . (3 *En.* 10, #894)

Enoch/Metatron was also robed as a high priest (3 *En.* 12, #896), crowned and given the name 'The Lesser Yahweh'. The Holy One then engraved upon the crown the letters by which heaven and earth were created (3 *En.* 13, #897). Enoch/Metatron was transformed into fire when he was taken to serve the throne of glory (3 *En.* 15, #900). Here the tradition of the high priesthood is beyond doubt.

Other Hekhalot collections, perhaps from different schools or different periods, record more of these traditions. The *Hekhalot Rabbati*, for example, is believed to be earlier than 3 *Enoch/Sepher Hekhalot*; it describes how the mystic, not named as Enoch, descends to behold the vision of the throne chariot and how the guardian angels try to bar his way (##258–9). God welcomes those who ascend to his throne (#218), and the mystic is thereby 'the favored one, not to say Israel's chosen, who undertakes the privilege of the heavenly journey and whose ascent to the throne of glory is passionately awaited by

---

[31] Or, 'on a great cherub with fiery chariots and fiery horses and glorious attendants'. Enoch's translation is like that of Elijah in 2 Kings 2:11.

God'. The mystic acquires knowledge so that he knows all the deeds of men; nothing is hidden from him. 'The greatest thing of all is the fact that he sees and recognizes all the deeds of men, even those that they do in the chamber of chambers, whether they are good or corrupt deeds.' The mystic has, in other words, the characteristics of the Messiah. The one who 'descends to the chariot' 'is Israel's emissary who by his heavenly journey constitutes anew the communion between God and Israel and sees to it that it can be realized continually in the liturgy'.[32]

Several details in these accounts call for comment. Given that there can be no question of Christian influence, it is surely significant that the exalted and transformed Enoch is given the name of the Creator and established as superior to the other heavenly beings, exactly what is said of Jesus in Philippians 2:9

> God has highly exalted him and bestowed upon him the name which is above every name, that at the name of Jesus every knee should bow, in heaven, on earth and under the earth and every tongue confess that Jesus Christ is LORD . . .

The name given to the ascended Enoch/Metatron was The Lesser Yahweh, and I have already shown in *The Great Angel* that when LORD was used of Jesus, it was used in the sense that Jesus was Yahweh. This was the name he was given after his ascent. Further, the ascended Enoch was described as the Servant, as was Jesus in Philippians 2. Enoch was also enthroned as the heavenly high priest, as is said of Jesus in Hebrews. In the *Hekhalot Rabbati* there was a clear connection of the mystic to the Messiah. Whatever the date at which these Hekhalot texts were deposited in their present forms, they are of such obvious and immediate relevance to the question of Christian origins that they cannot have originated in a Jewish community after the first century AD.[33]

These descriptions of the exalted Enoch would fit very well as the antecedent of the resurrection tradition detected by Nickelsburg in the intertestamental texts. He implied that the earliest tradition was of a wise man exalted to rule, a wise man whose situation resembled that of Isaiah's Servant. The descriptions of resurrection and ascent in the intertestamental period are evidence that the elaborate descriptions found in the hekhalot texts are deeply rooted in the earlier beliefs of

---

[32] (i) Schäfer, *The Hidden and Manifest God*, pp. 41, 143, 146. The mystic's circle were also introduced to the mysteries of the chariot.

[33] The conflict with Christianity is perhaps reflected in the account of the humbling and dethronement of Metatron. Elisha ben Abuyah (known as Aḥer) had ascended to heaven to behold the throne and had thought, when he saw the glory of Metatron, that there were two powers in heaven. The dethronement of Metatron was to prevent any further misconceptions. b.Ḥag 15a is probably the earliest account; a more elaborate version is in *3 Enoch* 16, Schäfer #856.

Israel.[34] The Servant motif, which recurs as a title for the exalted Enoch, suggests that the tradition could go back as far as the monarchy. The ultimate origin of the resurrection belief cannot concern us here; what is important is that it was well established as part of the royal and high priestly tradition, and is known to have existed both before and after the New Testament period.

The resurrected and exalted Jesus was not originally the post-Easter Jesus. The resurrection to which his should be compared is not that post-mortem phenomenon which was a sign of the last times; a vindication of the righteous and judgement on the wicked. Rather it should be understood in the light of the traditions of exaltation and transformation which have survived in the hekhalot texts but which originated in the Jerusalem temple. Enoch/Metatron was an enthroned high priestly figure, bearing the divine name.

The Ascent of the Priest-King

Philo shows one way in which this material was being used in the first century. He explained that when Moses ascended Sinai, he went into the presence of God: 'He was said to have entered into the darkness where God was, that is, into the formless and invisible and incorporeal archetypal essence of all things, perceiving things invisible to mortal nature' (*Life of Moses.* 1:158). There, in the darkness, he was named 'god and king'. It is unlikely that what Philo said of Moses was unrelated to what 3 *Enoch* said of the Enoch/Metatron figure who was enthroned and named as the Lesser Yahweh, and Philo is not necessarily evidence that the traditions in his time had become 'thoroughly syncretistic'.[35]

[34] (i) Is this what is commanded in Deuteronomy 29:29? . . . 'the secret things belong to the LORD our God'; and 30:11–12, 'For this commandment which I command you this day is not too hard for you, neither is it far off. It is not in heaven, that you should say, "Who will go up for us to heaven, and bring it to us, that we may hear it and do it?"' The Deuteronomists were temple reformers; was this ascent tradition one of the practices they tried to suppress?
(ii) Isaiah 14:12–20 and Ezekiel 28:14 presuppose a royal ascent, as does Zechariah 3:7 where the high priest Joshua, newly vested, is granted the right of access to the LORD. See also Wyatt, 'The Hollow Crown' and my *The Older Testament, passim.*
[35] (i) Meeks, 'Moses', p. 371: 'The traditions were closely connected with scripture and at the same time thoroughly syncretistic. Central to the midrashic themes is the notion that, when God gave to Moses his own name (*'elohim, theos*) he conveyed to him a divine status and a unique function among men. . . . Here the usual hellenistic conception of the 'divine man' was modified by combination with the Semitic notion of the agent (*šaliaḥ, apostolos*) as well as by the concept of the image of God.'
(ii) Hengel, *Studies*, p. 197, is perhaps unwise to dismiss this evidence about the 'divine' Moses on the grounds that 'the middle Platonist language and ideational world of Philo is not that of early christology . . .' Philo's world view was that of the temple; only the language was middle Platonist, and consequently his views are the primary source for understanding christology, as I showed in *The Great Angel*, pp. 114–33.
The most likely explanation for both Moses and Jesus would be the resurrected life of those who were living as angels after their ascent.

The language he uses may be that of his Greek contemporaries, but what he describes is the mystical experience of those who used to go into the presence of God, into the Holy of Holies. They too had become god and king. The experience ascribed by Philo to Moses had formerly and originally been that of the kings and high priests in Jerusalem, but such a mystical transformation had been transferred to Moses many years before the time of Philo. The compiler of the Pentateuch who knew that Moses' face shone when he had been talking to God (Exod. 34:29), knew this tradition of exaltation and transfiguration.

The high place to which Moses had ascended was, for obvious reasons, Sinai; but it had not always been so. The ascending priest kings had gone up to the holy mountain of God. If the Old Testament texts are read without pre-understanding, their mystical ascents soon reveal themselves.

> Of old thou didst speak in a vision to thy faithful one and say:
> I have set the crown on one who is mighty,
> I have raised up high one chosen from the people.
> I have found David my servant;
> with my holy oil I have anointed him . . . (Ps. 89:20–1)

Or

> The oracle of David, the son of Jesse,
> the oracle of the man who was raised on high,
> the anointed of the God of Jacob
> the sweet psalmist of Israel.
> the Spirit of the LORD speaks by me,
> His word is on my tongue. (2 Sam. 23:1–2)
> ('Was raised in high' is the word used elsewhere for raising the dead!)[36]

This ascent imagery is used of Jesus. 'God raised up his servant and sent him to you' (Acts 3:26). 'The God of our fathers raised Jesus whom you killed . . . God exalted him at his right hand (Acts 5:30). This was not raising from the dead as it happened, by implication, before the crucifixion. We find the ascending priest king in the Letter to the Hebrews which describes Jesus the new Melchizedek, the priest who was raised up (Heb. 7:11, 15) in contrast to the Aaronite priest who

---

[36] (i) There is also an enigmatic verse in the Chronicler's account of David's prayer after his meeting with Nathan the prophet. David thanks the LORD for something which is no longer clear; the Greek rendered it, 'You have looked upon me as the appearance of a man and you have raised me up' but the Hebrew seems to mean, 'You have caused me to see the form of the man who has been raised up' (1 Chron. 17:17).

(ii) Cf. *Pss. Sol* 18:5 (OTP 2) 'May God cleanse Israel in the day of mercy and blessing, in the day of election when he raises up his Messiah.' Charlesworth, *Messiah*, p. 30, wants to translate this, 'when he brings back his Messiah'. Why? The primary meaning of the verb *anago* is 'to lift up' or 'to raise up from the dead'.

(iii) Cf. LAB 61:8–9 (OTP 2): 'The Philistine looked and saw the angel and said, "Not you alone have killed me but also the one who is present with you, whose appearance is not like the appearance of a man" . . . Now the angel of the LORD had *changed* David's appearance. . . .' The text actually says *raised*; this is thought to reflect a confusion of *nś'*, *raised* and *šnh*, *changed*, but is this really the explanation?

was only 'named'. 'Raised up' is the verb used for resurrection. *It is ascent texts which are quoted of the resurrected Jesus* and not the customary resurrection texts such as Isaiah 26:19: 'Thy dead shall live; their bodies shall rise'; or Ezekiel 37, the valley of dry bones, or Daniel 12:2: 'Many of those who sleep in the dust of the earth shall awake.'[37] What the earliest church understood by the resurrection of Jesus was not the resuscitation of a body but the exaltation of the king, the Servant, the Melchizedek priest. There are allusions to Psalm 2:7 in several passages in the New Testament and it is quoted three times: 'You are my son, today I have begotten you', is the LORD's oracle to the king after he had been established in triumph on the holy hill. Psalm 110:1, 4: 'Sit at my right hand' and 'You are a priest for ever after the order of Melchizedek' are drawn from another ascent psalm which describes the enthronement of the king and these are the most frequently used texts in the New Testament. Isaiah's Servant Songs, which were important to the pre-Christian resurrection tradition, imply ascent as their setting rather than a post-mortem revival to receive one's just reward: the Servant of the LORD would be exalted, lifted up and made very high (Isa. 52:14); after his suffering he would see light and have knowledge (Isa. 53:11).

Clearest of all is the Christian use of Daniel 7, the vision in which the Man figure ascends and is enthroned.[38] The writer of Daniel 7 was a mystic, but one of the outer circle who knew of the ascent but could only describe it as an observer.[39] The writer of *1 Enoch*, however, described this same ascent experience as a participant. He was taken up by clouds to stand before the throne, the Great Glory. He did not see the man figure ascending; he was the man figure. *3 Enoch* shows that this is how the tradition was understood. When Jesus described

---

[37] (i) Proof texts for resurrection used in the early church were physical resurrection texts not ascent texts, e.g. Irenaeus, *Against Heresies*, V.15.1–2 PG vii 1163–65, on the resurrection uses Isaiah 26:19; 65:22; 66:13; Ezekiel 37. This suggests a change in the understanding of resurrection.

(ii) Also 4Q491.

[38] This must be the Man figure who has all but disappeared from David's prayer in 1 Chronicles 17, ascending to be enthroned.

[39] Those who ascended became divine; conversely, those who had been divine but were thrown down from the holy mountain became mortal and died. The king of Babylon was thrown down because of his pride; Isaiah described him as the Day Star who was cast out and buried (Isa. 14). Ezekiel's king of Tyre invites comment too. The enigmatic figure in the garden of God walked among the sons of fire as did Enoch. He wore precious stones which, in the Greek text, correspond to those of the high priest's breastplate. He was full of wisdom and seems to have worn the crown engraved with the sacred name. The text is obscure. What is quite clear is that he was thrown down to mortality. Had this once been an oracle against the high priest, perhaps explaining the destruction of the temple? It would certainly explain an equally enigmatic reassurance in Isaiah 41:9: 'You are my servant, I have chosen you, and not cast you off.'

himself as the Man figure, he located himself at the heart of the ascent tradition, not as an observer but as a participant.[40]

There are several passages in the New Testament which are best understood in this way. Jesus ascended as did Enoch; he was transformed by the experience and then returned to earth for a short period. He had become what later tradition ascribed to Enoch/Metatron; he had become the LORD. But the LORD was also the chief of the sons of God, the great angel of Israel, the Holy One, the heavenly high priest. John's Jesus said that he had been 'consecrated and sent into the world' (John 10:36).[41] 'Consecrated' must imply that Jesus had been made not holy but a holy one or a priest.[42] Similarly, Jesus claimed that he had been sent down from heaven (John 6:38, 42) and would return there (John 6:62). In the conversation with Nicodemus, Jesus spoke of being born from above (or born again), being born of the spirit and water, of the heavenly things he had seen and of the son of man who descended from heaven and would ascend also.

When Morton Smith discussed these ascent passages he found evidence of later accretions to an ascent tradition which had originally been a magical rite. The belief that Jesus was the pre-existent Logos was not, he thought, compatible with the original ascent tradition but this 'did not prevent John from preserving and reworking material which had come to him from an earlier and more historical tradition, and to such material we owe this recollection that Jesus in his lifetime claimed to have gone up to heaven and to speak of it from firsthand knowledge.[43] Whilst I agree with Morton Smith that there is evidence for Jesus practising ascent, this practice was far from being incompatible with the Logos tradition. The ascent to heaven was the way to the angelic state, and if Philo knew that the Logos was Yahweh, those who 'became' the LORD as the result of their ascent experience would have become the pre-existent Logos. This was the tradition of the temple and of the high priests who wore the sacred Name.

---

[40] Have our recent agonisings about the Son of Man been misguided? A Man figure certainly had a place in the pre-Christian visionary tradition. I suggest that Jesus identified himself as this figure, who was the high priest. Jesus' non-apocalyptic 'son of man' sayings, e.g. Mark 2:10, 'forgiving sins on earth'; or 2:28, 'Lord even of the Sabbath' make more sense read of a heavenly 'man', the high priest, than of Everyman. 'Son of Man' is a feature of all Mark's Passion predictions (8:31; 9:31; 10:33–4) because the heavenly high priest had to suffer to make the great atonement. Jesus as the Man returning on the clouds of heaven, Mark 14:62, rather than ascending to the throne, shows that he knew more about the 'Man' tradition than we do and that he was not dependent on one text in Daniel 7. (I shall deal with this in Chapter 4.)

[41] The context is significant: Jesus had claimed to be a son of God and justified this by reference to the 'elohim of Psalm 82, the sons of God Most High. The LORD was the chief of these sons, see my The Great Angel.

[42] Cf. LXX Leviticus 8:12 which has the same verb for 'consecrating' the high priest.

[43] M. Smith, Clement, p. 247.

Ascent and transformation is also the most natural explanation for some of the imagery in the *Odes of Solomon*, especially in passages where the speaker seems to be Jesus himself:

> (The Spirit) brought me forth before the Lord's face
> And because I was the Son of Man (or 'although I was a man')
> I was named the light, the son of God.
> Because I was the most glorified among the glorious ones
> And the greatest among the great ones
> For according to the greatness of the Most High, so She made me
> And according to His newness He renewed me.
> And he anointed me with his perfection;
> And I became one of those who are near him . . . (*Ode* 36)

Ode 38 begins:

> I went up into the light of Truth as into a chariot . . .[44]

The evidence is accumulating that resurrection was the rebirth experience which made a human being into a son of God. For some it was to be a post-mortem experience; the resurrected would be equal to the angels and sons of God (Luke 20:36).[45] For others, notably the high priests, it was achieved before death by ascent to the throne, where the Glory transformed or else destroyed any who looked on it. The son of God then returned to earth for a short time as a messenger from God, usually to announce judgement. If the transforming ascent of Jesus had been after the crucifixion, what tradition has come to call the ascension after forty days, this could explain Paul's quotation at the beginning of Romans: 'designated son of God in power according to the Spirit of holiness by his resurrection from the dead' (Rom. 1:4), but it would not explain very much else. If, however, Jesus' transforming ascent had occurred at the start of the ministry, it would invite a reconsideration of several crucial questions. Was Jesus conscious of being a son of God? Did he originate the teaching about himself which became the church's proclamation? Did he know who he was and what he was doing? These may seem excessively simple questions to ask, but a great deal of what has been written in the last two generations implies that 'Jesus' was the product of the early church's imagination, coming to terms with the disaster of the crucifixion.[46]

[44] Several of the *Odes* suggest that ascent and transformation was their original context. In *Ode* 17 the speaker is not unlike the servant, exalted and glorified. He then releases the bound and gives them resurrection. In *Ode* 21 the speaker is lifted up to the light. Throughout the *Odes* there is imagery of robing and crowning, cf. the promise to the sons of light in 1QS IV: they would have '. . . great peace . . . and a crown of glory and a garment of majesty in unending light'.

[45] Paul implies this in 1 Corinthians 13:12: '. . . but then face to face'.

[46] Hengel, *Studies*, p. 14: 'If Jesus never possessed a messianic claim of divine mission, rather sternly rejected every third-hand question in this regard, if he neither spoke of the coming, or present, 'Son of Man', nor was executed as a messianic pretender and

Let us return to the *Gospel of Philip* and ask whose voice we are hearing:

> Those who say that the LORD died first and then rose up are in error for he rose up first and then died (*Philip* 56).

The original 'raising' of Jesus, I suggest, was at his baptism and after that he was conscious of being the LORD. He then proclaimed himself as the heavenly high priest in whom the LORD was present with his people, bringing the great atonement.

alleged king of the Jews – as is maintained with astonishing certainty by radical criticism unencumbered by historical arguments – then the emergence of Christology, indeed, the entire early history of primitive Christianity, is completely baffling, nay incomprehensible.'

2

Rebirth

The irrational fullness of life has taught me never to discard anything even when it goes against all our theories (so short-lived at best) or otherwise admits of no immediate explanation. It is, of course, disquieting . . . but security, certitude and peace do not lead to discoveries.

C. G. JUNG
Foreword to the *I Ching*

ALL the gospels agree that the baptism of Jesus marked the beginning of his ministry. I want to explore the possibility that for Jesus this was the moment at which he 'became' son of God. His baptism was a merkavah ascent experience when he believed he had become the heavenly high priest, the LORD with his people. *This experience of transformation was his resurrection.*

The hope expressed in Deuteronomy 32:43 was very much alive in the first century CE; the LORD would come to his people to punish their enemies and atone the land. *The Assumption of Moses* reveals that the expected LORD was a great high priest coming forth from his holy place; a text from Qumran (11QMelch) names the heavenly high priest as Melchizedek, coming at the end of the tenth jubilee for the great Day of Atonement. Jesus saw himself as that heavenly high priest and his ministry was to be that of the LORD coming to his people to bring both judgement and atonement. I shall explore the question of the great atonement in the third chapter; for now I propose to concentrate on the question of baptism as ascent and resurrection, birth as a son of God and consecration as the great high priest. This is quite clear in the Letter to the Hebrews, but often lost in translation; Melchizedek, we are told, was made like the Son of God (7:3) and he was raised up (*anisteme*: the word also means resurrect) as a priest (7:11, 15). The sons of Aaron were only 'named' as priests.

Baptism as Resurrection

The strongest evidence for baptism as resurrection is in the New Testament itself, but it is not known where the teaching about Christian baptism originated. I suggest that it came from Jesus himself, based on his own experience, and that it was developed and altered in certain respects by Paul. The earliest teaching had been that baptism was the means of entering the kingdom of heaven, in other words, of accomplishing the heavenly ascent.[1] During Jesus' ministry, only a few of the disciples had the experience and for them, the kingdom was already present. They had been 'raised up' and thus were no longer of this world. Their account of Jesus forms the basis of the fourth gospel and goes back to Jesus himself.[2] Followers who were not part of the inner group, however, those who had not been given the secrets of the kingdom, continued to expect the kingdom as a future event when the LORD would appear with all his holy ones at the judgement. Paul is usually thought to give an earlier view of this than John;[3] it is more likely that Paul wrote later, but as one who had not been a part of Jesus' inner group.

[1] M. Smith, *Clement*, argued that 'the kingdom' was given to the disciples, pp. 211ff. and that the initiation rite had been baptism, pp. 178ff., given only to a few disciples, the inner group, pp. 209ff. He also suggests that the idea of participating in Jesus' death and resurrection was 'obviously later than those events' and must have been a secondary addition to the original teaching. Not necessarily; it depends on what was originally meant by the death and resurrection.
The Ebionites held that Jesus's baptism was the essential element in their belief, not the sacrificial death.

[2] Several theories point in this direction: e.g. Weeden, *Mark*, who identified the opponents in Mark's Gospel as the advocates of a *theios aner* theology; they were the people Jesus warned against in Mark 13:6. Mark's opponents would have been the 'inner' group. Similarly Goulder, *Tale*, identified two groups in the early church, the Paulines and the Petrines, the original Jewish Christians who 'were agreed about the supreme significance of Jesus but disagreed about almost everything else ... whether the kingdom of God had arrived or not ... visions ... Jesus' divinity, and the resurrection of the dead', p. x. The Jewish group were those whom Paul opposed in many of his letters, usually identified as gnostics. They claimed to have had visions which gave them knowledge and wisdom (Col. 2:16, 18), p. 50; they claimed that the resurrection was past, they had already been raised with Christ in baptism, p. 172. In 'The Visionaries', pp. 15–39, he suggested that Ephesians was written to counteract those who claimed to have had access to God, to have ascended through the heavens. On Goulder's hypothesis, though, the tradition in John would be reckoned on the Pauline side of the debate, on the grounds that 'the impossibility of divine vision is a recurring theme of the Johannine Gospel', 'Vision', p. 69. On the contrary, read in the light of the theory I set out in *The Great Angel*, that Jesus was recognized as the manifestation of the LORD, the fourth gospel says the vision of God is possible now that the Glory has been seen in Jesus. 'No man has seen God' refers to the Father, not to the LORD, the second God. Isaiah in his vision had seen Jesus' Glory when he saw the LORD (John 12:41). The fourth gospel therefore originates with the inner group.

[3] See Schweizer, 'Dying and Rising', p. 5.

Thus, in the interpretation of the pre-Johannine church, baptism, understood as a rebirth by water and spirit, guaranteed entry into the coming kingdom of God. John himself uses the same phrase in a different way. No longer does he expect a coming kingdom; for him, it is, as least primarily, a present reality, which the believer is already able to see.

The two most significant accounts of baptism are found in texts attributed to the two surviving members of the inner group, John and Peter.[4] In the conversation with Nicodemus, John's Jesus explains that only those who are born anew, or from above, can see the kingdom of God. That which is born of the flesh is flesh, that which is born of the spirit is spirit. It is birth by water and spirit which enables a person to enter the kingdom of God. This implies that 'entering' the kingdom was part of the primitive teaching,[5] perhaps going back to Jesus himself. Jesus then explains to Nicodemus that he bears witness to what he has seen, that he speaks of heavenly things. The Son of Man who has descended from heaven must ascend there again. This kingdom of God which is entered by baptism is a place which one sees and enters to learn of heavenly things (John 3:1–15). Have we here, as Morton Smith suggested, an authentic memory of the Jesus who had taught that baptism was the means by which one ascended to heaven?[6] John speaks of being born of God: Jesus gave to those who believed in him the power to become children of God, born not of flesh and blood but of God. John also speaks of those who have seen the Glory not in heaven but on earth as the Word become flesh, perhaps a reference to the transfiguration.[7] The most natural context for material such as this would be the mystical ascent; the kingdom of God is the place of God's throne, the place of the Glory and those who see the vision are transformed by it, resurrected, reborn. The Son of Man has been transformed and come back to reveal what he has seen; thus John can associate the transforming effect of the heavenly vision with the revelation of the Glory in Jesus.

1 Peter also has a baptismal setting. The newly baptized have been 'born anew to a living hope through the resurrection of Jesus Christ from the dead' (1 Pet. 1:3). They have been 'born anew, not of perishable seed, but of imperishable, through the living and abiding word of God' (1 Pet. 1:23). The association here seems to be different, admission into the royal priesthood (1 Pet. 2:9) rather than ascent to the presence of the throne, but they are in fact the same, for admission to the Holy of Holies in the temple, reserved for the high priests, was regarded as admission into the presence of God.

Paul is less clear; sometimes he implies that the baptized are already resurrected: 'If then you have been raised with Christ, seek the things that are above, where Christ is, seated at the right hand of God' (Col. 3:1); or, using different imagery: 'He has delivered us from the dominion of darkness and transferred us to the kingdom of his beloved son' (Col.

---

[4] According to Acts 12:2 James was martyred by Herod.

[5] 'To enter the kingdom of God' is probably a traditional formulation, since John does not use the expression elsewhere.

[6] M. Smith, *Clement*, p. 247. He also suggested that the 'man in Christ' of 2 Corinthians 12:1–7 was Jesus in 'Ascent'.

[7] Cf. 1 John 1:1–3.

1:13). At other times he says that the resurrection is yet to come: 'Let no one deceive you ... that the Day of the Lord has come' (2 Thess. 2:2); 'We shall all be united with him in a resurrection like his ... we shall also live with him (Rom. 6:5, 8). In Corinthians Paul insists that entry into the kingdom is a future event and the unrighteous will have no place there (1 Cor. 6:9–11). He was expecting his body to be transformed into the likeness of the glorified Christ only at the Parousia (Phil. 3:21) and yet he also believed that the process of change had already begun: 'We all are being changed into his likeness from one degree of glory to another' (2 Cor. 3:18; cf. Rom. 8:15, 23, where the adoption as sons is both a past and a future event).

There were Christians who believed that the resurrection had already happened, but Paul argues against them. The Christians at Corinth apparently believed that they were already resurrected to reign with Christ (1 Cor. 4:8); they baptized on behalf of the dead and had been given the gifts of the Spirit. The dispute in 1 Corinthians 15 was about the time of the resurrection; Paul argues that it was to happen in the future whereas the Corinthian Christians believed it had already happened.

> Paul fights Corinthian enthusiasm, an enthusiasm which leaves time and space behind it, by means of understanding baptism as the beginning of a way which leads to the final consummation; at the same time he will not deny that in baptism the old aeon of sin has been ended definitely and that the Spirit is the firstfruits of the coming life to have been given to the church.[8]

[8] (i) Schweizer, 'Dying and Rising', p. 7. We should perhaps give more weight to the description of resurrection in the Nag Hammadi, *Epistle to Rheginos*, CG I.4; and to the link between knowledge and apotheosis in Genesis 3.

(ii) Also Attridge, 'Angel' shows that those whom Paul opposed at Colossae believed that they had become angels through their baptism. He uses *Zostrianos* 4–8 (CG VIII.1) to show how a 'dipping and sealing' ritual transforms the seer into an angel, p. 484. The closing homily of the text shows how the seer returns to earth to preach deliverance ('awakening') to the race of Seth and warns then against 'baptism with death', surely a polemical comment on the Pauline teaching, p. 486.

(iii) Attridge, p. 487, compares also the *Gospel of the Egyptians* (CG III.2), which describes baptismal transformation into the angelic state and the gift of knowledge, and *Trimorphic Protennoia* 45 (CG XIII.1) which invites the baptized to 'enter the exalted, perfect light', to be enthroned and receive glorious robes of light. The gnostic evidence 'is but the tip of a significant iceberg', p. 489. Yes! But the iceberg is not derived from 'contemporary Platonism', p. 491. The heavenly journeys associated with baptism occur in gnostic texts replete with imagery drawn from temple tradition, as I showed in *The Great Angel*, pp. 162–89. The baptismal tradition which 'competed with what we know as the Pauline one', p. 493, was the original temple tradition going back to Jesus himself, the great high priest. Attridge is correct to locate the ultimate origin of these ideas in the second temple period and to link them to the Enochic materials. I suggest that the earliest evidence for them is found in Zechariah 3:5–7, where the high priest is robed and then permitted to enter the presence of the angels and given the mysterious 'stone' with which to make atonement. The baptism ritual of the atoning and ascending high priest almost breaks the surface in *m.Yoma*

Elsewhere the belief that the resurrection is already past is condemned as 'godless chatter' (2 Tim. 2:18).

Because Paul has a different understanding of resurrection, he uses different imagery to describe baptism. Whereas John speaks of birth from above and seeing the kingdom, and Peter of being born anew and entering the royal priesthood, Paul speaks of dying with Christ, being crucified and buried (Rom. 6:4–6) in order to rise with him, but when? *The confusion in Paul's thought is a sure sign that he is adapting an established pattern.*[9]

'Dying' was an original part of Jesus' own baptism experience but the death and ascent motifs of the original teaching about baptism derive not from Calvary but Jordan. Eliade has shown how widespread is the pattern of shamanic initiation involving an experience of death and

---

3:3, where he prepares to enter the Holy of Holies by five immersions (why five?), cf. the five seals in *Trimorphic Protennoia* 48, the robing, baptizing, enthroning, glorifying and rapture of the gnostic initiation. Cf. *Zostrianos* 53; after his fifth baptism, the seer becomes divine, enters the presence of Ioel (the Great Angel?) and is baptized again and anointed.

(iv) *The Epistle to Rheginos* was formerly thought to describe 'the intellect's escape and change of condition' Layton, *Gnostic*, p. 317, which was the Valentinian idea of resurrection in the second century. It is now thought to have affinities to the idea of resurrection which I am proposing. Thus Menard, 'Notion', pp. 113–15, who shows from the allusions to the Transfiguration that a resurrection of 'the flesh' was envisaged: 'Si notre auteur interprète ainsi la scène de la Transfiguration (Mc 9:14 ss) pour prouver la vérité de la résurrection, c'est qu'il conçoit que la chair terrestre peut être transfigurée en une chair céleste avec toutes les transformations que cette transfiguration peut comporter.' He draws parallels with *Gen R.* 14:10, which compares the resurrection to the first creation of Adam, when God breathed into him and transformed him, and the promised resurrection of Ezekiel 37:14; 'I will put my spirit in you.' The gift of the Spirit transforms as resurrection. Also Edwards, 'Epistle', p. 87: '*The Epistle to Rheginos* . . . while it promises an immediate translation to eternity, insists that this is not without the flesh.'

[9] (i) This is well illustrated by Barr, *Garden of Eden*, pp. 112–13, when he shows how hard it is to relate Paul's description of the resurrected body in 1 Corinthians 15 to anything found in the Hebrew Bible. This is certainly the case if one looks for evidence of the revival of corpses, however that may have been expressed. The origin of the Christian belief, however, is to be found elsewhere, in the ascent traditions and this is why Paul's thoughts on the subject are both confused and different. Paul was not a priest, and, I suggest, did not have any real knowledge of the priestly traditions.

(ii) I cannot agree with Barr's observation, p. 114: 'The particular concentration on resurrection, characteristic of Christianity, appears late and seems to be associated with martyrdom.' Martyrdom in Revelation 6:9, see Chapter 4, n. 13, was associated with the great Day of Atonement and there is no doubt that martyrdom, resurrection and atonement were associated see 4 Maccabees 6:28–9; 13:12; 16:20; 17:22, also Townshend, *4 Maccabees*, pp. 662–4, Vermes, *Scripture*, p. 198. The concept of resurrection relevant to Christian origins will prove to be apotheosis and to be as old as the Atonement rituals.

(iii) O'Collins, *Easter*, p. 51, is able to argue for the traditional sequence of death, resurrection, exaltation by assuming that Paul is the primary source because he is 'early' and John and the hymn in Philippians 2 are secondary because they are 'later'.

resurrection prior to ascent. Of more immediate relevance to the baptism of Jesus, though, is the evidence that the tradition of initiatory death was known to the rabbis of the third century and even the second. When the traditions can be clearly discerned in the third century and later, they are attached to the revelation at Sinai, but their roots are thought to lie in the esoteric teachings of the mystics who practised the ascent.[10] Now if Jesus' baptism had been an ascent experience, it would have been a mystical experience of death and resurrection and the original meaning of 'rising with Christ' would have been similar, like the experiences described in the Qumran hymns.

Before Paul, baptism had been rising with Christ to a heavenly life which transformed the believer into a son of God at that moment; the gift of the Spirit was a sign of this new state. Paul makes baptism into dying with Christ in order to rise with him at a future date. He understands resurrection in the same way as most of his contemporaries and so expects a post-mortem transformation except for those who are still alive at the Parousia (2 Thess. 2:2; cf. 1 Cor. 13:12 '... but then face to face'; 1 Cor. 15:51; 1 Thess. 4:17). Thus his teaching on baptism and resurrection is not consistent and the imagery is confused.

When Paul uses other imagery drawn from the older tradition, he modifies it: putting off the old nature and putting on the new (Col. 3:10) or putting on the new nature created after the likeness of God (Eph. 4:24; cf. Gal. 3:27) referred originally to the mystics' experience of being robed with glory before the throne, putting off the flesh and becoming an angel. When Paul associates baptism with entering a cloud, the original was presumably another reference to the ascent tradition, but he adapted it to refer to the pillar of cloud at the Exodus (1 Cor. 10:2). Characteristic of Paul, however, was this imagery of dying with Christ as sharing the crucifixion, and thus the significance of Jesus' own experience at baptism was lost.[11]

---

[10] (i) E.g. Eliade, *Shamanism*. For the importance of death and resurrection experiences see Chapters 2 and 4,
or Eliade, *Sacred*, p. 201.

> From one religion to another the immemorial theme of the second birth is enriched with new values, which sometimes profoundly change the content of the experience. Nevertheless, a common element, an invariable, remains. It could be defined as follows: access to spiritual life always entails death to the profane condition, followed by a new birth ...

or Eliade, *Myths*, p. 227.

> Initiatory death is thus a recommencement, never an end. In no rite or myth do we find the initiatory death as something final, but always as the condition *sine qua non* of a transition to another mode of being, a trial indispensable to regeneration; that is, to the beginning of a new life.

(ii) Chernus, *Mysticism*, Chapter 3.

[11] Kelly, *Doctrines*, p. 194. In the second century AD; 'The earlier Pauline conception of (baptism) as the application of Christ's atoning death to the believer seems to have faded.'

This would go some way towards explaining the old Eastern form of baptism which was a conscious imitation of Jesus' baptism in the Jordan. The newly baptized emerged from the water as a 'son of God' and there was no reference to Paul's teaching about dying and rising with Christ.[12] The earliest evidence is to be found in the *Didascalia*, which has preserved some significant terminology. It describes the bishop as the person 'through whom you were sealed, and through whom you became the sons of light, and through whom the Lord in baptism, by the imposition of the hand of the bishop, bore witness to each one of you and uttered in his holy voice, saying: "Thou art my son; I this day have begotten thee"'. 'Sealing', 'sons of light' and 'sons of God' are remnants of the earliest tradition. Other texts confirm that what happened in the Jordan was recalled and re-enacted at every baptism.

> So deeply did the baptism of Jesus impress itself upon Syrian liturgical imagination, that in the later liturgical books the font is named 'the Jordan'. Some commentators, in allusion to the idea of rebirth, refer to the font as a 'womb'. It is never called 'the grave' or 'the sepulchre'. The idea of Romans 6:3–5 in which St. Paul likens the baptismal ceremony to Christ's death and burial made no mark upon early Syrian thought about baptism.[13]

There have been various attempts to explain why Paul's imagery was not used,[14] but perhaps these early communities remembered that Paul's teaching about baptism had been his own and in their rituals they retained the original form and meaning of baptism.

We need to note another feature of these early descriptions of baptism. The *History of John* has two accounts. In the first the heavens open

[12] Connolly, *Didascalia Apostolorum*, ii.32, p. 93.
Cf. 1QS III: 'He shall be cleansed from all sins by the spirit of holiness uniting him to His truth, and his iniquity shall be expiated by the spirit of uprightness and humility. And when his flesh is sprinkled with purifying water and sanctified by cleansing water, it shall be made clean by the humble submission of his soul to all the precepts of God.'
Cf. Hippolytus, *On the Holy Theophany* 8, PG x 859: 'If, therefore, man has become immortal, he will also be God. And if he is made God by water, he is found to be also joint heir with Christ after the resurrection from the dead.'
[13] 'The Old Syrian Baptismal Tradition and its Resettlement under the influence of Jerusalem in the Fourth Century', in Ratcliff, *Studies*. Brock 'Ordines', p. 181:
> It would seem . . . that the whole emphasis of the Syrian (and Armenian) rite was on a charismatic rebirth to something new with little stress on death to something old: Christ's own baptism in the Jordan, with its public proclamation of his Sonship and (according to the Syrian tradition) the transference to him of the priesthood, serves as the primary basis of Christian baptism, rather than the Pauline idea of dying and rising with Christ.
[14] E.g. M. Smith, *Clement*, pp. 264–5: 'The material chosen by the triumphant party was predominantly Pauline. . . . The disappearance of Paul's theology of baptism from second-century Christianity cannot be explained . . . by ignorance. It must have been deliberate.' Smith suggests that Paul had 'substantially preserved' the teaching of Jesus about baptism but that this was considered dangerous since it was used by gnostics to support their libertine teachings. But see above n. 8(iii) where the gnostic tradition is thought to be at *variance* with Paul.

and angels appear to consecrate the oil and the water[15] and in the second
John prays that the baptized may become sons, as did Jesus in the
Jordan, and then fire and angels appear from heaven.[16] The Jordan
baptism, then, was remembered in tradition as a time when fire and
angels appeared; this was another characteristic of the merkavah ascent
experiences and it is found, as we shall see, in several other traditions
about the baptism of Jesus.

In these early rites the believer was anointed before being baptized,
and this was compared to the anointing of the ancient kings and
priests,[17] the giving of the Spirit. A pre-immersion anointing occurs
also in *The Testament of Levi,* which describes the vesting of the high
priest in a way that closely resembles Christian baptism. If the author
of the *Testament* was a Christian, s/he chose to describe the vesting as
a baptism, and if the author was not a Christian, the vesting of the
priest must in fact have been similar to early baptismal practice. In his
vision, Levi saw seven angels who offered him the tokens of high
priesthood. First he was anointed, then washed with pure water, then
fed bread and wine and robed in linen. He was given a purple girdle to
wear, a branch of olive to hold, and a wreath was placed on his head
and then the priestly diadem (*T.Lev.* 8). This was Levi's second vision
but his first had been equally significant. An angel had invited him to
enter the heavens. The second heaven was a place of brightness, where
the armies of holy ones waited for the day of judgement and the third
was the Holy of Holies, the place of the Great Glory where archangels
performed atonement rites before the throne. When Levi reached this
third heaven, he was able to become a priest of the LORD and reveal his
mysteries (*T.Lev.* 5). The first heaven, however, through which Levi
had had to pass before he could ascend to the Holy of Holies, was a
place of water and darkness (*T.Lev.* 3). Might this first heaven account

[15] In Wright, *Apocryphal Acts,* p. 39. After a place for baptizing had been constructed in the corner of the theatre: 'fire blazed forth over the oil and the oil did not take fire, for two angels had their wings spread over the oil and were crying, "Holy, holy, holy, Lord God Almighty"'. When the water was consecrated two angels appeared also.

[16] Ibid. p. 54, 'And in that hour fire blazed forth over the oil and the wings of the angels were spread over the oil' (the later manuscript has 'water').

[17] The *Manual of Discipline* 1QSIII.4 prescribes anointing before baptism; see n. 12 above. The imagery here is reminiscent of the Day of Atonement, but water takes the place of blood. *Didascalia* xvi, 'As of old the priests and kings were anointed in Israel, do thou in like manner, with the imposition of the hand, anoint the head of those who receive baptism . . .' Ratcliff, p. 141, 'The liturgical anointing, then, is not a confirmation or completion, but an inception; the giving of the Spirit is the beginning of initiation.' Brock, 'Ordines', p. 182: the pre-baptismal anointing carried the idea of 'anointing into the kingship and priesthood of Christ, the new Adam, with the proclamation of Sonship, this time for the Christian, who at baptism recovers the status that Adam and Eve had before the Fall (in Syriac terms he put on the robe of glory which was stripped from Adam and Eve at the Fall). Elsewhere, as we have seen, the robe of glory is the sign of resurrection.

for the water symbolism of baptism, the water through which the mystic had to pass before his ascent?

Finally, Levi foresaw the advent of a new priest in the last days, a messianic figure. The heavens would open and from the heavenly temple would come the Father's voice, consecrating him. 'And the glory of the Most High shall burst forth upon him and the Spirit of understanding and sanctification shall rest upon him in the water' (*T.Lev.* 18:6), the words 'in the water' usually being identified as a Christian addition. The messianic priest, by implication a son of God Most High, was to open the gates of paradise, give the saints access to the tree of life and bind Beliar. Whether these verses came originally from a Christian or a pre-Christian hand, and whether or not 'in the water' is a Christian addition, the baptism of Jesus can be seen to be remarkably similar to the consecration of the messianic priest. The voice came from the heavenly temple, the heavens opened and the Spirit was given. The *Testament of Levi* is further evidence that baptism was associated with ascent and also with the consecration of a high priest.[18]

The Baptism of Jesus as his Resurrection

All the gospels agree that Jesus' ministry began with the baptism; Acts also defined Jesus' ministry as the time 'from the baptism of John until the day he was taken up from us' (Acts 1:22). The synoptic gospels describe the scene at the Jordan when the heavens opened, the Spirit was given and a voice was heard.[19] Mark, usually thought to be the

[18] (i) 4Q213–14, an Aramaic *Testament of Levi*, also describes Levi's heavenly ascent to the gates of heaven which he was invited to enter.

(ii) Jansen, 'Kingship', argues that the ritual was drawn from life and reflected the rituals which would have been known to those for whom *T.Lev.* was written. 'The author is depending on a living pattern of cult . . . a feast for Yahweh as king and renewer of nature was still celebrated in late Jewish time', pp. 360–1. There was still a temple ceremony of covenant making, p. 362, and thus the heavenly ascent attributed to Levi was familiar to the second temple writer. 'The author is dependent on the cult pattern to such a degree that he writes things which are really out of place in this book', p. 353.

(iii) Murray, *Symbols*, pp. 55, 117, 178–80. The Syriac fathers hold a tradition that Christ received the Aaronic priesthood when he was baptized by John the Baptist, who was of the priestly family. . . . See n. 37 below.

[19] The details differ; Matthew makes the event a more public affair than do Mark and Luke. The voice from heaven addressed the crowd: 'This is my son with whom I am well pleased', and the heavens were opened, presumably for all to see. In Luke too, the open heaven was apparently for all to see but the voice addressed Jesus 'You are my Son . . .'

Lentzen-Deis, *Die Taufe*, is the most comprehensive study of the baptism accounts. He suggests that the vision narratives conveyed the meaning of the incident described. Using the Targums to Genesis 22 and 28 to show the role of the 'Deute-Vision' he concludes that the baptism vision was an explanation of the life of Jesus. More recently Vigne, *Christ au Jourdain*, links the New Testament traditions and early evidence for the Feast of the Epiphany.

most primitive version of the story, says that when Jesus came up from the water he saw the heavens open and heard a voice speaking to him: 'You are my beloved Son, with whom I am well pleased.' I shall examine four features of the baptism story: the gift of the Spirit, the immersion in the water, the open heavens and the voice.

First, the gift of the Spirit. The baptism of Jesus in the Jordan was far more than the rite of purification practised by some contemporary groups in Palestine;[20] more too than John's 'baptism of repentance for the forgiveness of sins' (Mark 1:4). Matthew's account of the conversation between Jesus and John before the baptism shows that Jesus' experience of baptism was distinguished from that of the others whom John baptized. It was the first time that the gift of the Spirit had been associated with baptism,[21] a gift which was to become the distinguishing

[20] (i) The Essenes purified themselves in cold water, Josephus, *War*, II.130. Josephus became the disciple of a certain Bannus, *Life* 11, 'using frequent ablutions of cold water day and night for purity's sake'. Cf. *Sibylline Oracles* 3:592 which extols the Jews who sanctify their flesh with water.

(ii) *Sibylline Oracles* 4:165–70, OTP 1, p. 283 thought to have originated in Jewish baptist circles, describes a baptism like John's: a baptism of repentance in 'perennial rivers' to avert the wrath of God.

(iii) 1QH VIII describes trees growing by a source of living water, not baptismal imagery as such, but linking water to the gift of discernment. The *Apocalypse of Adam* 8, OTP 1, p. 708, a non-Christian text originating perhaps in Palestine in the first or second century CE, describes 'the holy baptism of those who know the eternal knowledge through the ones born of the word and the imperishable illuminators . . .'

(iv) Ezekiel 36:25 was interpreted in the second century by R. Akiba in the context of atonement: 'Blessed are ye, O Israel. Before whom are ye made clean and who makes you clean? Your father in heaven; as it is written, And I will sprinkle clean water upon you and ye shall be clean.' *m. Yoma* 8.9.

[21] (i) Cf. John 1:33; *Gospel according to the Hebrews*; the *The Gospel of the Ebionites*.

(ii) The creation imagery is also known in later Jewish sources and linked to the Messiah in *Gen R.* 2:4: 'And the Spirit of God hovered: this alludes to the Spirit of Messiah as you read, And the Spirit of the LORD shall rest upon him (Isa. 11:2)'. The passage continues with an account of R. Simeon ben Zoma rapt in a merkavah trance and saying that the spirit of God hovered over the waters at the creation 'like a bird, flying and flapping with its wings'. The Holy Spirit hovering over the waters of the Jordan, understood in a merkavah context, would indicate an association with Genesis 1. The dove is the Spirit of Genesis 1:2 in *b.Hag* 15a and *T.N.* Genesis 1:1–2 has 'wisdom' and 'a Spirit of love from before the LORD' as the agents of the creation.

(iii) There are also links to an older and more violent account of the creation in which the LORD subdued and bound the forces of primeval chaos and established his cosmic covenant. The waters were terrified at the approach of Christ to his baptism. An Armenian baptismal prayer has: 'By thy dread command, thou didst close up the abysses and make them fast . . . thou didst bruise the head of the dragon upon the waters'; Psalm 77:17 (Eng, v. 16), 'When the waters saw thee, O God, they were afraid and the abyss trembled' and Psalm 114:3, 'The sea looked and fled, the Jordan turned back' are quoted as prophesying the baptism in the Jordan. Sperber 'Sealing', has traced these motifs in the *Talmuds*, where King David subdues the waters of chaos under Jerusalem, and linked them to the *Prayer of Manasseh* 3, to *Ode* 24, to several baptismal prayers and to a merkavah text (*Hekhalot Zutarti*, Schäfer #367). Murray has shown how this picture of creation was part of the cult of the first temple: 'A mythical picture

mark of Christian baptism. Paul was to meet disciples in Ephesus who knew only the baptism of John and had never heard of the gift of the Spirit (Acts 19:1–2). The first Christians believed that they became sons of God and received the gift of the Spirit at their own baptism and in the accounts they wrote of Jesus they said the same of his; he became a Son of God and received the Spirit. Did they read their own beliefs back into the life of Jesus *or did their beliefs about baptism stem from Jesus' own experience*? If their beliefs about baptism did originate with Jesus, then their belief in baptism as the moment of resurrection will have been his experience also.

Second, the immersion in the Jordan. There was a 'curious and remarkable connection' in early Christian thought between the baptism of Christ and his descent into Hades, wrote J. H. Bernard in his introduction to the *Odes of Solomon*.[22] No explanation has been offered of the extraordinary fact that imagery used to describe the death of Jesus on the cross followed by descent into hell and resurrection is reproduced exactly in the imagery used of his baptism. Paul wrote to the Colossians that Jesus had overcome the principalities and powers by his death on the cross (Col. 2:15); Peter wrote that Jesus descended after his death to 'the spirits in prison' (1 Pet. 3:18–20) and he explains that this corresponds to the Christian's baptism. Much of the imagery used in the early churches, however, suggests that the descent and conflict took place at the Jordan and that Jesus released the captives by his descent into the waters of the Jordan. The imagery of resurrection is applied both to Easter and to Epiphany, the feast of the Baptism.

The *Letter of Barnabas* treats the baptism and the cross together: Isaiah's oracle, 'I will break in pieces the doors of bronze and cut asunder the bars of iron' (Isa. 45:2–3 also Ps. 107:16), is applied equally to the descent following the baptism and the descent following the crucifixion.[23] The descent and ascent proved the identity of Jesus as the LORD

---

which we must suppose the priestly writer (of Gen. 1) decisively rejected'. The battle with Leviathan and all the links to the mythology of Ugarit were 'banished from the account which was carefully formulated to stand at the head of the edited Pentateuch', how such ancient motifs surfaced in early Christianity.

(iv) The dove was the symbol of wisdom: Philo, *Heir* 126–7, *Names* 248.

(v) Cf. 4Q521 where the eschatological Spirit hovers over the poor, clearly using the imagery of Genesis 1:2.

4Q287 fr3 seems to say that the Holy Spirit (?settled) on the Messiah.

(vi) The Spirit comes into Jesus in Mark 1:10, but upon him in Matthew and Luke. In Bezae and Eusebius, Matthew and Luke also have *into*.

[22] Bernard, *Odes*, p. 32.

[23] The descent of the Messiah to release the dead was a Jewish tradition. Bernard, *Odes*, p. 36, cites two extracts from *Gen R.* (which I cannot trace):

But when they that are bound, they that are in Gehinnom, saw the light of the Messiah, they rejoiced to receive Him. . . . This is that which stands written: We shall rejoice and exult in Thee. When? When the captives climb out of hell and the Shechinah at their head.

but the fundamental ambiguity is there even in the New Testament; was Jesus declared Son of God as he ascended from the waters of baptism, as is implied by the alternative text of Luke 3:22: 'You are my beloved son. Today I have begotten you'; or was he declared Son of God by the resurrection from the dead as is implied by Paul in Romans 1:4: 'designated Son of God in power according to the spirit of holiness by his resurrection from the dead'? Underlying the awkward Greek of Paul's statement may be a recollection of the baptism; the spirit of holiness is a semitism for 'the Holy Spirit' and the only time when Jesus was declared by the Holy Spirit to be the Son of God and thus empowered was at his baptism. Paul here calls it his resurrection from the dead.

It was the *Odes of Solomon* that prompted Bernard's remarks about the similarity of Baptism and Passion imagery. In *Ode* 22 the Lord's triumph in 'the regions below' is described as loosing bonds and triumphing over the dragon with seven heads. Although many of the *Odes* seem to have a baptismal setting, there is nothing in this particular poem to indicate that it was a triumph over the dragon at baptism; what it does show is that the evil which the Lord overcame was envisaged as the dragon with seven heads, something not explicit in

---

These are undateable, but an interesting sidelight.

The question remains: what point in the life of Jesus was believed to be his descent to release the dead?

In *Ode* 17 the doors and bars of iron are opened by Christ but there is no context in the ministry. Bernard, pp. 82–3, thought it was at the baptism. *Ode* 42 speaks of shattering Sheol and rescuing people from the bonds of darkness. The rescue is their baptism because Christ places his name on their foreheads, but again there is no indication when Christ shattered death. Harris, *Odes and Psalms*, p. 123: '(*Ode* 24) may refer to the descent into Hades and to the Baptism as events happening in close connexion. I mean that it is not out of the region of reasonable criticism to suggest that in the earliest times the Baptism of Christ was the occasion of his triumph over Hades.' Melito's *Homily on the Pasch* 102 links the Passion to the triumph over the enemy. The Eucharistic prayer in Hippolytus' *Apostolic Tradition* is similar: Christ destroyed death, broke the chains of the devil and brought the righteous to the light by his Passion. The undateable *Descensus ad Inferos*, which may incorporate early material, is confused. The resurrected Rabbi Karinus reported that whilst he was still dead he had seen Satan and his ministers trying to make fast their doors as the King of Glory approached. Michael assured Seth: 'For the most beloved Son of God shall come down from heaven into the world and shall be baptized of John in the river Jordan: and then shall thy father Adam receive of this oil of mercy, and all they that believe in him.' Later John the Baptist recalled the baptism of Jesus: 'I baptized him in the river Jordan. I heard the voice of the Father out of heaven thundering upon him and proclaiming: This is my beloved Son in whom I am well pleased. I have received an answer from him that he would himself descend into hell.' There is no unambiguous reference here to descent at the Baptism. Murray, *Symbols*, pp. 325–9, has several examples from the Syrian church of the descent after the crucifixion, but observes that in iconography the resurrection is not depicted as breaking down the doors until the sixth century. In Revelation 1:17, the Living One who has the keys of Death and Hades suggests that this image of the resurrection goes back to the earliest period.

the New Testament as we usually read it. *Ode* 24 is equally enigmatic but seems to describe the terror inspired in the underworld by the baptism of Jesus; the chasms were submerged and perished. Other texts, both baptismal liturgies and the liturgies for Epiphany, are quite clear that the dragon was overcome in the waters of the Jordan at the moment of Jesus' baptism, fulfilling Psalm 74:13: 'Thou didst break the head of the dragons on the waters.' Cyril of Jerusalem explained to his catechumens: 'Since it was necessary to crush the heads of the dragon, he went down into the water to bind the strong man so that we should take authority to tread on serpents and scorpions.'[24] An Epiphany hymn attributed to Severus of Antioch says that Christ by his baptism opened the way to heaven, brought down the Holy Spirit and crushed the head of the evil serpent on the waters. Coptic and Ethiopian prayers to consecrate the baptismal water recall how the Lord bound the seas and sealed the deeps and shattered the heads of the dragon in the water.[25]

[24] Cyril (mid fourth century), *Catechesis III, De Baptismo,* PG xxxiii 441. The dragon of Job 40:23 was the devil whom Christ overcame at his baptism. From early in the third century there is Hippolytus, *On the Holy Theophany* 2, PG x 853: 'For the waters saw him and were afraid. They almost broke from their place and burst their boundary. . . .' We have seen the creator of all things in the form of a servant'; and ibid. 4: Jesus at the baptism 'hid the dignity of his divinity to elude the snares of the dragon'. Origen's free rendering of Psalm 77:17 (Eng, 77:16) is: 'The abysses revealed the subterranean powers who were thrown into disorder by the Parousia of Christ', PG xii 1540. Theodoret saw Psalm 74:13 as prefiguring the overthrow of demonic powers by the grace of baptism. Pseudo-Epiphanius describes the descent of Christ in terms of Psalm 24:8: 'Who is the King of Glory?' and the reply is, 'It is he who has broken the heads of your dragons in the waters of the Jordan,' PG xliii 460. An Epiphany hymn of Cosmos of Jerusalem, PG xcviii 465: 'Adam renews what was corrupted in the streams of the Jordan and the King of Eternity breaks the heads of the writhing dragon.'

[25] A Greek baptismal liturgy has: 'You sanctified the streams of the Jordan having sent your Holy Spirit from heaven and shattered the head of the dragon writhing there.' A Coptic prayer for the consecration of the baptismal water includes: 'You have broken the head of the dragon on the waters.' An Armenian baptismal prayer has: . . . 'thou didst close up the abysses and make them fast . . . thou didst bruise the head of the dragon upon the waters'.

All these examples are taken from Bernard, *Odes,* pp. 32–9 and 93–6. He drew his examples from Denzinger, *Ritus Orientalium* and Conybeare, *Rituale Armenorum.*

There is also the mysterious *Hymn of the Pearl* in the *Acts of Thomas.* A prince from the east has been sent by his father to recover a pearl which is guarded by a serpent. When he has recovered the pearl he will be able to wear the royal robe again and to become joint heir with his brother. He forgets his identity and his mission but his memory is restored by reading a letter from his father which flies to him. He then recovers the pearl by overcoming the serpent with the name of his father, leaves behind the filthy garment he has been wearing as a disguise and is guided back home by the light of the mysterious letter. He is reunited with his royal robe and becomes his former self. The *Hymn* is an early composition, possibly known in the second century. It describes perfectly the baptism experience of Jesus as I am reconstructing it; whether a sequence such as this was known in first-century Palestine and whether the *Hymn* is a vestige of Jesus' own experience is beyond our knowing. (But see Chapter 4, p. 106, suggesting that the parable of the pearl of great price was autobiographical and recorded Jesus'

Less explicit, but on the same theme, is the imagery in *Hermas*. The stones of the living temple have been brought up from the depths (*Vis.* 3.5.2); the apostles and teachers have descended into the waters to preach to the dead (*Sim.* 9.16.5) and presumably Christ had done the same (cf. *Gospel of Peter* 10). The most striking evidence of all, however, is to be found in the Book of Revelation, a topic to which I shall return.[26]

Per Lundberg has also shown that the image of Jesus as the rising Sun appears in the liturgies for Epiphany and for Easter.[27] The association of baptism and resurrection is thus carried by several distinct

---

discovery of his identity as the LORD and what this was to cost him.) The parable of the Prodigal Son seems to be the exoteric version of the same teaching (the two sons, the far country, the fallen state of the second son, the return and the gift of the best robe) adapted by Luke's community to express their relationship with Judaism.

[26] Passages such as 2 Timothy 1:10 suggest that Christ abolished death and this implies a conflict. It seems likely that the idea of Jesus overcoming the power of Satan, and therefore of death, at his baptism, was part of the early tradition, a descent into the waters of the abyss to release the dead. Per Lundberg concluded his study, *La Typologie Baptismale*, by noting that Paul's description of the resurrection 'exclut toute activité de la part de Christ dans l'Hades', p. 26. He makes resurrection an act of God and Jesus the passive recipient: God raised him (Rom. 6:4). This implies that Paul has altered the understanding both of baptism and of resurrection, something we have suspected already. The conquest of hostile powers was part of the ancient rites of kingship, the preliminary to exaltation and enthronement. The imagery of baptism confirms what we have seen elsewhere; that the earliest New Testament resurrection tradition is based not on that of reviving the dead but on that of the triumph and ascent of the priest-king. The sequence of ideas in Hebrews 2 implies that the conflict with death happened before the high priest made the atonement: '. . . that through death he might destroy . . . the devil . . . so that he might become . . . a high priest . . . to make expiation' (Heb. 2:14–17).

[27] (i) Per Lundberg argued that it was fruitless to compare the baptismal liturgies of Epiphany and Easter, since the words were the same on both occasions. Rather, it was necessary to compare prayers peculiar to each feast: 'Car il apparait . . . qu'ainsi que dans les formules liturgiques de l'Epiphanie Jésus est figuré sous l'image du Soleil, la même image . . . et souvent appliqué au Ressuscité au temps du Pâques,' p. 168. For Easter he cites, among others, the Easter homily of Pseudo Epiphanius, where Christ is the Sun and Clement of Alexandria, who speaks of the Sun of the resurrection. For Epiphany he cites a Greek hymn: 'Today the never-setting Sun is born and the world is illuminated by the light of the Lord' . . . 'the dark mist of the world is cleared by your appearance', Conybeare, pp. 429, 433; and a Nestorian hymn: 'The Excellent and desired Sun: its light hath shone forth in the world . . . and the error of Satan was extinguished before the brightness of his rays: and the dominion of the demons was taken away', Conybeare, *Rituale*, p. 354. One might add from Hippolytus, *On the Holy Theophany*, 10, PG x 861 that the newly baptized emerged shining like the sun.

(ii) Selwyn, 'Tabernacles', discussing the imagery of the *Odes*, remarked, p. 225: '. . . the question arises, how all this wealth of symbolic phrase and usage can be found in its flourishing exuberance around the ceremony of Christian baptism.' He argued that all three great Jewish festivals were taken into the Church; Passover became Easter, Weeks became Whitsun and Tabernacles became the feast of Theophany and Epiphany of the Eastern churches. He suggested that the original setting of Isaiah 60–2 was Tabernacles, the day when the LORD was to become king over all the earth (Zech. 14.9). This would explain how the white robes of Tabernacles became the white robes of the great multitude before the throne of the Lamb in Revelation 7.9–10 and will prove important for the discussion of the Transfiguration in Chapter 4.

patterns of imagery and must raise the question: had there been a tradition which, from the very beginning, understood that Jesus' resurrection was his baptism? Had the death of Jesus originally been understood by some of his followers as something other than his crucifixion? And how could this have come about if it did not originate with Jesus?

Baptism and ascent as Son of God is also implicit in 2 *Esdras* 13, a Jewish text from the end of the first century reworked by a Christian hand. In his vision, Ezra sees a Man rising from the sea and flying on clouds to the top of a great mountain. A fiery stream from his mouth destroys the enemies who mass against him. The vision is similar to the Man vision in Daniel 7, but Daniel says nothing of the origin of the Man figure, whereas 2 *Esdras* shows that he rose to heaven from the water. Both Daniel and 2 *Esdras* give interpretations, but in neither case does the explanation exactly fit with all the details of the vision, a sign that older material was being reworked. What that older material might have been is another question which cannot be answered, but 2 *Esdras* shows that this older material was understood at the end of the first Christian century to refer to the Son of God Most High rising from the water and going up to heaven (2 *Esd.* 13:32). After his triumph in heaven he comes back down to earth and draws to himself another multitude, in this case the ten lost tribes.

Baptism and the Mystical Tradition of the Temple

There were, as we have seen, mystics who believed that human beings could be transformed into angels, sons of God, when they ascended to the presence of God and that this state is what the earliest Christian sources described as the resurrection. There are also indications that Jesus had such experiences and that he ascended to heaven at his baptism and became a son of God. A variety of evidence in early tradition links the baptism with merkavah phenomena and with the priesthood where these secret practices had their origin.[28]

First there is tradition of the fire or the light on the Jordan. Justin told Trypho of a fire which was kindled in the Jordan when Jesus went into the water, before the Spirit came upon him (*Trypho 88*, PG vi 685). Other second-century sources describe the fire but only the *Sibylline Oracles* suggest that this was a hostile fire from which Jesus escaped.[29] The *Gospel of the Ebionites* describes a light which appeared

---

[28] See my *The Gate of Heaven*, Chapter 4.

[29] Other second-century sources describe the fire but only the *Sibylline Oracles* (OTP 1) 6:6 suggest that this was a hostile fire from which Jesus escaped: 'He will escape the fire and be the first to see delightful God coming in the spirit in the wings of a dove', 'Vaincu par l'eau et par le baptême de Jésus', Bertrand, *Le Baptême*, p. 128.

Or was this the fire through which all who approached the throne had to pass? See below n. 33. *Sib* 7:84 has '. . . your baptism through which you were revealed out of fire'.

after the descent of the Spirit and the voice from heaven. John's reaction is like Saul's on the road to Damascus; he asks the LORD to baptize him. The *Gospel of the Ebionites*, described thus by Epiphanius, was clearly a compilation of several New Testament traditions, but his comments on the Ebionites show that they believed Jesus became the Son of God at his baptism.[30] The light that shone around and the recognition of Jesus as LORD would have been consistent with this belief. Two witnesses to the Old Latin of Matthew 3:15 add to the text that a great light shone from the water at the moment of the baptism and the crowd were afraid.[31]

There have been various attempts to explain this phenomenon; one attempt may be found in Origen's remarks on Luke 3:16: 'He will baptize you with the Holy Spirit and with fire' (*Homily 24 on Luke*, PG xiii 1864). John, he said, predicted that Jesus would baptize with Spirit and with fire; the baptism by the Spirit was at Pentecost but scripture does not record the baptism by fire. This, he says, was the third baptism, the means by which those who had received the baptisms of water and Spirit were able to enter the heavenly glory. Jesus himself stood in the river of fire, next to the flaming sword which barred the way to the presence of God, ready to baptize them into the presence. The river of fire, then, was the boundary between earth and heaven. The fire in the Jordan could well have been a sign, for those who recognized it, that this was Jesus' fiery baptism, his passage into the presence of God when he became a son

---

[30] 'They say that Jesus was begotten of the seed of a man, and was chosen; and so by the choice of God he was called the Son of God from the Christ that came into him from above in the likeness of a dove. They deny that he was begotten of God the Father and say that he was created as one the archangels, yet greater . . .' Epiphanius, *Against Heresies* I.ii.30.16, PG xli 431.

[31] (i) Codex Vercellensis, fourth or fifth century has 'et cum baptizaretur, lumen ingens circumfulsit de aqua, ita ut timerent omnes qui advenerant'. Codex Sangermanensis, seventh century, has 'et cum baptizaretur Jesus, lumen magnum fulgebat de aqua, ita ut timerent omnes qui congregati sunt'.

(ii) Also known in Epiphanius I.ii.16, PG xli 432, and in Ephrem's *Commentary on the Diatessaron* IV.5; 'And when he had seen from the bright light upon the water and by the voice from heaven. . . .' Petersen, *Diatessaron*, argues that the combined evidence of Justin and the Syriac tradition points to an early tradition, p. 20: 'It shows that traditions in the Diatessaron are sometimes connected with primitive recensions which were either so obscure that they failed to be included in the main Greek manuscript tradition, or, alternately, were actively rejected by later Christians'; cf. also his note: 'In the case of the light at Jesus' baptism, the presence of the tradition in both eastern and western Christendom in the second century seems to point more towards rejection rather than ignorance.' This is exactly Ehrman's conclusion, see below n. 43(ii); 'Today I have begotten you' was also the older reading but removed by later 'orthodoxy'. See also on the fire/light tradition, Bammel 'Die Täufertraditionen'.

(iii) Scholem, *Jewish Gnosticism*, p. 78, quotes from the *Hekhalot Zutarti* (Schäfer #350) a passage describing the *yored merkavah* as a Man who is able to walk in rivers of fire.

of God.[32] This theme appears elsewhere in Origen and also in Theodotus who describes a river of fire through which the 'seed' must pass if it is to reach the Pleroma (*Excerpts* 38, PG ix 677). The veil of the temple shielded 'things' from its brightness and Jesus, the high priest, stood behind the veil in the Holy of Holies to assist those who passed through. The *hylikon*, the material, was burned away 'in its passage through the fire' (*Excerpts* 52, PG ix 683) and renewed. Thus, according to Theodotus, the river of fire was the final purification. If his account is accurate, the river of fire would have been known to Valentinus in the middle of the second century and thus could well have been what Paul had in mind when he wrote: 'the fire will test what sort of work each man has done . . . If any man's work is burned up he will suffer loss, though he himself will be saved, but only as through fire' (1 Cor. 3:13, 15). Theodotus describes the high priest/archangel entering the place of fire; for him this fire imagery was located in the temple tradition of Israel and Jesus was the high priest.

The river of fire flowing from the throne of God is mentioned in other Jewish texts; the earliest is Daniel 7:10: 'A stream of fire issued and came forth from before him.' Nothing more is said in Daniel, but there is Malachi's prophecy that when the LORD appeared in his temple he would be like a fire to purify the sons of Levi, the priests who thought of themselves as the angels on earth (Mal. 3:2–3). Later texts describe the angels around the throne purifying themselves in a river of fire before joining the heavenly liturgy (3 *En.* 36, Schäfer #920). Enoch himself was transformed by fire into the angel prince Metatron, but a river is not mentioned.[33] These texts are impossible to date but as similar ideas

---

[32] (i) Alter, *Biblical Narrative*, Chapter 3, shows the necessity for reading any work within the grid of conventions upon which it operates. 'One of the chief difficulties we encounter as modern readers in perceiving the artistry of biblical narrative is precisely that we have lost most of the keys to the conventions out of which it was shaped. The professional biblical scholars have not offered much help in this regard . . .' p. 47. 'Reading any body of literature involves a specialised mode of perception in which every culture trains its members from childhood. As modern readers of the Bible we need to relearn something of this mode of perception that was second nature to the original audiences', p. 62.

(ii) Lodahl, *Shekinah*, p. 154, makes a similar point, '. . . it is worth remembering that the creeds of Chalcedon and Nicea gave no attention to Jewish context of Jesus'.

[33] (i) See Edsman, *Le Baptême de Feu*, esp. pp. 19–31, which survey the evidence for fiery baptism in Jewish sources. Most texts cited are too late to be directly relevant to Christian origins. The mediaeval Ma'ayan Hokmah (text in A. Jellinek, *Bet Ha Midrasch*, p. 60) describes the river of fire, named Rigyon, which was the breath of the four living creatures, flowing from the throne of Glory. When the Holy One has judged his angel servants they dip themselves in the river of fire and are renewed. The hot charcoal which remains is tipped on the heads of sinners (!) The baptism of fire transforms them so that they are no longer 'sons of Adam'. Gaster, *Studies and Texts*, vol. 1, pp. 124ff. suggests that this material could have been a source of the Christian *Apocalypse of Peter*. A similar tradition appears in *Gen R.* 78:1: new angels are created daily from the river of fire, the perspiration of the living creatures. Cf. *b.Hag* 13b. I suspect that the original passage through the river of fire can be detected in Isaiah 33:13–22: the righteous

were known to Theodotus who recorded the teachings of Valentinus, they could have been known in the middle of the second century.

The most obvious similarities to the account of the fire in the Jordan are in the stories of R. Johannan ben Zakkai and his disciples, who were contemporaries of the first Christians. R. Johannan saw fire burning around one of his disciples, R. Eleazar, as he expounded the mysteries of the merkavah. Other phenomena which accompanied the exposition of the mysteries were earth tremors, a rainbow appearing in a darkened sky, dancing angels and a voice from heaven. Halperin suggested that the tongues of fire at Pentecost had their origin in a merkavah experience such as this, but there are other points of contact too. The voice from heaven, according to the accounts in the Palestinian and Babylonian Targums, invited the master and his disciples to ascend to a place above, where couches were prepared for them and cushions spread out. They had been allocated a special position. Compare here the account in Mark 10:35–40 where James and John, two of the three who had witnessed the Transfiguration, ask to be given the places of honour when their Rabbi ('Teacher') has his place in glory. Jesus replies by asking if they can endure the baptism with which he is baptized, implying that this is the means of access to such glory.[34] Halperin's comments on the traditions about R. Johannan and his disciples are worth pondering. Why, he asked, did the narrators say nothing about the merkavah which these sages were expounding? It was not their purpose: 'What they wanted was to show the wondrous

---

person can dwell with the devouring fire and will stand on the heights to see the king in his beauty. It may also lie behind the enigmatic references in the Old Testament to 'passing through the fire to Moloch', i.e. to the King.

Edsman suggested that baptism of fire was the rite of transition to the heavenly state:

'Si donc le passage de l'existence terrestre à l'existence céleste, et si donc les formes sous lesquelles s'effectue ce passage, sont conditionées par l'action réciproque entre culte et eschatologie, cette réciprocité présente une égale valeur pour l'état consecutif à ce passage. D'un côté la vie céleste se voit realisée dans l'assemblée cultuelle, d'un autre côté l'existence éternelle peut étre definie comme le culte pur et parfait comme la louange céleste sans fin', p. 135.

(ii) Hippolytus, *On the Holy Theophany* 4, PG x 856, has John the Baptist ask Jesus: 'Baptize me with the fire of divinity.' An *agraphon* recorded in Didymus on Psalm 88:8, PG xxxix 1488: 'He that is near me is near the fire. He that is far from me is far from the kingdom.'

[34] D. J. Halperin, *The Faces*, pp. 13–14.

(i) The fire on R. Eleazar, quoting *y.Ḥag* 2:1, *b.Ḥag* 14b, and the Geniza Fragment of *Mekhilta de R. Simeon ben Yoḥai*: '... R. Eleazar b. Arakh expounded until fire burned all around him. When R. Johannan b. Zakkai saw that fire was burning all around him, he descended from his ass, kissed him and said to him: R. Eleazar b. Arakh, happy is she who bore you. . . .' Parallels to the story suggest that R. Eleazar had asked his teacher to expound the merkavah and R. Johannan had refused because the merkavah could not be expounded by an individual unless he was a scholar who understood on his own.

(ii) The places of honour, quoting *b.Ḥag* 14b.

greatness of the ancient sages. They did this by describing the vivid tokens by which God and the angels showed their regard for the way these men expounded Scripture'.[35] These stories about the sages of the merkavah were circulating in the period of Christian origins and may well explain why Jesus' baptism was described in a similar way. Reticence about the actual merkavah experience may account for the secret tradition mentioned especially in Clement and Origen.[36]

Origen offers other evidence that the baptism of Jesus was linked to the merkavah, and this brings us to the third theme, that of the open heavens. In his *Homily 1 on Ezekiel* 4–7, PG xiii 672–4, he compares Ezekiel's vision of the merkavah to the baptism of Jesus, implying that what the prophet saw, Jesus also saw.[37] He gives an extraordinary account of the baptism. The heavens were opened. They had been shut, but were opened, unlocked, at the coming of Christ, so that the Spirit could come upon him in the form of a dove. He then quotes Psalm 68:19: Jesus ascended to heaven and received gifts (not the version quoted in Eph. 4:8 which has 'he gave gifts'). He then completes the quotation from Ephesians to the effect that Jesus distributed the gifts of the Spirit which he had received on his ascent when the heavens opened at his baptism. After Jesus had thus opened the heavens, the angels were able to ascend and descend upon him (John 1:51) and to serve him (Matt. 4:11; Mark 1:13). Halperin suggests that Origen's account of the baptism was the result of his contacts with Jewish scholars in Caesarea[38] and derived from the association of the merkavah and the Sinai revelation which had by his time become established. The ascent of Jesus at his baptism was modelled on the ascent of Moses at Sinai, he said, and all the traditions about Moses as the heavenly hero were transferred to Jesus. Further, the Israelites at Sinai were believed to have experienced a death and resurrection experience at Sinai, dying at the sound of the voice of God, but being revived by the dew of Resurrection. This is suggested as the link to Christian baptism. That there are similarities is beyond question, but I suspect that the point of contact with the merkavah tradition goes back to the time of Jesus himself and that Origen, far from having recently discovered these

[35] Halperin, *The Faces*, p. 15.

[36] E.g. Clement, *Misc* v. 10 *passim*, PG ix 93–101; vi.7, PG ix 284; Origen, *Celsus* 3:37, 60; PG xi 969, 1000; *Celsus* 5.19, PG xi 1208; *Celsus* 6.6 *passim*, PG xi 1297; *First Principles*, Preface 3, PG xi 116; *On Matthew* 7.2, PG xiii 833; *On John* II.174, PG xiv 164; VI.76, 83, PG xiv 223, 226. Especially *On John* VI.23–4, PG xiv 205: Isaiah and Ezekiel saw the throne and its mysteries and 'Those who have been perfected in former generations have known no less than the things which were revealed to the apostles by Christ, since the one who taught the apostles revealed the unspeakable mysteries of religion to them.' See also Chapter 4.

[37] Both vision (Ezek. 1:1) and baptism (Epiphany) happened in the fourth month of the Jewish year reckoned from the autumn. Both Jesus and Ezekiel were thirty years old (Ezek. 1:1; Luke 3:23), the age when priests began to serve (Num. 4:3).

[38] Halperin, *The Faces*, p. 328.

ideas through contact with the Rabbis of Caesarea, was recording accurately what many had known for a long time.[39]

Mark's account of the opening heavens differs from those of Matthew and Luke; for Mark, the vision was granted to Jesus alone and he alone saw the heavens 'rent'.[40] Those who understood the symbolism of the temple would have linked this with the rending of the temple curtain at the moment of Jesus' death, because the curtain was hung across the entrance to the Holy of Holies, the heavens. Access to the holy place implies the Day of Atonement. The Letter to the Hebrews says Jesus the high priest entered the sanctuary after the crucifixion (Heb. 10:19–20) but Hippolytus (early third century), in his *On the Holy Theophany* 6, PG x 857, uses Day of Atonement images in his description of the baptism.

> For the heavens were shut before this (i.e. the baptism of Jesus); the region above was inaccessible. We would in that case descend to the lower parts but we would not ascend to the upper. He also renewed the old man and committed to him again the sceptre of adoption. For straightway 'the heavens were opened to him'. A reconciliation took place of the visible and the invisible; the celestial orders were filled with joy, the diseases of the earth were healed; secret things were made known; those at enmity were restored to amity.

[39] The association of merkavah practices with Christianity would explain why there was a change in attitude towards the merkavah mystics in the second and third centuries. Halperin suggests that the merkavah had become linked to Sinai because Ezekiel 1 was read in the synagogues at Shabuot together with the account of Sinai. In second- century Palestine, he said, 'the preachers fed their people's hungry imaginations on the glories of the God who had given them his Torah', p. 37. Those who edited the Mishnah, however, had an attitude of 'chilly and apprehensive reserve', p. 25, and so they warned against the merkavah and all associated with it. The 'merkavah scare' of the early third century, p. 28, was followed by a flowering of mysticism in Babylonia in the fourth century where the character of merkavah experience changed into something more magical. Chernus offers a different explanation; that the rabbis chose to 'depict the Sinai event in terms drawn from that (i.e. the merkavah) tradition', p. 13, in order to legitimate the merkavah. The tradition of ecstatic experience already existed and there was a danger that the experience 'might become schismatic and even heretical, leading out of Judaism and into Gnosticism' . . . 'The problem, then, (and it may have been the over-riding problem for the second-century tannaim) was to integrate these new experiences into the total gestalt of Jewish religiosity as the tannaim were attempting to shape it', p. 13. Now if the reshaping of Judaism needed to redefine the associations of the merkavah, can we be sure that the threat was from Gnosticism? Chernus rightly observes that the nature of merkavah and gnostic ascents differed, the latter being a post-mortem hope and the former an experience of this life. It was the Christians who were telling of an experience very similar to that of the mystics, the experience of being raised with Christ. The 'merkavah scare' of the early third century coincided with Origen's use of the merkavah to describe Jesus' baptism. Was Origen introducing the merkavah to Christianity? (I think not!)

[40] Matthew 3:16 has 'the heavens were opened', Luke 3:22 has the singular. Davies and Allison, *Matthew*, p. 329, suggest that the change from 'rent' to 'opened' may be a sign of the influence of Ezekiel 1:1 and that a distinction be made between 'this type of revelation and that in which the heaven opens in order to allow the seer to journey into the upper regions as in Revelation 4:1, *T.Lev.* 2:6, 5:1'. They offer no supporting

The heavens are first opened by the baptism, not by post-crucifixion ascent, and although he does not mention the blood and the temple curtain, the imagery of reconciliation and healing which Hippolytus uses is drawn from the Day of Atonement.[41]

The voice at the baptism, the fourth theme, was another merkavah feature, as can be seen from the stories of R. Johannan and his disciples.[42] Again, the accounts differ. In Mark and Matthew the words are a conflation of Psalm 2:7, 'You are my son', and Isaiah 42:1, 'in whom my soul delights'. Jesus is presented as the Son and the Servant to whom the Spirit is given. The variant reading in several texts of Luke has only Psalm 2:7, 'Today I have begotten you.' It is obvious why such a reading might have been removed from the text in the interests of later orthodoxy, but it is perhaps too simplistic to say that it crept into the text as a result of scribal error, completing the familiar quotation from Psalm 2:7 instead of conflating with Isaiah 42:1. Psalm 2:7 in its entirety was applied to Jesus elsewhere in the New Testament, but in all other cases (Acts 13:33; Heb. 1:5; 5:5; cf. Rom. 1:4) 'Today I have begotten you' referred to the resurrection. There must have been some in the early church who thought that a resurrection text was appropriate to the baptism[43] and perhaps some who thought it better removed.

---

evidence. Rowland, *Open Heaven*, pp. 52–8, distinguishes between ascent visions and those experiences which communicate a revealed truth, often in dialogue with an angel. The examples he gives of visions without ascents are both post-Christian texts: 2 *Esdras* (OTP 1) from the end of the first century CE and *Syriac Baruch* (OTP 1) from the early second. This is significant as ascent was a sensitive issue at this time, possibly because of Christian claims. Daniel 7 describes an ascent, but from the point of view of an observer. Some texts of Matthew 3:16 (Bezae, Freerianus and several Latin) read 'The heavens were opened to him.' One wonders what this implies.

[41] Cf. Origen, *Homily 27 on Luke*, PG xiii 187, which also links the baptism with Jesus' ascent to heaven to bring down spiritual gifts.

[42] Halperin, *The Faces*, p. 14: When his disciples were expounding the merkavah a rainbow appeared in the sky, and a voice from heaven invited them to ascend to the places prepared for them. *b.Hag* 14b.

[43] (i) *Contra* Fitzmyer, *St. Luke*, p. 480:

Neither the descent of the Spirit upon Jesus, nor the recognition of him as 'Son,' nor the implication of his being Yahweh's Servant connote a messianic function. There is simply no evidence that the titles 'Son of God' or 'Servant of Yahweh' were regarded as messianic (i.e. belonging to an expected, future anointed agent of Yahweh) in pre-Christian Judaism. Hence Jesus' consecration must be understood more strictly as the Synoptic evangelists have themselves proposed it.

But is this so? If the resurrection had no messianic significance either (Lapide, *Resurrection*, p. 15), were the first Christians making an entirely new construction?

The words at the baptism present a major problem. The form which appears in the synoptic gospels is a conflation of Psalm 2:7 and an allusion to the Servant Songs, especially Isaiah 42:1.

(ii) Ehrman, *Corruption*, has argued that the Codex Bezae text of Luke 3:22, 'You are my Son, today I have begotten you', was the original and that 'orthodox scribes who could not abide its adoptivistic overtones "corrected" it into conformity with the parallel in Mark', p. 62. He shows that the reading was the ancestor of the old Latin of

THE RISEN LORD

There is also some doubt as to whose voice was heard: the Gospel of
the Hebrews (quoted by Jerome on Isa. 11:2) says that the Holy Spirit

Luke and was in the text known to Justin (*Trypho* 88), Clement of Alexandria
(*Instructor* 1.25.2), *The Gospel according to the Hebrews*, *The Gospel of the
Ebionites*, the *Didascalia*, Origen (*On John* 1:29, *Against Celsus* 1:41), Methodius
(*Symposium* 9). It is also found in Lactantius, Juvencus, Hilary, Tyconius, Augustine,
Acts of Peter and Paul 29. 'Except for the third-century manuscript 𝔓⁴, there is no
certain attestation of the other reading, the reading of a later manuscript, in this early
period', p. 62.

(iii) There are two other indications that Psalm 2:7 may have been original:

(a) The reading of 1Q28a II.11, *yolid*, begets, is almost certainly God 'begetting'
the Messiah. Barthelemy, *DJD* I, p. 117, said '. . . la lecture de ce mot apparait
pratiquement certaine', but there was agonized hesitation. Even Vermes, *Scrolls*, p.
121, now concedes that this is the reading and translates, 'When God will have
engendered the (priest)-Messiah. . . .' The allusion to Psalm 2:7 is apparent, as is
the link to Christian traditions of Jesus the priest-messiah from the time of his
baptism.

(b) Two of Jesus' temptations relate to the expectations of Psalm 2; Jesus was
taken to the pinnacle of the temple in Jerusalem – cf. 'I have set my king on Zion,
my holy hill,' Psalm 2:7; and Jesus was tempted by the power of the kingdoms of
the world – cf. 'Ask of me and I will make the nations your heritage', Psalm 2:8.
The rulers of the world are ordered to kiss the enthroned son, Psalm 2:12. One
cannot but be reminded of 3 *Enoch* 10, where the enthroned Metatron receives the
homage of the angel rulers and Mark 1:13: '. . . the Angels served him' and
Philippians 2:10: '. . . every knee should bow, in heaven . . .' In addition, there is
the undateable but possibly late first century AD *Life of Adam and Eve* (OTP 2)
chapters 12–16 which echoes these traditions. Satan was expelled from heaven
because he would not worship Adam who had been made in the image of God.
Some MSS of 14:2 say that the image of God was named Yahweh. Thus Satan fell
from heaven because he would not acknowledge Adam the Man who had received
the breath of God which made him into Yahweh, his image. There is here the same
double attribution of the Name as in 3 *Enoch*; both the divinity and the one who
becomes divine are named Yahweh. Enthronement is the moment of transformation
or apotheosis and Satan falls from heaven – cf. Luke 10:18: 'I saw Satan fall from
heaven . . .' All these suggest that Psalm 2:7 could well have been the original words
at the baptism and that the traditions of the first temple are not far beneath the
surface of the New Testament. Marcus,'Baptismal Vision', links Luke 10:18 to the
baptism: 'About the authenticity of this detached saying there can be little doubt;
the tradition would not have preserved such a "bolt out of the blue" if it were not
authentic, and the short vivid comparison of Satan's fall to . . . a flash of lightning
suggests a visionary experience. . . . Moreover, in contrast to other *NT* passages
dealing with the overthrow of Satan (John 12:31; 16:11; Rev. 12:7–12) *this one
does not connect that overthrow with Christ's death and exaltation to heaven*, but
implicitly ascribes it to a purely *theo*-logical cause' (my emphases). If the baptism
had been the original death and exaltation experience, this would fit perfectly with
the other *NT* evidence!

(iv) But how are we to account for the conflations with Isaiah 42:1, which is not used
in its LXX form but rather as a free translation into Greek? The *agapetos* of Mark and
Matthew is found also in Matthew 12:18 and is clearly another available rendering of
Isaiah 42:1. Since a primitive reading of John 1:34 has 'this is my Chosen Son' (𝔓⁵ and
the original text of Sinaiticus), like the 'Chosen' of LXX Isaiah 42:1, the Servant motif
was equally a part of the primitive tradition (see Davies and Allison, *Matthew*, pp.
337–8).

spoke and that Jesus was her first begotten son who would reign for ever. It also says that Jesus called the Holy Spirit his mother and that she took him by the hair and transported him up to Mount Tabor (Origen, *On John* II.87, PG xiv 132). This mode of travel was traditional for visionaries (e.g. Ezek. 8:3) and probably described Jesus' departure into the wilderness after the baptism. Mark says Jesus was 'driven by the Spirit' into the wilderness where he was tried by Satan. Mark's brief account adds that he was with the wild beasts and that angels were his servants. Some scholars have seen here a reference to the new Adam at peace with the wild beasts, others have suggested that the beasts were satanic forces which he overcame with the help of the angels.[44]

The account of the temptations in Matthew and Luke has details of the encounter with Satan and reveals that Jesus had been fasting, like the mystics. Two of the experiences are reminiscent of ascents: Jesus is taken to a pinnacle of the temple like Habakkuk and Enoch. He is also taken to a high mountain (Matt. 4:8) where he sees all the kingdoms of the world in a moment of time (Luke 4:5), like Ezekiel or Abraham in

---

(v) It is perhaps inappropriate to speak of deliberate conflation and so forth. Allusion to scripture, rather than quotation, is the characteristic of the apocalypses. The Book of Revelation is steeped in the Old Testament and yet has no verbatim quotation.

The conflation of texts might be better understood in the light of a story about R. Akiba and Ben Azzai.

> When they were stringing together words of the Torah, and from the words of the Torah to the Prophets and from the Prophets to the Writings, and the fire was burning around them and the words were rejoicing at their revelation at Sinai ... Ben Azzai was sitting and expounding and the fire burned around him ... (R. Akiba) said to him, 'Perhaps you were involved with the sections of the chariot?' He said to him, 'No, rather I was sitting and stringing together words of the Torah, and from the Torah to the Prophets and from the Prophets to the Writings and the words were rejoicing as at their revelation at Sinai, and they were as sweet as at their original revelation'. (*Song R.* 1:10.2)

The dangerous secrets of the tradition lay in the way the various parts of scripture were combined. Cf. also Underhill, *Mystic Way*, p. 87, that Jesus 'heard' the two texts at his baptism and gave them a special meaning and authority.

(vi) Vermes, *Scripture*, suggests that the words were derived from Genesis 22 and Isaiah 42; while one cannot agree that attempts to link the words to Psalms 2:7 are 'entirely useless and inconclusive' in view of the history of the text, an association with the Akedah, see below Chapter 3, n. 22, is quite possible. Such a link need not exclude associations with Psalm 2:7.

[44] Murray, *Covenant*, pp. 127–8 and notes.

T.Naphtali 2.4 (OTP 1): 'If you achieve the good, my children, men and angels will bless you, and God will be glorified through you among the gentiles. The devil will flee from you, wild animals will be afraid of you and the angels will stand by you.' The Christian character of this whole section of *T.Naphtali* makes it more likely that it depends on Mark 1:13 rather than vice versa. Murray favours the new Adam, at peace with the animals.

the *Apocalypse of Abraham*, or Enoch again.[45] When Mark wrote that Jesus was with the beasts and that the angels served him, he may well have been revealing the true nature of this desert experience, even if he was only the faithful recorder of what he did not fully understand. Beasts would be a normal experience for a man in the desert, but angels suggest something more. I suspect that the beasts and angels were around the throne of God and that the experience in the desert resembled that in Revelation 5.[46]

The Book of Revelation is largely pre-Christian; the material was known to Jesus in his formative years, and the visions not only inspired him but were the framework within which he interpreted his own experiences.[47] The original core of Revelation was a description of the Day of Atonement at the end of the tenth Jubilee, as were the three visions which are now the *Similitudes of Enoch*. Jesus had originally been caught up in the fervent expectations of the Baptist, expecting an imminent outpouring of wrath. The vision of the one hundred and forty four thousand sealed from the twelve tribes was John's vision of those who would be saved by the seal of God on their foreheads to protect them from the wrath, that is, by his baptism (Rev. 7:1–8; cf.

[45] Habakkuk was set on a tower, i.e. the temple, to see his vision (Hab. 2:1); Enoch was taken by three angels to a high tower to see all history unfolding before him (*1 En.* 87:3) or, as Metatron, he showed Ishmael the curtain before the throne with all history depicted on it (*3 En.* 45). Ezekiel was placed on a high mountain to receive his vision (Ezek. 40:2). Abraham was taken up to stand before the throne and then looked down to see all the history of the world, in effect in a moment of time (*Apoc. Abr.* chapters 21–30; OTP 1).

[46] There are problems with the Greek words. The beasts in Mark are *theria*, as in Daniel 7 (LXX and Theod.); the beasts in Revelation 4 are *zoa*, as in LXX Ezekiel 1. But the Hebrew of Ezekiel 1 has *ḥayyot* and the Aramaic of Daniel 7 has *ḥeywan*. Halperin, *The Faces*, p. 95: 'In the Hebrew or Aramaic substrate that many scholars detect behind the bizarre Greek of Revelation, I cannot imagine how the two would have been distinguished.'

[47] (i) The Book of Revelation is far from being the unsealed prophecy it was intended to be (Rev. 22:10). A traditional account of its origins still prevails: that John, not the evangelist, received the visions on Patmos during a time of persecution. It is recognised that it contains many allusions to the Old Testament and much pre-Christian material. The only significant challenge to this consensus was made by Ford, *Revelation*, but her suggestions have been largely ignored or dismissed. Revelation 4–11, she said, came from the circle of John the Baptist before the time of Jesus and Revelation 12–22, though of a later date, also originated with his disciples. She is broadly correct. I would not agree that the visions originated with John the Baptist, p. 37, but they certainly shaped his preaching and the expectations of his contemporaries, one of whom was Jesus. The visions were enriched by Jesus and by the inner group of his disciples, those who had been given the secrets of the kingdom. One of these was John the Evangelist, and I suspect that it was his interpretation of Jesus' visions which ensured that the Book of Revelation was used by the Church. See Chapter 5.

(ii) Charlesworth, *Jesus*, p. 38, said: 'Certainly, Jesus was not one of the apocalyptists' but then concluded that 'the impact of Jewish apocalypticism and apocalyptic thought upon Jesus is undeniable and pervasive', p. 42.

Ps. Sol 15:1–9).[48] Jesus had gone to John to receive the seal but John had recognized him as One who was to come. Justin (*Trypho* 8, PG vi 493) records a Jewish belief that 'the Messiah is unknown and does not even know himself and has no power until Elijah comes to anoint him and make him manifest to all'. This tradition is unknown elsewhere, but fits well with John 1:26, that the Messiah was already among his people but unknown to them.[49] John revealed the Messiah not only to the people but also to Jesus himself. The prophetic word: 'Behold the Lamb of God who takes away the sin of the world' (John 1:29) was the moment of revelation for Jesus, who then found himself caught up in the vision recorded in Revelation 4–5.

The slain Lamb of Revelation 5, filled with the sevenfold spirit of God, is the royal high priest, the Servant who has poured out his life as a sin offering and then approached the throne. In the second temple this had become the ritual of taking blood into the Holy of Holies and sprinkling it where the throne had been. The beasts and the elders in the vision acknowledge the Servant/Lamb and worship, as the heavenly host in *3 Enoch* worship Metatron, the exalted Enoch who has been enthroned (*3 En.* 10, Schäfer #894). The Lamb then takes the scroll of heavenly secrets, just as Metatron is given the secrets after his enthronement (*3 En.* 11, Schäfer #895) and the Servant becomes wise[50] after his exaltation: 'Behold my servant shall become wise, he shall be exalted and lifted up and shall be very high (Isa. 52:14). The seven angels with their trumpets release the wrath and this section ends at Revelation 11:18 with the song of triumph: 'Thou hast taken thy great power and begun to reign.'

This vision showed what Jesus had to accomplish: the sacrifice of the Servant, the Lamb, which would inaugurate the Atonement and save his people from the imminent wrath. (This will be the theme of Chapter 3.) His followers saw the vision fulfilled in the crucifixion, but

---

[48] Thus Davies and Allison, *Matthew*, p. 322, but also CD VII MS B: 'The humble of the flock are those who watch for Him. They shall be saved at the time of the visitation whereas the others shall be delivered up to the sword when the Anointed of Aaron and Israel shall come, as it came to pass at the time of the former Visitation concerning which God said by the hand of Ezekiel: They shall put a mark on the foreheads of those who sigh and groan (Ezek. ix.4). But the others were delivered up to the avenging sword of the Covenant.'

[49] (i) Justin might have made up the tradition to fit the evidence of John's gospel, but Enoch was also 'hidden'. 'Before these things Enoch was hidden, and no-one of the children of men knew where he was hidden and where he abode and what had become of him' (*1 En.* 12:1).
(ii) Ezra's vision of the Man from the sea: 'As for your seeing a man come up from the heart of the sea, this is he whom the Most High has been keeping for many ages, who will himself deliver his creation. . . . When these things come to pass and the signs occur which I showed you before, then my Son will be revealed whom you saw as a man coming up from the sea. . . .' 2 Esdras 13, vv. 25–6, 32.

[50] The verb is *śkl*, which in Daniel 12:3 is used for 'the wise' who will shine like the brightness of the firmament.

it did not originate with them. The accounts of the temptations in the desert faithfully reflect Jesus' struggle with this vision; he was with the beasts and the elders before the throne and then Satan offered him other ways to take power and begin his reign, to have authority over the kingdoms of the world. 'If you are the Son of God', the words of Satan, are also an accurate recollection of this struggle. The vision of the Lamb did determine the way he took and he finally accepted its implications in Gethsemane.[51]

'And God's temple in heaven was opened and the ark of the covenant was seen' (Rev. 11:19) is the start of another sequence which describes the making of the royal high priest, his initial ascent rather than the Day of Atonement. The ancient kingmaking is described in Psalm 89:

> Of old thou didst speak in a vision to thy faithful one and say:
> 'I have set the crown upon one who is mighty,
> I have exalted one chosen from the people.
> I have found David, my servant;
> With my holy oil I have anointed him . . . (Ps. 89:19–20)

Psalm 2 has the king set on the LORD's holy hill and declared to be his son: 'Today I have begotten you . . . I will make the nations your heritage . . . you shall break them with a rod of iron' (Ps. 2:7–9). It has also been suggested that Psalm 74 gives a glimpse of the kingmaking:[52]

> Thou didst break the heads of the dragons on the waters;
> Thou didst crush the heads of Leviathan (Ps. 74:13–14)

The king then re-established the cosmic covenant.

---

[51] The Man Figure in Daniel 7 was enthroned and given an everlasting dominion over all nations but there is no indication of what the Man did before he was taken up to the throne.

[52] (i) Day, *Conflict*, p. 194, suggested that the *Chaoskampf* was part of the Autumn Festival:

> Since both the Feast of Tabernacles (cf. Jud. 9:27) and the festal theme of the king-god in conflict with the chaos waters were appointed from the Canaanites, it is reasonable to suppose that this motif was also a feature of the Canaanite Autumn Festival (p. 2).

The Leviathan of Psalm 74:14 could have been the Ugaritic dragon which had seven heads (another Ugaritic link to Revelation 12).

(ii) Bauckham, *Climax*, pp. 185–98, discusses the dragon. He is dubious about the Ugaritic link in the first century AD, p. 186 and suggests Isaiah 26:16–27:1 as the likely source; the woman giving birth and the defeat of Leviathan. The conflict between the woman and the dragon derives from the enmity between the woman and the snake in Genesis 3:15. If we knew who Eve had been before she was historicized, it might be possible to locate this piece of mythology also!

Bauckham's dragon has many roots, deriving 'not so much from a single living myth on which John depended as from a fresh combination of associations creating a new symbol', p. 198. The dragon may have acquired all sorts of associations – that is how apocalyptic literature renewed itself – but for the Palestinian Christians among whom the book of Revelation almost certainly originated, the dragon was the monster who opposed Yahweh at the creation and the king at his inauguration.

The sequence from Revelation 11:19–12:10 is the kingmaking as recalled by the visionaries with whom Jesus spent his formative years. First the heavens opened and the temple was seen as in Levi's vision (*T.Lev.* 18). The ark was seen, which means that the sanctuary was open to admit the high priest. The ark had been hidden for centuries but, they believed, in the day of the Anointed One it would be restored, along with the fire, the lamp, the Spirit and the Cherubim.[53]

Then there are the signs of theophany: thunder and lightning, voices and earthquake and hail. In the old tradition this had been a sign of the LORD coming to rescue his faithful one from a strong enemy in the waters.

> From his temple he heard my voice,
> And my cry to him reached his ears.
> Then the earth reeled and rocked;
> The foundations also of the mountains trembled . . .
> The LORD thundered in the heavens,
> . . . He reached from on high and took me,
> He drew me out of many waters,
> He delivered me from my strong enemy
> And from those who hated me (Ps. 18:6, 13, 16, 17).[54]

The divine figure who appears in this theophany (and the context suggests that she emerges from the temple) is a woman clothed with the sun. According to Ben Sira 24:10 the woman who served in the tabernacle on Zion was Wisdom, and here, embedded in the Book of Revelation, is a vision of the birth of her son, the king. *The Gospel According to the Hebrews* knew this:

> And it came to pass when the LORD was come up out of the water the whole fount of the Holy Spirit descended and rested upon him, and said unto him: My Son, in all the prophets was I waiting for thee that thou shouldst come, and I might rest in thee. For thou art my rest, thou art my first begotten son, that reignest for ever.

In the earliest strata of the gospels, we are told, Jesus was presented as the child of Wisdom or her envoy and this was the earliest Christology to 'embrace the idea of pre-existence'.[55] The earliest traditions also said that the Spirit came on Jesus like a dove, which was the symbol of Wisdom.

In the pantheon of Ugarit the woman clothed with the sun had been the sun goddess, the virgin mother and consort of El, heavenly counterpart of the chief queen.[56] In Jerusalem she had been the Queen of

---

[53] *Numbers R.* 15:10.
[54] Other texts describe how the LORD came with earthquake and rain (Ps. 67:7–9) or with lightning, plague and pestilence (Hab. 3:3–4).
[55] See Dunn, *Christology*, pp. 198, 209.
[56] Wyatt, 'Stela', pp. 271–7; also Wyatt, 'Liturgical Context' suggests that Psalm 19 originally described the marriage of El and the sun goddess whose chariots had been removed from the temple during Josiah's reform. The role of this goddess can be

Heaven, the woman of Isaiah's oracle who would give birth to Immanuel, God with his people.[57] When Malachi prophesied the day of fiery judgement he said that Elijah would warn of its coming, as did John the Baptist, and that the sun of righteousness would arise with healing in *her* wings (Mal. 3:20; Eng. 4:2). This significant reference is overlooked because of the customary translation, but the mythology of Ugarit represented the sun goddess as a winged sun, protecting her people.[58] She was officially abandoned after the Deuteronomic reform, but never forgotten.[59] The Queen of Heaven was also known as Wisdom, or the Spirit, and her most recent encomium had been the Book of Wisdom. The Solomon who wrote it still remembered her as the one who shared the throne of God (Wisd. 9:4) made the kings more than human (Wisd. 7:5–7; cf. Gen. 2–3), and gave them secret knowledge (Wisd. 7:21) and immortality (Wisd. 8:13). Embedded in the *Similitudes of Enoch* is a fragment about Wisdom's despair; she could find no place to live on earth and so she returned to heaven to take her place among the angels (*1 En.* 42).

How this mythology known from Ugarit had survived to reappear in Revelation is a question for another time, but it is there. The son of the sun goddess of Ugarit was the divine counterpart of the king and he was known as the Morning Star.[60] In the Book of Revelation Jesus her son is also called the Morning Star: 'I am the root and offspring of David, the bright Morning Star (Rev. 22:16).[61]

---

reconstructed to some degree from Ugaritic texts which show the Morning and Evening Stars as the geminated forms of the son of the goddess. Psalm 19 describes a sacred marriage from which the king is born, 'mythologically Athtar, the Morning Star'. This birth was the king's coronation ritual.

[57] (i) She also figures in Micah 5:3 as the one who gives birth to the divine ruler.

(ii) Bauckham, *Climax*, p. 197, favours the suggestion that Revelation 12:1–4 derives from the myth of the birth of Apollo, as does Yarbro-Collins, *Combat*, pp. 63–7. But did Revelation originate in Asia Minor where this myth was well known?

[58] Wyatt, 'Stela', pp. 272–4.

[59] The *Apocalypse of Weeks* says those who abandoned Wisdom were "blinded" (*1 En.* 93:8) a description reserved elsewhere for the followers of the fallen angels (*1 En.* 90:25–6). The prophecy which Jesus claimed to fulfil (Luke 4:18–19) included releasing captives and giving sight to the blind.

[60] Wyatt, 'Stela', p. 277.

[61] Cf. Revelation 2:28 where the reading, 'I will give him the Morning Star' probably indicates the Hebrew use of *ntn*, give, in the sense of 'appoint', so 'I will make him the Morning Star'. There is a remarkable parallel to this usage in a merkavah text which Schäfer designates N8128 and prints as ##384–400. A 'Youth' ascends to the throne. He is identified as the Prince 'written' with seven voices, seven letters and seventy names who serves before the fire. He is 'given' to Moses. (The text #396 only has *ntn* with no object, but one, e.g. 'his Name' could be implied.) It seems that 'the Youth' who has been sealed with the one letter by which the heavens and the earth were created somehow 'became' Moses. This is an obscure and undateable text, but the most obvious similarity is to Ezekiel 28:12ff. where a heavenly being who 'was' the seal is cast out. The LXX version of the precious stones he wore suggests that this disgraced figure was the high

The red dragon with seven heads, waiting to devour the newly born child of the Wisdom is the dragon of ancient Semitic myth, the Leviathan whom the king had to conquer before he claimed his throne. When Jesus speaks of binding the strong one (Matt. 12:29) before plundering his house, this is a recollection of his baptism as shaped by this vision, an experience remembered in the early baptismal liturgies, but originating with Jesus. This probably accounts for another of Jesus' cryptic sayings also: the old era ended with John the Baptist and since then the kingdom has been taken by force (Matt. 11:12/Luke 16:16). The original is lost beyond recovery, but the struggle to overcome hostile forces and thus ascend to the throne of God is a reasonable context.

The woman's child was then caught up[62] to the throne of God just as Philip was caught up by the Spirit after he had baptized the Ethiopian (Acts 8:39) and Paul's 'man in Christ' was caught up to the third heaven (2 Cor. 12:2; cf. 1 Thess. 4:17). This was the ascent of one who was to rule the nations with a rod of iron. Psalm 2 describes him, set on the holy hill and acknowledged by the LORD, with the words 'You are my son', the words which Jesus heard at his baptism.

The simplest explanation of the traditions associated with Jesus' baptism would be that there had originally been a merkavah connection and that the baptism was for Jesus the formative experience when he had been raised up as Son of God, the Servant of the LORD. His ministry was the outworking of that original vision and thus, as we find in the *Gospel of Philip*, 'Those who say that the LORD died first and then rose up are in error for he rose up first and then he died.'

---

priest in his heavenly aspect, wearing the seal of the sacred name. We shall return to this in Chapter 3. The 'Youth' text N8128 echoes what is said of Jesus in Philippians 2:9–11.

[62] (i) The same verb is used of taking the kingdom by force.

(ii) Methodius, *Symposium* 10, PG xviii 152–3, seems to have known this interpretation of Revelation 12, linking it to baptism: 'The great red dragon with seven heads . . . (which) lies in wait to devour the child of the woman in labour, is the devil who lies in ambush to abuse the mind of the illuminated faithful. But he misses and loses his prey, for the reborn are snatched up on high to the throne of God.'

3

Renewal

For Paul and John – and not only for them – the voluntary self-sacrifice of the sinless Son of God which took place once and for all, was the unsurpassable expression of God's free love. . . . Here we are concerned not simply with a mythical view which has now become obsolete and which could be put aside without further ado; here – we may confidently affirm – perhaps in a mythical form which at first seems strange to us, we come up against the heart of the gospel which grounds and supports our faith as it did of the first witnesses. It is the prime task of theology to show what lies at this heart in the language of our own time.

MARTIN HENGEL
Conclusion to *The Atonement*

ANY Christology must lead to a Soteriology and both must be firmly rooted in first-century Palestine.[1] Both must also take seriously the Christian claim that Jesus had been the fulfilment of the Old Testament. Prophecies, cult and sacred history all culminated in the person and work of Jesus Christ. In other words, the New Testament must be read as the last chapter of the Old; to say that the New Testament is a re-reading of the Old Testament, or a new interpretation of the Old Testament is to make several assumptions. The first Christians did not see it that way and if we are to understand Christian origins we must try to read with their eyes.[2]

---

[1] (i) The second major question addressed by the First Princeton Symposium on Judaism and Christian Origins was: 'What is the relation between the confession that Jesus is the Christ and Jesus' death? Charlesworth, *The Messiah*, p. 10.

(ii) *Doctrine Commission*, p. 97: 'Yet this message (of atonement and justification) which lies at the heart of the gospel raises numerous consequential questions. The most obvious of these is *why the death of Christ should have this astonishing result.*'

[2] (i) Ricoeur, *Essays*, 'Preface to Bultmann' (originally his preface to Bultmann's *Jesus, Mythologie et demythologisation,* 1968): 'Why has Christian preaching chosen to be hermeneutic by binding itself to the rereading of the Old Testament? Essentially to make the event itself *appear*, not as an irrational irruption, but *as the fulfilment of an antecedent meaning* which remained in suspense' (my emphases). Such an approach assumes that it was the Christians who re-read the Old Testament to create their new faith. The opposite is probably nearer the truth.

57

The origin of any Soteriology must be sought in the mysterious and bloody rites of the Day of Atonement when sin was 'atoned' and the earth was renewed at the start of another year. Images from the Day of Atonement rituals are to be found in many early Christian writings; in the Letter to the Hebrews Jesus is presented as the high priest making the atonement offering, but any reference to Jesus passing through the curtain of the sanctuary, be it entering with the blood or emerging with secret knowledge[3] must have the Day of Atonement as its context as this was the only occasion when anyone entered the Holy of Holies. Performing the blood rite was the distinctive role of the high priest and the messianic high priest was expected to perform the great atonement at the end of the seventy weeks of years.

Jesus saw himself as the anointed high priest[4] (the starting point for any Christology) and his death as the great atonement sacrifice (the starting point for any Soteriology). His formative experience of ascent and transformation, resurrection as Son of God and LORD had cast him in the role of the new priest who was to be raised up at the end of the seventy weeks of years. *The Testament of Levi* 18 describes this priest as one whose star will rise in heaven, upon whom the Spirit of the LORD will rest. The account of the new priest's inauguration bears a distinct, perhaps intentional, resemblance to the account of Jesus'

(ii) J. Neusner, *Incarnation*, says that when the Jerusalem Talmud had taken shape within the Palestinian community it had been addressing the threat of Christianity in the fourth century. The Judaic response to the Christian way of reading the Old Testament was 'a counterpart exegesis', p. 107. The Jewish sages adapted the Scripture to their new situation. When they 'read and expounded Scripture it was to spell out how one thing stood for something else. . . . The as-if frame of mind brought to Scripture renews Scripture with the sage seeing everything with fresh eyes', p. 125. Such studies should make us less confident that it was the *Christians* who were 're-reading' the Old Testament.

[3] E.g. Ignatius, *Philadelphians* 9, PG v 703–4: 'To (Jesus) alone as our High Priest were the secret things of God committed.' *Contra* Staniforth who suggests that the secret things were the sanctuary treasures such as the Ark. Clement, *Misc* vii.3, PG ix 417: 'This is the function of the gnostic who has been perfected, to have converse with God through the Great High Priest' and '. . . they do not enter in as we enter in, through the tradition of the Lord by drawing aside the curtain . . .' *Misc* vii.17, PG ix 548.

[4] (i) The anointed high priest was distinguished from the high priest of many garments, *m.Horayoth* 3:4, the priest who wore eight garments rather than the four of the regular priests. Since the oil for anointing the high priests had been removed from the temple during Josiah's reform, according to *b.Horayoth* 12a, there had been no anointed high priest in the second temple period and his restoration was to be a sign of the last times.

(ii) *Contra* Dunn, 'Messianic Ideas', p. 373: 'We can dismiss at once . . . the priest messiah. There is no indication whatsoever that this was ever canvassed as a possibility or seen as an option in the case of Jesus. Presumably Jesus was known to lack the basic qualification of belonging to the tribe of Levi . . . Significantly, when the attempt is *subsequently* made to present Jesus as High Priest, it is done by using the quite different and extraordinary order of Melchizedek rather than that of Aaron (Heb. 7:5).' (My emphases; was not Psalm 110, the Melchizedek Psalm, the basis of the earliest Christology and common to most strands of the New Testament?)

baptism. The new priest restores peace to the earth and brings joy in heaven. He will open again the gates of paradise and bind Beliar, giving his followers power to trample on the evil angels. Much of the description is drawn from the prophecies of the messianic king, but here he is clearly a priest. The origin of the passage is a mystery; some scholars have found allusions to the Maccabean priest kings, others suspect a Christian hand. Whatever the truth of the matter, other pre-Christian material from Qumran confirms that such a messianic priest was expected and if *The Testament of Levi* is a Christian composition, it is clear evidence for Jesus being recognized as that priest. If it is pre-Christian, it is additional evidence for the ideas current in first-century Palestine.

The Day of Atonement

The Day of Atonement rituals at the end of the second temple period are described in the *Mishnah* and they appear very similar to those prescribed in Leviticus. After purification and preparation the high priest sacrificed a young bull and then cast lots over two goats, one for Azazel and one for the LORD. The blood of the bull was taken into the Holy of Holies and sprinkled on the *kapporeth* and in other parts of the sanctuary. He then sacrificed the goat 'for the LORD' and the blood was taken into the Holy of Holies. He sprinkled it first on the *kapporeth* and then as he emerged from the sanctuary, the blood was smeared and sprinkled on significant places in the temple. Finally he placed all the sins of Israel on the head of the goat 'for Azazel' and it was led off into the desert.[5] Minute details of procedure are carefully preserved in

---

[5] (i) The prescriptions for the Day of Atonement in 11QT 25–7 are a compilation of Leviticus and Numbers with some points clarified, e.g. that three rams were required for the offerings.

(ii) *Jubilees* 43:18–19 has its own account of the origin of the ritual; the blood of the goat reminded the people of the sin against Jacob when he had been told that Joseph was dead. In the second century BCE, then, the origin of the Day of Atonement needed explanation; either the older meaning was no longer known or the tale in *Jubilees* was a deliberate substitute.

(iii) The bull was the original offering for cleansing the sanctuary, Ezekiel 45:18, and for the sin offering at Passover, Ezekiel 45:22. A bull was also the sin offering for the high priest and his house on the Day of Atonement; its blood was taken into the Holy of Holies and sprinkled. The two identical goats seem to have been added to the ritual after this time, suggesting that they replaced something in the cult of the first temple. A vestige of what they replaced can be seen in the stories of Abraham's two sons who had fates exactly similar to those of the two goats; Ishmael was sent into the desert and Isaac was taken to the temple mount to be sacrificed, but a substitute was offered. Isaac was associated in later tradition with Isaiah's Servant, see below n. 22.

(iv) The blood of the young bull was sprinkled on the *kapporeth* and then kept until the blood of the goat had been similarly sprinkled. The two bowls of blood were then mixed and sprinkled on the altar of incense and poured at the foot of the altar of sacrifice (*m.Yoma* 5:4–5). This mixing of the bloods, which is not mentioned in Leviticus, must have been significant since the practice was unique to the Day of Atonement. The

the *Mishnah*: how the blood was to be stirred to prevent clotting, how it was to be sprinkled, how the goats were to be identical in every way but distinguished by red wool tied on the head of the Azazel goat but around the throat of the sacrifice. The movement of the ritual was outwards from the Holy of Holies which represented the place of the heavenly throne; the blood was used only after it had been brought from the presence of the LORD. Since Leviticus also says that blood is effective for atonement because it is life (Lev. 17:11), the ritual must have brought out life from the presence of the LORD into the temple. In rituals as elaborate as these every detail will have been important yet there is absolutely no indication in these texts of what any of it meant. Since the Day of Atonement was 'the keystone of the sacrificial system of post-exilic Judaism' the extent of our ignorance about it is a measure of our ignorance about Israel's religion and about Christian origins. It is also thought to be one of the most ancient rituals yet seems to be unmentioned in the surviving accounts of pre-exilic worship.[6]

---

life of the bull (i.e. of what the bull represented) was joined with life of the goat (i.e. the LORD) in the act of atonement. The logic of the ritual, if there can be such a thing, would suggest that the bull represented the high priest, whose life was joined with that of the LORD in the act of atonement. Cf. Engnell, *Essays*, p. 235n, who suggests that the bull represented the priest king but he has no suggestion as to the role of the goat *lyhwh*, see below n. 8(ii). The Christians had no place in their scheme for the bull sacrifice. Whatever it represented cannot have been a part of the claim made for Jesus. If it represented the earthly, the human, figure of the high priest, this would explain why the Christians made no use of it. The ritual of mingling bloods, i.e. mingling lives, may account for the otherwise inexplicable command at the Last Supper, to drink the blood. The separate treatment of bread and wine as body and blood makes sacrifice the only possible context for the sayings; see below, nn. 36, 37. If the eating of the 'body' indicated that the disciples were the new priests, then their part in the act of atonement would have necessitated mingling their blood/life with that of the LORD, see Chapter 4 n. 13.

(v) There is a curious fossil in Clement's *Excerpts from Theodotus* 27, PG ix 672, which mentions a Day of Atonement custom not recorded elsewhere. Before entering the Holy of Holies, the high priest removed the gold plate inscribed with the Name, see below, nn. 8, 28, 29. Was this the Name which was worn by the goat who was sacrificed 'as the LORD'? (The description of the golden plate in Exodus 28:36 does suggest it was a seal.) The elaborate purification before entering the sanctuary and the terror with which the high priest entered would suggest that he was not at the time wearing the Name to protect him from the wrath, cf. Wisdom 18:24–5. He was not entering heaven as the LORD but 'became' the earthly aspect of the LORD again when he emerged from 'heaven', symbolized and effected by the mingling of the bloods. The high priest losing his 'divinity' at the moment of entering the sanctuary might account for Jesus' cry of dereliction and explain why the heavenly Christ in Revelation 5:6 approaches the throne as a slain Lamb (i.e. as a human being in the code of the apocalypses). The Jesus of Philippians 2 is exalted ('again' is implied, as he had been 'in the form of God') and then receives the Name. The king in the Babylonian ritual was *reinvested* with his regalia. In the *Hymn of the Pearl* the traveller *resumed* his former state.

[6] Quotation is from *The Jewish Encyclopaedia*, 'Atonement', p. 286.

(i) The problems begin with the meaning of *kpr*; 'smear', 'wipe' or 'cover' describe only the ritual action, not what it represented. The object of *kpr* was a place or an

The LORD as the Priest-King

Temple worship was a copy of the worship in heaven. The earliest evidence for the ordering of the cult is incorporated into the instructions given on Sinai; everything had to be made and done according to what Moses had been shown on the mountain (Exod. 25:9, 40; 26:30). He

---

object, not a person. They were cleansed, consecrated and *kpr* from the uncleannesses of the people. The cleansing and restoration was represented by smearing and sprinkling blood. Milgrom, *Leviticus*, p. 1037 on Leviticus 16:1: 'The reason for these two discrete acts is given in the verse; to purify it and to consecrate it. The order of the verbs is crucial ... the daubing ... purifies ... and the sevenfold sprinkling ... consecrates.'

(ii) The evidence divides as to who performed *kpr*; some texts, e.g. Deuteronomy 32:43, indicate the LORD, others the priests. Ezekiel, a priest in the first temple, shows that *kpr* was performed by priests to purify and cleanse the altar, Ezekiel 43:18–27. Milgrom, *Leviticus*, p. 1083: 'Outside the cult, *kipper* undergoes a vast change which is immediately apparent from its new grammar and syntax. Whereas in rituals the subject of *kipper* is usually a priest and the direct object is a contaminated thing, in non-ritual literature the subject is usually the deity and the direct object is sin (Isa. 6:7; 22:14; Jer. 18:23; Ezek. 16:63; Pss. 65:4; 78:38; 79:9). Actually this represents no rupture.' Cf. Smith, *Old Testament*, p. 381 n. 'the most important point (about *kpr*) is that except in the Priests' Code, it is God not the priest who atones. . . .' This suggests that the priests 'were' the LORD as they performed the rituals.

(iii) *The Jewish Encyclopaedia*, 'Atonement', draws the wrong conclusion: 'In the prophetic language the original idea of the atonement offering had become lost and instead of the offended person (God) the offense or guilt became the object of atonement . . .' God was *never* the object of atonement, but the subject, however this was represented.

(iv) Offerings of animals, cereals, oil and drink were also used to *kpr*, Ezekiel 45:13–17, cf. 11QT 22; it was not only a blood rite.

(v) Blood was smeared on the doorposts to *kpr* the temple in preparation for Passover, Ezekiel 45:18–20. This suggests that *kpr* was apotropaic, as do Numbers 8:19; 17:11ff.; 25:13, where *kpr* by priests or Levites averts the plague or the wrath. Ezekiel 16:59–63 associates *kpr* with the LORD re-establishing his covenant.

(vi) 1 Samuel 12:3 and Amos 5:12 require 'bribe' as the meaning of *kpr*. 2 Samuel 21:3, 14 implies that *kpr* by sacrificing seven of Saul's sons would restore fertility to the land. *kpr* was part of the ordination rites, Leviticus 8:34 and of the readmission of a leper to the community, Leviticus 14:31.

(vii) It is impossible to find one concept which covers cleansing, protecting, consecrating and admitting to community. The term suggests that impurity laid one open to danger and excluded both from the community and from contact with holy things.

(viii) We have at least moved away from the confidence of Cheyne who asserted in 1898 (*Religious Life*, pp. 75–6) that the rituals 'probably are among the passages which are late insertions into the levitical legislation'. The scapegoat was evidence of 'the low spiritual state of the mass of the Jews'. Ezra, a 'church-statesman', had to make a few carefully guarded concessions to the weakness of human nature, and thus the 'miserable ceremony of the scapegoat' was established (!) As late as 1957 (ET 1961) De Vaux, *Israel*, p. 509, could write that it was a 'new feast', 'the combination of Levitical customs with popular superstitions'. On the contrary, the strongest argument for the antiquity of the rituals must be that they are unlikely to have been invented in the second-temple period. Milgrom, *Leviticus*, pp. 1063ff., argues that the ritual could be very old indeed.

was told not only how to build the tabernacle but also how to clothe the priests, how to make the incense and the oils, how to perform the sacrifices. Other texts show how literally this was understood: the king sat on the throne of the LORD (1 Chron. 29:23), he could speak the words of the LORD (Ps. 2:7). Someone who was both God and king processed into the sanctuary (Ps. 68:25; Eng. 24; cf. Ps. 45:7; Eng. 6). Evidence from Qumran corroborates this; at the end of the second temple period the priests were regarded as angels and we can only assume that the rituals on earth were still regarded as the worship of heaven.[7]

The high priest must have represented the LORD; this is the first point to establish in reconstructing the high priestly Christology. No explicit statement to this effect has survived in materials which could have been known in the first century CE, but there is plenty of indirect evidence. First, the system of correspondences in temple lore means that the high priest would have been the chief of the angels, the LORD. The Melchizedek text found at Qumran shows that Melchizedek, the great high priest, was a divine figure who would appear on the great Day of Atonement at the end of the tenth jubilee, to rescue his people from the power of Belial. Second, both Aristeas in the second century BCE and Philo in the first century CE say unambiguously that the high priest wore the sacred Name on his diadem. The customary translation of Exodus 28:38 is that the golden plate on the high priest's forehead was inscribed with the words 'Holy to the LORD', but there is good reason to believe that the whole issue was rather sensitive and that the identity of the

---

Gray, 'Atonement', p. 70, also thought an ancient origin more likely, comparing it to the sufferings of Ba'al. 'It is generally admitted that the desert demon Azazel was incompatible with the last development of the Jewish cult in the P source of the Pentateuch. It must thus be the survival of a very early conception, and certainly has much more in common with the conception of Ba'al's atoning suffering at the hands of the Devourers and Renders in the desert than anything with which we are familiar in the religion of Israel in historical times.' Wyatt, 'Atonement', p. 419, interprets the evidence differently. What seems to emerge is that the twin gods, the Devourers, were a threat to the natural order and Ba'al acted to prevent this threat. In the Old Testament the Devourers appear as the wrath of the LORD which devours and consumes; Atonement is protection against this wrath. *What Ba'al does in conflict with the Devourers, the high priest does in Israel.*

[7] (i) Priests as angels; 1QH III, VII, IX; 1Q Sb IV; *Jub.* 3:18; 31:13–15. In Merkavah texts, see Elior, 'Mysticism', pp. 45–8.

(ii) Origen, *On John* II.188–90, PG xiv 169, quotes from a lost '*Prayer of Joseph*' in which Jacob has inherited many of the titles which elsewhere are given to the Logos. He is called the Man, the First-born, the Archangel of the power of the LORD, the man who looks on God. He is also simultaneously human and divine: 'I, Jacob, who am speaking to you, am also Israel, an angel of God and a ruling spirit.'

(iii) Christian worship also kept this idea; Ignatius, *Magnesians* 6, PG v 668, explains: 'Let the bishop preside in the place of God ...'

officiating high priest was a matter of some dispute.[8] Third, the description of Aaron in Wisdom 18:24 says that he wore the divine majesty itself on his diadem, which does imply rather more than an inscription of dedication. Fourth, the king had been a divine figure in the cult of the first temple and the high priest, as we have seen in *The Testament of Levi*, took over his role. Finally, there is the evidence of Philo whose Logos is clearly the LORD of the Old Testament; when he describes the events of Exodus 24:9–10, for example, he says that the elders ascended Mount Sinai and there saw not the God of Israel but the Logos (*On the Confusion of Tongues* 95–7).[9] Philo describes the Logos as the high priest of the universe. He uses this title throughout his writings and the information he gives about the role of the high priest shows that he bore all the titles which appear in early Christologies and several more besides. He was the Judge and Mediator, he was set before the face of God, he was the King, he was the First-born, he was the Man, he stood at the border of the material and divine worlds, he was the Branch, Zechariah's title for the Messiah. He was also the Archangel, the Bond of the universe, the Name of God, the Seal and the Covenant.[10] He not only entered the heavenly sanctuary but also emerged and became visible when he clothed himself in the material world. Philo used a text of Leviticus 16 which differs from any other known version. His translation of verse 17 is not, 'There shall be no

---

[8] (i) Aristeas, *Letter* 98: 'the royal diadem full of glory with the name of God inscribed in sacred letters on a plate of gold. . . .' Philo, *Life of Moses*, II.114: 'a name which only those whose ears and tongues are purified may hear or speak in the holy place and no other person nor in any other place at all. That Name has four letters . . . *On the Migration of Abraham* 103: the golden plate represented 'the original principle . . . by which God shaped or formed the universe.'

(ii) Cf. the description of the golden name plate in Exodus 28:36 and 39:30 which could be read, 'you shall engrave on it the engravings of a sacred seal *lyhwh*', exactly what was worn by the sacrificed goat on the Day of Atonement.

(iii) A literal reading of the third commandment indicates that it applied originally to the high priest: 'You shall not bear the Name of the LORD your God worthlessly, for the LORD will not leave unpunished the one who bears his name worthlessly.'

(iv) Diodorus Siculus, xl 3:5–6 quoting Hecataeus of Abdera, a fourth-century source, describes the high priest as 'an angel of the commandments of God. The Jews fall to the ground and worship, *proskunein*, the high priest'. This could establish that the high priest was believed to be divine, but this alone would not show that he was believed to 'be' the LORD, unless 'worship' indicates this.

(v) Newsom, *Songs*, p. 33, wonders whether there is one 'superior angel who presides over the angelic priestly hierarchy'. The text is broken but 'it appears highly likely, however, that a reference to Melchizedek was originally contained in 4Q401.11.3 . . . A second possible reference to Melchizedek occurs in 4Q401.22.3 . . . in a line immediately following a reference to the ordination of angelic priests'.

(vi) This reconstruction of the role of the high priest is very different from what is usually proposed, e.g. Jenson, *Graded*, p. 200: '. . . on the Day of Atonement the high priest is *closely identified with the rest of Israel*'.

[9] See my *The Great Angel*, pp. 114–33.

[10] (i) Philo, *Questions on Exodus* II.13; *On Flight* 12, 112, 118; *On Dreams* I.215; II.237; *Who is the Heir?* 205; *On the Confusion of Tongues* 41, 62, 137, 146.

man in the tent of meeting when he (the high priest) enters to make atonement' but, 'When he enters the (Holy of Holies) he shall not be a man until he comes out.'[11] He continues: 'And if he becomes no man . . . he retains this midway place until he comes out again to the realm of body and flesh' (*On Dreams* II.189, 231). The linen robes worn by the high priest in the Holy of Holies are described as 'radiant' and 'imperishable', 'not made from a mortal creature' (*On Dreams* I.216–17). The language implies that the linen robe is the garment of glory which appears in the ascent texts as the garment of the resurrected. There is no means of knowing how wide-spread were Philo's beliefs about the Logos and the high priest; we do know, however, that he went to Rome as spokesman for the Alexandrian Jews and so his views must have been acceptable in the community who chose him. Jerome (*De Vir Ill* xi) even says he was *de genere sacerdotum*.

Other Traces of Temple Tradition

Not only were the priests the counterpart of the angels; the whole temple was sacred space in sacred time. It represented the created order and was the point of contact between time and eternity. The Holy of Holies was heaven, the place of God's throne, concealed from the world by the great curtain which represented the material world. The four colours from which it was woven represented the four elements from which the world was created[12] and the high priest, wearing an identical fabric, was the LORD made visible in the creation. This accounts for the

[11] *Lev R.* 21:12 implies that the high priest was more than human; '. . . when the Holy Spirit rested upon Phineas, his face flamed like torches about him. Hence it is written: the Priest's lips should keep knowledge . . . for he is the angel of the Lord of Hosts (Mal. 2:7)'.

[12] (i) For the symbolism of temple architecture, see my *Gate of Heaven*, pp. 65–77. An identical pattern appears centuries later in the Kabbalists' doctrine of the four worlds: Atsiluth, world of emanation and divinity, Beriah, the world of creation, the throne and the highest angels, Yestirah, the world of formation and the chief domain of the angels, and Asiyah, 'the spiritual archetype of the material world of the senses', Scholem, *Major Trends*, p. 272.

(ii) Philo, *On Flight* 112. The tradition on which Philo bases this idea is implicit in the Old Testament but never spelled out. The sanctuary curtain, he says, represented the material world 'the materials woven together which are four in number (he refers to the white linen and the red, blue and purple threads) . . . are the symbols of the four elements: earth, water, air and fire, *Questions on Exodus* II.85. Josephus, himself of a priestly family, has the same explanation: 'Nor was this mixture without its mystic meaning; it typified the universe', *War* V.212. The high priest was robed in a similar fabric: Exodus 26:5–8; cf. 26:31; and Exodus 36:8; cf. 39:2–4. Philo says the vestments were 'a copy of the universe', *Special Laws* I.96; cf. Josephus, *Antiquities* III.184 and Wisdom 18:24: 'Upon (Aaron's) long robe the whole world was depicted.' The vested high priest symbolized the Incarnation, the material world both concealing the divinity and making it visible, cf. Hebrews 10:20.

(ii) For the same imagery in the Syrian church see Murray, *Symbols*, pp. 310–11.

(iii) *Exodus R.* 38:8; Aaron was given garments like those of God 'after the pattern of the holy garments' revealed on Sinai.

otherwise cryptic comment in Hebrews 10:20: 'The new and living way which he opened for us through the curtain, that is, through his flesh.' The 'nave' of the temple was the Garden of Eden, the completed creation, and the courtyards were the world of mortality and pain to which Adam and Eve were banished. The role of the messianic priest was to reopen the way to the Garden of Eden and restore humankind to the angelic life they had lost. Rituals in the various areas of the temple affected the corresponding parts of the creation. Thus a sin committed anywhere in the land caused pollution in the temple and the land had to be atoned and restored by means of rituals in the temple.[13]

The divine order was envisaged as a system of bonds known as the covenant of peace or the covenant of eternity, by which the LORD had subdued the powers of the universe and thus secured the creation. The bonds were sealed with the sacred Name.[14] When God's laws were broken, the corresponding bonds of the covenant were broken and the stability of creation was threatened. Wrath broke in through the breach and the priests with their rituals had to repair the damage by making atonement.[15] Aaron protected the people from wrath after the rebellion of Korah (Num. 16:47); Phineas protected them from wrath after the apostasy with the Baal of Peor (Num. 25:13) and was given the covenant of *šlm*, the covenant of the priesthood of eternity, because he had acted in this way. Thus the priests by their atonement rituals maintained the covenant which secured the created order and they protected their people from wrath. Ezekiel's LORD promises to re-establish the covenant of eternity with his people when he has atoned all they have done (Ezek. 16:59–63). He will purge out rebels and bring his people back into the bond of the covenant (Ezek. 20:37–8).

[13] (i) *T.Lev.* 18:10 (OTP 1); cf. Revelation 2:7.
(ii) Milgrom, *Leviticus*, pp. 260–1, aptly compares the long distance effect of sin on the temple to the portrait of Dorian Grey. The parts of the temple deemed polluted were open only to the priests and so there can have been no idea of direct or literal pollution.
[14] This belief was widespread; *Prayer of Manasseh* 3; *1 Enoch* 69; *b.Sukkah* 53a; *3 Enoch* 13 (Schäfer #897) tells how Metatron, the angel prince, is given a crown bearing the letters which created the world; originally these must have been the Name on the crown of the high priest. This is why the golden plate worn on his forehead was called the 'seal', Exodus 28:36. See Sperber, 'Sealing'; Murray, *Covenant*, pp. 11–13.
[15] Douglas, 'Atonement', pp. 117–18:

> Terms derived from cleansing, washing and purging have imported into biblical scholarship distractions which have occluded Leviticus' own very specific and clear description of atonement. According to the illustrative cases from Leviticus, to atone means to cover or recover, cover again, to repair a hole, cure a sickness, mend a rift, make good a torn or broken covering. As a noun, what is translated atonement, expiation or purgation means integument made good; conversely, the examples in the book indicate that defilement means integument torn. Atonement does not mean covering a sin so as to hide it from the sight of God; it means making good an outer layer which has rotted or been pierced.

The Hebrew verb *ḥll* means both to pierce and to defile! In a personal letter of 18 June 1994 Professor Douglas expressed delight that I had pointed this out to her.

The prophets described vividly what happened when the system collapsed completely; the earth withered away and primeval chaos returned. 'The earth mourns and withers', said Isaiah, 'because they have transgressed the laws, violated the statutes and broken the everlasting covenant' (Isa. 24:4–5). Murray, in his book *The Cosmic Covenant*, has reconstructed the processes by which this covenant was established, broken and then restored.[16] He suggested that the king performed rituals to counter hostile powers and affirm right order, both cosmic and earthly. The priestly theology of our present Old Testament has left no obvious sign of this priest king, but traces of the figure can be discerned.[17] He then shows how this pattern survived the demise of the monarchy and became the fundamental concern of the second temple cult. Whether represented by priest king or high priest, the LORD himself was at the centre of this system in the first temple (according to Ezekiel who was a priest) and in the second (according to Philo who described the high priest as the Bond, the Covenant and the Seal).[18]

Atonement was an apotropaic ritual, protecting from the consequences of sin. This understanding of atonement was current as late as the first century BCE when Numbers 17 was retold in the Wisdom of Solomon. Aaron protected the people from the wrath by placing himself between them and danger; thus he showed he was the LORD's Servant (Wisd. 18:20–5). It seems that the high priest himself deflected the danger, perhaps by absorbing or bearing the sin. At Qumran too, atonement 'was not merely a synonym for cleansing or even for forgiveness. It always carried overtones of the abolition of divine wrath.'[19] There is a similar idea in accounts of the Passover; the blood on the doorposts was a sign that the lamb had been killed and this protected the first-born of Israel from the plague which the LORD sent on Egypt, just as Aaron and Phineas were later to withstand the plague, the wrath of the LORD, with acts of atonement. Later tradition associated the redemption of the first-born son with the tenth

[16] See Murray, *Covenant*, pp. 14–26. Also p. 139, where he suggests that the 'cosmic covenant' was the ultimate origin of the Kabbalists' teaching of *tiqqun*; Isaac Luria's insights 'released once again the essential meaning and power of very ancient ideas inspiring Israel's religious thought and ritual'.
Scholem, *Major Trends*, p. 268; 'The restoration of the ideal order, which forms the original aim of creation, is also the secret purpose of existence. Salvation actually means nothing but restitution, the re-integration of the original whole, or *tiqqun*. . . .' *Kabbalah*, p. 127; 'For a *tiqqun* that is regarded as a restoration of unity from multiplicity is necessarily related in some way to redemption.'
[17] Murray, pp. 68–93.
[18] (i) Cf. Ezekiel 28:12 where the heavenly being thrown from the mountain of God is described as the Seal. According to the LXX he is dressed in the precious stones which correspond to those of the high priest's breastplate.
(ii) Again the Kabbalah; 'The *tiqqun* restores the unity of God's name.' Scholem, *Major Trends*, p. 275, does suggest that the original the Name which was being restored was the Bond of the cosmic covenant, the original purpose of the atonement ritual.
[19] Garnet, *Salvation*, p. 115.

plague; the LORD had destroyed all the first-born except those of Israel, implying that the blood of the Passover had been a substitute to avert the wrath (Exod. 12:13). Ezekiel prescribed identical rites for both autumn and spring atonements; his 'Passover' is not recognizable as such, but the atonement element is quite clear (Ezek. 45:18–20). The similarity of Passover and Atonement is also clear from later opinions about the Akedah; the atoning nature of Isaac's sacrifice was recognized but linked by some to Passover and by others to the autumn Atonement.[20]

The Letter to the Hebrews describes Jesus as the great high priest who offered blood on the Day of Atonement; like the Qumran Melchizedek he had inaugurated the great atonement at the end of the age (Heb. 9:26). Jesus had passed through the heavens (Heb. 4:14) and like the Qumran figure he was also divine (Heb. 1:5; 7:3). He had taken his own blood into the Holy of Holies (Heb. 9:12) and become the mediator of a new covenant (Heb. 9:15). He had been enthroned in glory (Heb. 8:1) and was waiting there until his enemies were destroyed (Heb. 10:13). In his presentation of Jesus the writer is making a point by point comparison with the temple rituals. He knows that the temple rituals were only 'copies of heavenly things' (Heb. 9:23) and argues that Jesus' death had been the true atonement sacrifice, not just the earthly copy repeated every year by the high priest. Other emphases in the comparison should be noted: Jesus takes his own blood into the sanctuary, not the blood of animals, implying that the animal blood used in the annual ritual had been recognized as a substitute and that the true atonement, the heavenly reality, required the blood of the high priest. Jesus was also the mediator of a new covenant, implying that atonement in the first century CE was still a priestly covenant ritual and that the Christians' new covenant must be understood in this context.[21] Matthew's Jesus also links covenant and atonement: '. . . my blood of the new covenant poured out for many for the forgiveness of sins' (Matt. 26:28), implies that its context was the same high priestly sacrifice.

Traces survive from the first temple which suggest that the Servant had been associated with human sacrifice or a ritual which represented it. Isaiah 53 had been used to interpret Genesis 22 independently of Christian influence, and thus some Servant traditions may have survived in Akedah texts. Even when the Pentateuch was being compiled, Genesis

---

[20] Spiegel, *Trial*, esp. pp. 38–59; Riesenfeld, *Jésus*, pp. 86–96, suggested that the Akedah echoed the ritual suffering of the Babylonian king in the New Year festival and therefore was a relic of first temple practice in Jerusalem; Vermes, *Scripture*, pp. 214–18: the Akedah was associated with Passover before the Christian era.

[21] Later Jewish tradition associates the Day of Atonement with renewing the Sinai covenant, Exodus 34. It was calculated that the second tablets of the Law were given on the tenth day of the seventh month and thus the renewal of the covenant was associated with the Day of Atonement (*Lam R. Proem* 30).

22 has a ram offered on the temple mount as a substitute for the son who had been demanded by the LORD and this sacrifice was regarded as an atonement which was recalled in all subsequent offerings.[22] Micah 6:7, 'Shall I give my first-born for my transgression?' was read as a reference to Isaac as a sin offering.

[22] (i) Vermes, *Scripture*, p. 202, shows that the leading ideas of Isaiah 53 (the freely offered sacrifice, the motif of the lamb) are paralleled in Genesis 22: 'On the targumic level, the resemblances are plainly realised and the nature and effect of the Servant's passion are applied to the sacrifice of Isaac so that Genesis 22 becomes the story of a just man who offered himself for the sake of sinners.' He suggests that the targumic motif of Isaac's vision may have originated from *yhwh yr'h*, Genesis 22:14 being read in the light of Isaiah 53:11 'because of the travail of his soul he shall see. . . .' The real significance of the association of Isaac and the Servant, however, lies not in the story of the martyr, which Vermes suggests was the origin of the association, but in who the Servant might originally have been. The blood of martyrs came to be seen as an atonement, but there could be another explanation for Isaac having become associated with atonement. One has to ask: *Why should the Akedah have been a reworking of the Servant?* Did Isaac replace whatever the Servant had formerly been? Put in that way the question becomes very interesting indeed, in the light of Wyatt's observation ('Atonement', p. 430) that the fate of the two goats on the Day of Atonement corresponded to the fate of Abraham's two sons. The goats had originally been the geminated forms of 'Attar-Mot. The sacrificed goat would have been whatever Isaac replaced. Vermes notes p. 203, that *Sotah* 14a links Isaiah 53:12 and the incident of Moses offering himself as an atonement, Exodus 32:32, another indication that the human sacrifice of the priest-king lay behind these traditions. Vermes notes also that *Sifre* on Numbers 25:13 links Isaiah 53:12 to Phineas and the priestly atonement.

(ii) Vermes, *Scripture*, pp. 206–8, gives evidence from the Targums to show the saving power of the Akedah: it saved the first-born in Egypt as the blood reminded the LORD of the blood of the Akedah; it was recalled when Israel was saved at the Sea; when Jerusalem was about to be destroyed after David's census, the LORD saw the blood of the Akedah and spared the city. The earliest evidence in the Fragment Targum associated the Akedah not only with deliverance but also with forgiveness of sins. 'The Akedah, although ritually incomplete, was indeed considered a true sacrifice and Israel's chief title to forgiveness and redemption', p. 217. He agrees with Jeremias, *Words*, pp. 244–55, that Jesus' 'Do this in remembrance of me' should be understood in a similar way: God was entreated to remember Jesus' sacrifice. 'By far the most frequent practice in Judaism in the time of Jesus . . . is to use *eis anamnesin* and its equivalents of God's remembrance', Jeremias, p. 247. Vermes concludes, p. 223; '. . . the Akedah theme, bound, as in Judaism, to the Servant motif, belongs to the oldest pre-Marcan stratum of Christian kerygma'. Perhaps one may shift the paradigm a little and suggest that the sacrifice of the Servant and whoever he represented, belonged to the earliest stratum; whatever gave rise to the Akedah resurfaced in Christianity and was recalled in the Eucharist.

(iii) Vermes wondered how much the use of Akedah theology by early Christians contributed to the suppression of the link between Akedah and Passover.

(iv) *T.Isa.* 53:12 does not exclude the possibility that the Messiah would die, see Chilton, *Glory*, p. 94, an interesting further link to the ambiguous Akedah traditions about the fate of Isaac.

(v) The Palestinian Targums, which preserve pre-Christian traditions, suggest that the Akedah – Passover link was superimposed on older traditions. *F.T.* on Exodus 12:40–2 describes the *Four Nights* 'written in the Book of Memorials': the night of Creation , the night of the Akedah, the night of the Passover and the night of the end of the world when the Messiah will appear. *T.N.* is broadly similar but *T.Ps.J.* does not mention the Akedah. In addition, *F.T.* links the Akedah to Abraham's covenant sacrifice in Genesis

Day of Atonement Texts

Rituals are closely tied to myth and, since there is no theological treatise on atonement surviving from the second temple period (apart from the New Testament!), we have to glean here also for evidence that has survived in other texts. The Qumran Melchizedek text shows that there were some in first-century Palestine expecting a divine high priest at the end of time bringing the day of the LORD which was also the great Day of Atonement. He would come to Zion as the anointed one prophesied by Daniel and proclaim the kingdom of God (I shall return to this theme in Chapter 4).

Several other texts can be located on the basis of this Melchizedek pattern from Qumran. The Letter to the Hebrews begins by establishing the identity of Jesus, using several Old Testament texts, one of which is a fuller version of Deuteronomy 32:43 than is found in the Masoretic Hebrew. 'Let all God's angels worship him' (Heb. 1:6) was formerly thought to be a reading unique to the Septuagint but something very

---

15. Each of the four nights describes a revelation: the Creation, the Akedah and the Passover were all revelations of the LORD. The fourth was to be the revelation of the Messiah; according to F.T. he would come 'from on high' with a cloud going before him, reminiscent of the Man figure of Daniel 7. (Thus Le Déaut, *Nuit*, pp. 359–69, Diez Macho, *Neofiti, ad loc.*, rather than 'from Rome', the other possible reading.) The sequence suggests that the fourth revelation would also be a revelation of the LORD, the Messiah coming for the Judgement, the hope associated elsewhere with the Day of Atonement. The *Four Nights* indicates an alternative pattern of sacred history with no mention of Sinai or the fall of Jerusalem. The four themes suggest an origin in the pre-exilic Atonement rituals which have been 'historicized' and linked somewhat artificially to Passover. The LORD appearing to create, the covenant sacrifice of 'Isaac' (i.e. the Servant), the blood protecting from the plague of the Destroyer (i.e. the Wrath) and the emergence of the Messiah to bring Judgement and Renewal were originally part of the Day of Atonement.

The *Four Nights* is an attempt to incorporate the essentials of the ancient festival into (a) a sacred history and (b) a Passover setting. Both indicate the hand of the Deuteronomists. Le Déaut, *Nuit*, p. 101, has shown how the themes of the *Four Nights* can be detected in, e.g., Genesis 15 where Abraham has a preview of the history of his descendants, but this passage too betrays its author!

The Akedah is not mentioned elsewhere in the Old Testament even though in 2 Chronicles 3:1, Mount Moriah recalls Genesis 22. The Passover cannot have been linked to the Jerusalem Akedah sacrifice before the Passover itself was centralized in Jerusalem yet its theme is that of Isaiah 53: Isaac, I suggest, took over the role of 'the Servant' whose sacrifice renewed the covenant. The Akedah thus became linked to Isaiah 53, to the Servant who is the Covenant of the People (42:6; 49:8). The *Four Nights* links the Abraham covenant sacrifice to the Akedah, and the Akedah to Atonement. The original matrix of Atonement and Covenant had been the pre-exilic Day of Atonement whose central theme was rejected by the writer of Exodus 32:30–3.

(vi) At the moment of his sacrifice, according to the Palestinian Targums to Genesis 22:10, Isaac saw the Glory; the Servant, too according to the LXX and 1QIsᵃ 53:11 saw the 'light' after his ordeal.

(vii) Theophrastus, fourth century BCE, *De Pietate* quoted in Porphyry *De Abstinentia* II.26 says the Jews offer human sacrifices.

similar has been found at Qumran, showing that the fuller text was known in first-century Palestine.

> Heavens praise his people,
> *All 'elohim bow down to him.*
> for he avenges the blood of his sons,
> and takes vengeance on his adversaries,
> and requites those who hate him,
> and *atones* the land of his people.[23]

C. H. Dodd demonstrated some time ago that the so-called proof texts of the New Testament were to be 'understood as wholes, and particular verses or sentences were quoted from them rather as pointers to the whole context than as constituting testimonies in and for themselves'. The Letter to the Hebrews uses the verse 'Let all God's angels worship him' to describe the advent of Jesus but *the original passage in Deuteronomy from which it was taken described the coming of the* LORD, *like the Qumran Melchizedek, to bring judgement and atonement.* Hebrews therefore presents Jesus not only as the high priest at the great atonement but also as the LORD who brings the day of judgement, in fact the same figure.[24]

The Assumption of Moses is an expansion of part of Deuteronomy 32 and shows how it was understood in the first century BCE.

> Then his kingdom will appear throughout his whole creation.
> Then the evil one will have an end.
> Sorrow will be led away with him.
> Then will be filled the hands of the angel
> who is in the highest place appointed;
> he will at once avenge them of their enemies.
> The heavenly one will go forth from his kingly throne
> he will go forth from his holy habitation with indignation and wrath on
> behalf of his sons. (*Ass Mos* 10)

The key figure in the Testament is not named as the LORD but is simply described as an angel high priest who comes forth from his royal throne to take vengeance on his people's enemies. This is the appearance of his kingdom, the time when the evil one is destroyed. The angel high priest emerging from his holy place was probably the 'angel of the covenant' of whom Malachi had spoken (Mal. 3:1–5), the one who was to appear in the temple like refiner's fire, purifying the sons of Levi.

These texts show that the key figure in the atonement ritual was the LORD; named either as the LORD, the angel of the covenant, the great

---

[23] Details in Skehan, 'Fragment'.
[24] Quotation from Dodd, *Scriptures*, p. 126. Origen, *On John* XX.152, PG xiv 614 commenting on John 8:42, 'I proceeded and came forth from God', links it to Micah 1:3, the LORD coming forth from his place. Thus he too links the coming of the LORD and the Incarnation.

Holy One, or Melchizedek, he emerged at the appointed time to establish his kingdom and save his people from their enemies, to banish Satan and make atonement. Other texts add detail: *1 Enoch* describes how the LORD comes forth from his dwelling with ten thousands of holy ones to bring judgement on the ungodly. The text resembles Deuteronomy 33:2–5, where the LORD comes with ten thousand holy ones *on the day he becomes King*. *1 Enoch* 10 describes the judgement; the four archangels are sent out to bind Azazel and imprison him and then to destroy the fallen angels and their children. They then heal the earth, purify it from all defilement, oppression and sin and inaugurate an era of righteousness and fertility: 'And he will proclaim life to the earth that he is giving life to her' (*1 En.* 10:7). *Here, at last, is a text which gives the meaning of atonement; it was the process by which the effects of sin were removed so that the earth could be healed and restored.* It was a rite of recreation when the LORD came forth from his holy place and established his kingdom.[25]

Several other texts have the Day of Atonement as their setting and elements of the ritual can thus be reconstructed. The *Similitudes of Enoch*, for example, are three parallel accounts of the heavenly judgement. No trace of them has been found at Qumran and so there is no proof of their age, but the detail they record shows that their setting was almost certainly the Day of Atonement. The heavenly events they depict were the reality reflected in the temple rituals. The key figure has various names; he is called the Chosen One, the Righteous One and the Son of Man. He looks like a man but has the face of a holy angel and he goes to up to the heavenly throne where he is seated as the judge. One enigmatic passage in the second *Similitude* suggests that this figure was the one whom the high priest represented in the Day of Atonement ritual. The blood of the Righteous One is brought up from the earth to heaven so that the judgement can begin. Since the Day of Atonement was the only occasion when blood was taken into the Holy of Holies, this text must be describing what happened when the blood was taken behind the curtain. It had originally been the enthronement ceremony which preceded the judgement. It has been suggested that elements of this passage in the *Similitudes* invite comparison with the fourth Servant Song, a possibility to which we shall return.[26]

The account of the blood ceremony follows a passage which has been compared to the Son of Man vision in Daniel, suggesting that Daniel's vision is yet another text whose original context was the Day

---

[25] Underhill, *Mysticism*, p. 141: 'The Incarnation, which is for popular Christianity synonymous with the historical birth and earthly life of Christ, is for the mystic not only this but also a perpetual Cosmic and personal process. It is an everlasting bringing forth, in the universe and also in the individual ascending soul, of the divine and perfect Life, the pure character of God, of which the one historical life dramatized the essential constituents.'

[26] Black, *Enoch*, p. 209. See Chapter 5 n. 24.

of Atonement. The entry of the high priest into the Holy of Holies was the heavenly Man going up to his enthronement. Scholars have shown how closely the vision in Daniel 7 resembles Psalm 2, the enthronement psalm in which the anointed one is set on the holy hill and declared to be the LORD's son: 'Today I have begotten you.'[27] Psalm 2, *1 Enoch* 46 and Daniel 7 all describe what was represented when the high priest entered the Holy of Holies and put the blood on the *kapporeth*; *The Assumption of Moses*, the Qumran Melchizedek text and Deuteronomy 32:43 describe what happened when he emerged bringing judgement and atonement.

Almost contemporary with Daniel's vision, *The Assumption of Moses* and the Melchizedek text, is an account of the Day of Atonement in Ben Sira who described the high priest Simon 'coming out of the house of the veil', the Holy of Holies. The description is very interesting indeed. The reappearance of the high priest is described as a theophany; Simon emerges like the morning star, like the moon and the sun, clothed in perfection and making the sanctuary glorious with his presence. (Ben Sira 50:5, 6, 11.)

Central to the argument of Hebrews is the blood which was used for the great atonement. Jesus, it is emphasized, used his own blood, implying that the blood of the annual ritual had been regarded as a substitute for that of the high priest. One line in Origen may be the evidence we need to reconstruct the detail here. He said that on the Day of Atonement the goat sent into the desert was not 'for Azazel' the customary translation at this point, but that it was named Azazel.[28] In other words, the goat was chosen to represent Azazel who was banished on the Day of Judgement; *1 Enoch* describes how he was cast into a desert place (*1 En.* 10:4) before the earth was healed.[29] *The Assumption of Moses* says, significantly, that evil will be led away on the Day of Judgement.

[27] Bentzen, *King*, pp. 74–5; Emerton, 'Origin', p. 230: Bentzen's proposal 'has the advantage of explaining all the principal features of the imagery as organically related in a single whole.'

[28] Origen, *Celsus* 6.43, PG xi 1364, identifies Satan as the snake in the Garden of Eden and as the goat named Azazel sent out into the desert. This is clear in both the Greek and the Latin versions.

[29] (i) Several texts suggest that the goat was Azazel, but there is a complex relationship between Leviticus 16, *1 Enoch* 10 which describes the fate of Azazel and the Palestinian Targum to Leviticus 16. *1 Enoch* describes how Azazel is bound by the archangel Raphael and imprisoned in Dudael. He has corrupted the earth by teaching humankind the heavenly secrets and the LORD says: 'Write upon him all sin.' The Targum says all the sins of Israel are put on the head of the goat, as in Leviticus, and the goat is then led to the desert where a strong wind from the LORD carries it away to its death.

(ii) Nickelsburg, 'Apocalyptic' gives reasons why the goat could not possibly have been Azazel and why *1 Enoch* did not 'reflect' Leviticus 16: (a) in the Targum the expulsion of the goat results in atonement and in *1 Enoch* the burial (his word; it was in fact imprisonment) of Azazel results in the healing of the earth; (b) in *1 Enoch* Azazel

If Origen was correct in his reading of Leviticus (and he did have many contacts with the rabbis of Caesarea at this time) then the other goat of the Day of Atonement ritual was not 'for the LORD', an expression not used of sacrificial animals elsewhere in the Old Testament, but 'as the LORD'. The construction of the Hebrew is identical for both goats. *The goat sacrificed on the day of Atonement represented the LORD*, explaining perfectly the comparison is made in the Letter to the Hebrews: 'taking not the blood of goats and calves but his own blood . . .' (Heb. 9:12) Jesus was the LORD, the heavenly high priest making the final great atonement.

Taken together, the evidence suggests that at the heart of the second temple cult had been a ritual in which the LORD offered his own blood, his life. Philo knew this; he says that the high priest on the Day of Atonement 'pours as a libation the blood of the soul' (literally 'spiritual – *psuchikon* – blood', *Allegorical Interpretation* II.56). The context implies that it is the blood of his own soul,

---

is destroyed but in the Targum the goat is destroyed; (c) in *1 Enoch* 10:8 the sin is written on Azazel but in the Targum and Leviticus it is placed on the head of the goat. He thought the Prometheus myth a more likely root of the Azazel material and could see no link between atonement and healing.

(iii) The complex arguments used to try to distinguish various demons on the basis of the many spellings of Azazel seem to be misdirected ingenuity and even Azazel and Semihazah were probably variants of the one name; see Cheyne, 'Date' and Charles, *Enoch*, p. 16, also Ginzberg, *Legends*, V, p. 152: 'The identity of Azzael with Azazel does not require any proof; but it has not hitherto been noticed that Uzza or Azza were originally the same as Shemhazai', the '*l* element of the angel name being replaced by *šm*'.

(iv) In contrast, Grabbe, 'Scapegoat', concluded that the scapegoat was symbolic of Azazel, but he worked without reference to Origen's *Celsus* which would have added weight to what he was saying.

(v) Other arguments to identify the goat and Azazel are based on the name of the desert place to which the goat was sent: these were first (and best) set out in Charles, *Enoch*, p. 22 notes, but other versions have been offered by Milik in *DJD* and in *Enoch*, pp. 29–30.

(vi) Another relevant text is 4Q En. Giants a where Ohyan, one of the giants, explains, 'Then he punished not us but Azazel . . .'; the text is a fragment but the context is clear enough.

(vii) Grabbe also cites *The Apocalypse of Abraham* 13, where Azazel, in the form of an unclean bird, tries to prevent Abraham's ascent to heaven. The angel Iaoel drives him away and says that his heavenly garment will now be given to Abraham and all the corruption which was on Abraham would be put on Azazel. The context here, though, is slightly different; the corruption of Abraham which is given to Azazel probably refers to his mortal state since he exchanges it for Azazel's garment of glory, the angelic state from which he has been banished.

(viii) The Zohar reflects this understanding of the scapegoat; 'The Zohar declares that the other side, (evil) has its legitimate place . . . these rites serve to contain it within the proper limits, but not to destroy it, for this is possible only in the Messianic age. It is in this sense that the Zohar interprets the scapegoat that is sent out into the wilderness on the Day of Atonement.' Scholem, *Kabbalah*, p. 129.

i.e. himself, that is being poured out.[30] Philo was an exact contemporary of Jesus and I suggest that Jesus also understood his high priesthood in this way. As he accepted that he was the anointed high priest come to his people, so too he accepted that his death was necessary if the great atonement was to be made. The synoptic predictions of the passion in their present form may incorporate details from a later period, but the conviction that death was the necessary culmination of his work originated with Jesus himself.[31]

When the high priest emerged from the Holy of Holies he sprinkled the blood to cleanse and renew the creation and in a similar way Jesus, the high priest who had entered the Holy of Holies, was expected to return bringing judgement and renewal. This became the Parousia, and the Day of the LORD imagery associated with the Parousia in the New Testament confirms this as its context. The Man figure in Daniel 7, who has attracted so much attention from New Testament scholars, is the high priest entering the Holy of Holies; *but the returning Man figure in the Parousia passages of the New Testament is the returning high priest, the LORD emerging from his holy place.* He returns with his

---

[30] The atonement sacrifice of the divine ruler, however this was represented, was part of the ritual of the first temple. Exodus 32:30–5 shows that the practice was buried beneath the Mosaic religion of individual responsibility. After the sin of the golden calf, Moses ascends to the LORD and asks if he can offer himself as atonement for the people's sin. The LORD refuses and says, in effect, that such atonement is not possible. Each bears his own sin, cf. Jeremiah 31:30; Ezekiel 18:4, 20. After Moses' failure to make atonement, the people suffer a plague, a sure sign that the wrath has broken out, and yet even as late as Wisdom of Solomon 18, Aaron was said to stop the plague by atonement. Here is evidence that the older temple differed from that represented in the final form of the Pentateuch on the crucial issue of atonement and how it was effected. There may be other Day of Atonement motifs in Exodus 33–4, but Moses has replaced the king at the centre of the cult; Moses experiences the presence of the LORD and the Glory whilst standing by a great rock (Exod. 33:21; cf. the *'eben shetiyyah* in the Holy of Holies). The LORD proclaims his name, an odd thing to do unless this is a memory of a ritual which proclaimed the Name, cf. *m.Yoma* 6:2, where the high priest speaks the Name only on the Day of Atonement). Moses returned from the mountain with a shining face; Simon the high priest emerged radiant from the sanctuary, Ben Sira 50:5–7, the face of Phineas flamed like a torch, *Leviticus R.* 21:12.

[31] (i) There are several indications that Jesus predicted his own death; three underlying forms of the Son of Man sayings (that he will suffer/be delivered up, that this is what has been predicted for him, and that he will give his life (a ransom) for many) were originally separate from the resurrection prediction, rising after three days. Lindars, *Jesus*, pp. 60–84, shows this well, even if his arguments as to the meaning of 'son of man' are unconvincing. 'A man may be delivered up in the course of his duty', p. 81, or 'the resolution and deliberation with which he faced the inevitable march of events', p. 84, are sentiments from another age!

(ii) The parable of the Tenants in the Vineyard also suggests that Jesus predicted his death, albeit not by crucifixion, but the fact that there is no mention of resurrection must call into question whether Jesus spoke of his resurrection as a future event.

(iii) The passion predictions are closely related to the fourth Servant Song and this also came from Jesus himself. It must be significant that the Servant is exalted before he suffers, Isaiah 52:13, and 'sees light' (v. 11, LXX and Qumran) afterwards.

angel reapers to gather the elect and to cast sin and evil into the furnace of fire. Peter explains this in his sermon in the temple: 'Repent therefore and turn again that your sins may be blotted out and times of refreshing may come from the presence of the LORD and that he may send the Christ appointed for you, Jesus whom heaven must receive until the time for establishing all that God spoke by the mouth of his holy prophets from of old' (Acts 3:19–21).[32]

'Bearing' Sin

When he had performed the blood rituals, the high priest laid all the sin of Israel on the scapegoat, on Azazel, and he was banished. This raises several questions: first, how is it that the early Christians saw Jesus as the scapegoat as well as the high priest and second, how was it possible for the high priest to transfer all the sins of Israel onto the scapegoat? The answer to the first of these questions may be found in the *Epistle of Barnabas*, an early Christian writing attributed to St. Paul's companion, who was a Levite from Cyprus. Presumably a Levite would have been acquainted with the temple practices of his time and yet his description of the Day of Atonement rites does not accord with the regulations in Leviticus.[33] *Barnabas* says that the two goats for the ceremony had to be identical in every respect, a detail found in the *Mishnah* but not in Leviticus, but he identifies Jesus as the scapegoat rather than as the sacrifice. There follows a passage of considerable interest: 'The point of there being two similar goats . . . is that when they see him coming on the Day, they are going to be struck with terror at the manifest parallel between him and the goat' (*Barnabas* 7). The one who emerges on the Day of Judgement is closely identified, in the mind of Barnabas the Levite, with the goat who was banished and presumably also with the goat who was sacrificed. This suggests that the two animals had originally represented two aspects of one figure who not only bore away evil but also emerged on the Day of the LORD and was recognized as the one who

---

[32] (i) Cf. 2 Thessalonians 1:7, where it is the LORD Jesus who is revealed with his fiery angels; Revelation 19:13 where the Word emerges wearing a robe sprinkled with blood, a Day of Atonement image, followed by the armies of heaven. *1 Enoch* 1, Jude 14 and Hebrews 10:13 are all similar.

(ii) Origen, *On John* I.258, PG xiv 94: 'For this reason he is a great high priest since he restores all things to the kingdom of the Father. . . .' Origen knew that the role of the high priest was to restore, to bring in.

(iii) This future aspect of the resurrection, the Day of Judgement and the renewal of the creation, accords well with Moltmann's intuition that the real significance of the resurrection is in the future, in the new creation and the new being which is yet to be.

[33] Horbury, 'Priesthood', pp. 50–2, shows that early Christian writers had accurate knowledge of contemporary Jewish practices on the Day of Atonement where these had developed beyond the Pentateuchal regulations, e.g. the use of the ashes of the red heifer, mentioned in Hebrews 9:13 but not in Leviticus 16.

had borne the sins.[34] Now the recognition of the persecuted one is a theme not only of the Fourth Servant song in Isaiah but also of other texts such as the *Similitudes of Enoch* and the Wisdom of Solomon (*1 En.* 62:3; Wisd. 5:5). *Barnabas*' comments about the scapegoat agree with what is implied elsewhere and this increases the possibility that what he writes is an accurate account of first-century belief and practice.

Barnabas includes other information about the Day of Atonement which is not known in any other source; the scapegoat was goaded

[34] (i) The two goats and what they represented may point towards one of the greatest problems in the Old Testament; the nature of the LORD. There is plenty of evidence that there had been a dark side to the ancient Yahweh. Job knew the source of his troubles (Job 12:9; 16:9), one of the few places where the name Yahweh occurs in the text. The later prose framework makes Satan the source. Satan tempts David, according to 1 Chronicles 21:1, but in 2 Samuel 24:1 it is the anger of Yahweh which tempts him. Jacob wrestled with a mysterious being whom he recognized as God (Gen. 32:30). Yahweh tried to kill Moses (Exod. 4:24). Yahweh is not entirely distinct from the Destroyer in Exodus 12:23, and Isaiah, establishing that the LORD is one God, emphasizes that he creates light and darkness, weal and woe (Isa. 45:7). Had Azazel and Yahweh been geminated forms of one God? Such deities were known at Ugarit, e.g. 'Attar, with his two forms as the morning and evening stars, later developed into two distinct deities, an arch demon and a saviour figure', Wyatt, 'Attar', p. 94.

(ii) In Genesis 3 the snake is not entirely evil nor is the LORD entirely good; the gnostics remembered this when they described the God of the Old Testament as an evil figure and exalted the snake. There was a bronze snake in the temple in Jerusalem, removed by Hezekiah, 2 Kings 18:4. The snake had been a deity, because 'until those days the people of Israel had burned incense to it'. The snake had absorbed evil, a priestly role; those who turned to the snake were protected from snake bites, Numbers 21:9. The bronze snake *Nehushtan* and the great snake *Leviathan* are words of similar form, but the Levi element cannot be overlooked in a temple context. What was the 'idolatry' for which the Levites were demoted, Ezekiel 44:9–14? And who were those 'skilled to rouse Leviathan', Job 3:8? (I am grateful to Dr R. Price for drawing my attention to this). The text suggests that they were people who could pronounce a curse, perhaps a priestly group? Most extraordinary is the similarity between the Servant in Isaiah 53, the scapegoat and the serpent in Genesis 3. All are sin-bearing figures who invite our sympathy; the Servant because he bears the sins of others, the snake in Eden because he was punished for telling the truth about the tree of knowledge and the scapegoat who is driven out to a miserable end.

(iii) Jesus at his crucifixion is compared favourably to the bronze serpent in John 3:14, Jesus is called the Morning Star in Revelation 22:16, he is presented as the Servant throughout the New Testament and as the scapegoat in the *Letter of Barnabas* 7. *What are we reading?* The first Christians knew and used some very old ideas about the LORD, whose double nature has survived elsewhere as the tradition that Yahweh and Elohim were two different aspects of the one divinity, see Marmorstein, 'Philo' and *Doctrine*, pp. 45ff.; Dahl and Segal, 'Rabbis'. Philo knew that *Kyrios* represented the divine justice and judgement, the *kolastezos*, and '*elohim* represented the goodness and mercy, the *euergetes*, equivalents which appeared in the older Haggadah but were exactly reversed in the later due to 'religious movements which necessitated such a discarding of an older teaching', 'Philo', p. 296. Was this gemination the reason for the two identical goats?

(iv) Justin, *Trypho* 49, PG vi 584, knows of the two comings of the Anointed One. 'Scripture compels you to admit that two advents of Christ were predicted to take place – one in which He would appear suffering and dishonoured and without comeliness; but the other in which He would come glorious and Judge of all. . . .'

and spat upon as it was driven away, another clear reference to the Suffering Servant,[35] and the sacrificed goat, whose carcase had to be burned according to the rules in Leviticus, was eaten by the priests whilst the people were keeping the fast.[36] *Barnabas* links this to the offering of Jesus' body as a sacrifice. If his account is accurate, then the high priest who represented the LORD would have regarded the sacrificed goat as a substitute for himself and, if it was eaten by the priests, *he could well have uttered the words over the goat which Jesus used over the bread at the Last Supper as he gave it to his disciples to eat: This is my body.*[37] *Barnabas*, then, gives us three valuable pieces of information: that the two goats were aspects of one figure, that the figure had probably been the Servant, and that the body of the sacrifice was eaten by the priests.

The second question is equally intriguing; how was it possible for the high priest to transfer all the sins of Israel onto the head of the Azazel goat? The Yahweh goat, described in Leviticus 16:9 as a sin offering, clearly did not do away with sin as this remained to be put on the head of the other goat. In order to understand the workings of the Day of Atonement ritual it is necessary to look closely at what the Old Testament actually says about the role of the priests. They were said to 'bear the guilt' of the sinner after they had performed an atonement ritual (e.g. Lev. 10:17), and this was done by eating the flesh of the sacrifice. The implication is that by eating the flesh they absorbed the iniquity into themselves, not unlike the process for purifying the temple in Babylon, where the carcase of a ram was used to absorb impurities.[38] The verb used for this 'bearing' of the sins is *nasa'*, but when the same

---

[35] *m. Yoma* 6:4 mentions only the pulling of its hair, another reference to the Servant, Isaiah 50:6.

[36] This could be another example of a practice which differed from that prescribed in Leviticus or even in the *Mishnah* (see n. 33). Barnabas seems to be quoting from a written source: 'What does it say in the prophet? "Let them eat of the goat which is offered for their sins at the fast . . . let all the priests, but nobody else, eat of its inward parts, unwashed and with vinegar."' This is related directly to the institution of the Eucharist. Hebrews 13:11, on the other hand, compares Jesus' death outside the walls of the city to the custom of burning there the carcases of sin offerings whose blood had been taken into the Holy of Holies.

[37] Morton Smith, *Clement*, pp. 218–19, suggests that both Eucharist and Baptism derived from magical practices and 'show a similar break with traditional Judaism'. 'That a man should undertake to identify his own blood with wine and give it to his followers to drink in order to unite them with himself – this goes far beyond the mysteries; its only close parallels are in magic.' This conclusion is perhaps premature; our knowledge of first-century Judaism, though vastly increased in recent years, is still painfully fragmented, and absence of evidence is not necessarily evidence of absence. There are significant points of contact with temple theology, and the origin of the Eucharist may yet be explained entirely within this context.

[38] The texts in ANET, pp. 331–4, are from the Seleucid period but the ritual is thought to be more ancient. The priests sprinkle water, burn incense and beat a drum. The doors of the sanctuary are smeared with cedar resin and aromatics are burned in a silver censer. The ram is then decapitated and the body is used to perform the *kuppuru*

verb is used of the LORD it is translated differently and an element of interpretation creeps into the text which effectively obscures the meaning of the atonement ritual. The LORD is said to 'forgive' iniquity when the text says literally that he 'bears', e.g. Micah 7:18: 'Who is a God like you, bearing [that is, forgiving] sin?' There are many examples;[39] what emerges is that bearing iniquity was the role of the LORD, of the priests and of the scapegoat. Now if the temple ritual mirrored the rituals of heaven, it is unlikely that a distinction would have been made between the role of the LORD forgiving and the role of the high priest 'bearing' the iniquities.

When the high priest, the LORD, emerged from the Holy of Holies on the Day of Atonement he must have absorbed into himself, by means of the blood rite, all the iniquities of the people, all the effects of their sin. Once absorbed, the iniquity no longer breached the covenant bond

---

ritual for the temple, absorbing the impurities. The body of the ram is thrown into the river. The king then has to undergo the ritual humiliation before being reinvested with his regalia.

[39] (i) *nś'* means literally carry or bear but in certain contexts the meaning must be forgive or bear guilt. Why should 'carry' have been used when there is *slḥ* which means, forgive, and nothing else? *slḥ* is only used with God as subject and would have been the obvious choice for a cultic context. *BDB* observes that *slḥ* is used in D and Kgs, P and Chron, Jer and Lam, D-Isa. and Dan. *nś'* is characteristic of earlier texts, though the division is not absolute. This suggests that *nś'* was an older way of describing forgiveness.

(ii) The high priest 'bears' the guilt of holy things when he wears the sacred name and they become acceptable, Exodus 28:38. Aaron and his sons 'bear' the guilt of the sanctuary and the priesthood, Numbers 18:1, the Levites 'bear' the guilt in the tent of meeting, Numbers 18:23. By eating the sacrifice offered for another's sin, the priests 'bore' the guilt to *kpr*, Numbers 10:17; the implication is that by eating the sacrifice they absorbed the guilt and this enabled the offender to return to the community, cf. Leviticus 22:15 which implies that if the offerings are not correctly eaten, the people continue to bear their own guilt. This 'bearing' of guilt must underlie the scapegoat ritual and also the ritual of the two birds for cleansing a leper, Leviticus 14. Note that the priest bore the guilt when he was wearing the sacred name, but the goat bore it when he wore the name of Azazel.

(iii) The LORD also bore guilt: Hosea 14:2; Psalm 25:18; Psalm 32:1 (which does not have the word *kpr* but perfectly describes the process; bearing transgression is parallel to covering sin); Psalm 99:8 is similar; literally: You were a 'bearing' God for them and took vengeance. . . .' Also Micah 7:18; Job 7:21; Isaiah 33:24. These are relatively early texts; is it possible that beneath the later metaphorical use of *nś'* there lies the memory of an older ritual when the LORD bore away the guilt, sin and transgression of his people which would otherwise have laid them open to the dangers of sickness, enemies and other disasters?

(iv) Taking too narrow or 'recent' a view of what was relevant to understanding New Testament can produce such statements as, 'There is no text in the Jewish tradition which contains a teaching that a righteous man can vicariously atone for the sin of others by becoming accursed and sinful . . . no theological or textual justification can be found for a sacrificial interpretation of atonement passages in Paul's letters', McLean, 'Absence', pp. 551, 552; or Hengel, *Atonement*, p. 8; 'A representative death to atone for the guilt of others can be found at best on the periphery of the Old Testament, for example in Isaiah 53, which K. Koch rightly describes as an "erratic block"'. See also Chapter 5 n. 10.

and thus the creation was renewed and the people protected from the wrath. This was the blood of the covenant which took away sin. Bearing these iniquities, the high priest transferred them to the Azazel goat and thus they were banished. Barnabas knew this, and he also would have known how the emerging high priest related to the goat who was to be banished. We do not. He, and presumably the other Jewish Christians of his time, associated this ritual of expulsion with the humiliation of the Suffering Servant and they used Servant texts when they described the role of Jesus.

Those whose sins were not borne by the priest were condemned to bear their own and this meant that they were cut off from their people. (Lev. 19:8; 20:17, etc.). They were outside the covenant bond and its protection. Any breach in the covenant not only affected the sinner, it also exposed the whole people to wrath, which could break out where the bond had been destroyed. The wrath, which often took the form of plague, was held back by atonement, which restored the security of the created order. This suggests that 'bearing' the iniquity of the people was an important temple ritual to unite the community and protect the cosmos. As custodians of the eternal covenant, the priesthood had to maintain the standards of cult purity but also the wholeness of the community and the cosmos. It is interesting that the purity laws of Leviticus do not serve to divide the community; the code of priestly practice was designed to overcome impurities and restore wholeness both to individuals, to the community and to the whole creation, and to protect from the ever present danger of wrath. Ezekiel, who was a priest (Ezek. 1:3) describes the process at the beginning of the second temple period: '. . . I will establish with you an everlasting covenant . . . when I atone all you have done, says the LORD God' (Ezek. 20:60, 63); or, 'I will be king over you . . . I will bring you into the bond of the covenant' (Ezek. 20:33, 37). This is an important association of ideas; establishing the kingdom of God, even in the time of Ezekiel, was the process of bringing people into the covenant bond. Paul called it justification and Jesus enacted it by bringing in the outcast and the sinner.[40]

In the first century we find the same ideas in Philo; in his role as high priest the Logos was the bond of the creation.

---

[40] Mary Douglas, 'Stranger', casts interesting light on this. She suggests that the stranger, *ger*, who had special rights was 'only an outsider to the extent that the ancient ties of kinship had recently broken down', p. 286. The priestly editors of Numbers and Leviticus had a strong sympathy for these half-brothers but others were hostile to those who had not shared the exile. (Cf. my *The Older Testament*, pp. 184–200.) She sees the old priesthood opposed to the Ezra-Nehemiah programme, committed rather to the older and more inclusive ways. 'Ezra-Nehemiah claim to be restoring the ancient cult according to the sacred books, but what they prescribe is not actually in the sacred books at all and makes nonsense of what is there', p. 288. If this is correct, then Jesus' going to the 'outcasts' would have been in accordance with the older priestly tradition.

And the oldest Logos of God has put on the universe as a garment . . . ' he does not tear his garments' . . . for the Logos of God is the bond of all things, as has been said, and holds together all parts, and prevents them by its constriction from breaking apart and becoming separated (*On Flight* 112).

According to John, Jesus wore a seamless robe (John 19:23).

The Servant Songs, I suggest, were inspired by the most ancient form of the atonement ritual. The Servant was the figure whose role was taken over by the two goats in the rituals of the second temple. There are considerable problems with the text of the Servant Songs in both the Hebrew and the versions, and so a few indications must suffice here.[41] The fourth song is the most enigmatic of them all; it describes a disfigured and suffering Servant of the LORD and his eventual triumph. The Targum at this point translates so as to give a rather different impression of the Servant; he is not disfigured but rather distinguished by his holiness, he brings judgement on Israel's enemies, he purifies and cleanses the remnant, restores the sanctuary and has a kingdom. This is all Day of Atonement imagery. Now there is nothing in the text of Isaiah 52–3 as usually read to associate it directly with these rituals, apart from the reference to the sin offering. How, then did such a complex set of allusions 'reappear' in the Targum after several centuries unless there had been an unbroken tradition of understanding the text in that way? Presumably such an understanding was available to the first Christians.

A literal reading of the fourth Song, however, gives interesting possibilities. Isaiah 52:13 says that the Servant will be raised up and made wise and this wisdom, as the serpent in Eden knew well, made one like the gods. Isaiah 52:15 says that the Servant 'sprinkles' many nations. This is usually amended to 'he shall startle many nations' but the Hebrew 'sprinkles' is recognizable as the action of the high priest on the Day of Atonement. Like the high priest and the later scapegoat the servant carries the sickness and weakness of the people and enables them to be made whole again (53:4). Two details of this fourth Song require comment; first that the servant makes himself a sin offering and pours out his soul, and second that he makes intercession. The blood used in atonement rituals was the life or soul of the animal; Leviticus explains that 'Blood makes atonement by reason of the life' (Lev. 17:11). This means that on the Day of Atonement the blood of the Yahweh goat was not only the life of the goat but also the life of the LORD and the life of the high priest. The blood was brought from the Holy of Holies, from heaven, and was used to cleanse and renew the earth. This was a ritual of re-creation, when the LORD gave his life not for his people but to his people. *When the Servant pours out his soul and makes it a sin offering, the poem records what the ritual represents.*

[41] I shall consider to the Servant in more detail in Chapter 5.

80

Atonement Patterns in the New Testament

Jesus saw himself as the great high priest. The paradigm of high priesthood explains both the Christology and the Soteriology of the New Testament. He had been raised up to the vision of the throne at his baptism and began his ministry as the LORD, the Holy One, the high priest come to his people to rescue them on the great Day of Atonement at the end of the tenth jubilee. The seventy weeks of years had passed and the time had come for the establishing of the Kingdom of God. The high priest would restore the eternal covenant and bring in those who had been cut off; his own blood would be offered on the Day of Atonement and he would enter the Holy of Holies to be enthroned. When he emerged he would bring healing and renewal for the creation and judgement on Azazel.

Such a hypothesis explains many features of the New Testament. First, it explains the importance of Psalm 110, which appears in the New Testament, either in quotation or allusion, more frequently than any other Old Testament text. Jesus' exaltation is consistently connected with this text and it is the exaltation of the Melchizedek priest. The idea occurs throughout the New Testament: in the Synoptic Gospels, the Acts, the Pauline letters, 1 Peter, Hebrews, and if one allows that to be seated on the heavenly throne is the same idea, it is the theme of Revelation. In Philippians 2, Paul shows that exaltation to receive the Sacred Name was another way of expressing the same idea. Thus the 'place' and function of the Resurrected One was quite clear from the very beginning[42] and the reason for this, I suggest, is that it was Jesus' own teaching about himself.

Second, it explains the pattern of the ministry; Jesus the high priest goes to those who have become outcasts, those who have been cut off from the covenant bond. He removes whatever impurities have cut them off: bleeding, leprosy, physical disability or unspecified sins. He exorcises or, in the words of the Melchizedek text, rescues the children of light 'from the hand of the spirits of Satan's lot'. Matthew sees both healings

---

[42] (i) See, most recently, Hengel, *Studies*, p. 134: '... the significant majority of the New Testament texts ... evidences the influence of Psalm 110:1, from which an apparently basic Christological statement originated'. The text, or an allusion to it, occurs at: Matthew 22:44; 26:64; Mark 12:36; 14:62 (16:19); Luke 20:42–4; 22:69; Acts 2:34–6; Romans 8:34; 1 Corinthians 15:25; Ephesians 1:20; Colossians 3:1; Hebrews 1:3, 13; 8:1; 10:12–13. We find exaltation to the right hand at: Acts 2:33; 5:31; 7:55–6; Hebrews 12:2; 1 Peter 3:22. The use of Psalm 110 to describe a historical person, recently put to death in Jerusalem but then declared to be enthroned in heaven, is, p. 203, 'the greatest mystery in the origin of the earliest Christology. Doesn't this unspeakably audacious and at the same time provocative step necessarily have a basis in the teaching and the bearing of Jesus himself?'

(ii) *1 Clement* uses the high-priest tradition with an addition not found in the New Testament. Jesus is 'the High Priest ... the Protector' (*1 Clem.* 36 and 58, PG i 281, 328), an exact description of the role of the high priest protecting against the wrath.

and exorcisms as the work of the Servant: 'He cast out the spirits with a word and healed all who were sick. This was to fulfil what was spoken by the prophet Isaiah: "He took our infirmities and bore our diseases"' (Matt. 8:16–17; cf. Luke 11:20).

Third, it explains the New Testament's emphasis on unity and reconciliation. The high priest's renewal of the cosmic covenant is the natural context in which to understand Ephesians 1:10: '. . . a plan for the fullness of time, to unite all things in him, things in heaven and things on earth'. The great Christological statement in Colossians 1 has not simply been drawn from the thought of Philo or an ill-defined group called gnostics. The one who is the image of the invisible God, who reconciles all things on earth and in heaven, who makes peace by means of blood, is the high priest. In 2 Corinthians 5, Paul speaks of the ministry of reconciliation which is part of the new creation; again the original context of such ideas is the Day of Atonement.

Fourth, it explains the kenotic hymn in Philippians 2, which is widely recognized as one of the earliest statements about Jesus. Paul seems to be quoting an established sequence, perhaps a hymn, and for some time it has been the fashion to read it as a comparison of Jesus and Adam, even though the key theme of self-emptying is not an Adam motif. The poem reads more naturally as a comparison of Jesus and the Servant since the key phrases of the passage echo the Fourth Servant Song.[43] One example must suffice: the enigmatic phrase, 'he emptied himself', which has prompted much speculation, is a reference to the pouring out of the blood on the Day of Atonement. The ancient belief that blood was the life or the soul meant the high priest's sacrifice was a pouring out of himself. Philo, as we have seen, says that the high priest poured out the blood of the soul (or spiritual blood) (*Allegorical Interpretation* II.56) and he was an exact contemporary of those who described Jesus in this way.

Fifth, it explains Peter's sermons. At Pentecost, Peter told the crowd that they were seeing the fulfilment of Joel's prophecy; the Spirit had been poured out on all, and in the original prophecy this gift of the Spirit had been a sign that the LORD had renewed the cosmic covenant. The implication of what Peter said is that the last times had come and the renewal of the covenant had begun. In his temple sermon Peter spoke of Jesus as the Servant who had been glorified, as the Holy and Righteous one and as the Author of life, a reference to the life-giving blood. If they repented, he told them, sins could be blotted out and times of refreshment come from the presence of the LORD, together with Jesus, who had been appointed as the Anointed One. Blotting out sins, times of refreshment coming from the presence of the LORD and

---

[43] Jeremias, *Servant*, p. 97: 'The connection of Philippians 2:6–11 with Isaiah 53 becomes plain as soon as it is recognized that not the LXX but the Hebrew text of Isaiah 53 is used . . .', what we should expect if the ideas in the passage originated in the Palestinian community. See also Chapter 5, n. 65(ii).

the sending forth of the Anointed One all point to the Day of Atonement. The high priest who had entered the Holy of Holies would return again bringing the Day of the LORD. This accounts for the otherwise inexplicable picture of the two comings of the Messiah and all the associated problems. Jesus would have seen himself as the high priest who entered heaven to emerge again on the Last Day.

Sixth, it enables us to trace back to its origin one of the many tangled threads in the Letter to the Romans. 'Justification' is Paul's way of speaking about bringing the sinner back into the covenant bond; his other imagery follows. When he says that the righteousness of God is manifested he is referring to the appearance of the Righteous One, that is, the One who makes Righteous, the Servant who restores the covenant (cf. Isa. 53:11). Justification brings peace, the original *shalom* of the covenant (Rom. 5:1); it also protects from the wrath (Rom. 5:9). The reference to Jesus as the *hilasterion*, the mercy seat, in Romans 3:25, is probably a reference to the place whence the atoning process came and the quotation in Romans 4:7, 'Blessed is the man whose iniquities are forgiven and whose sin is covered' is from Psalm 32, which is the clearest description of atonement in the Old Testament. While he carries his own sin, the guilty one wastes away, says the psalmist, but when he confesses, the LORD carries the sin and it is covered over. Paul's great exposition ends by asking, 'Who shall separate us from the love of Christ?' (Rom. 8:35), another reference to the renewed covenant bond from which the believer can no longer be cut off, either by sin or by the influence of the heavenly powers.

Seventh, it clarifies the saying attributed to Jesus in Mark 10:45; 'The Son of Man also came not to be served but to serve and to give his life as a ransom for many.' Much has been written about the word ransom, but underlying the Greek *lutron* there must have been *kopher*, a word which means not only 'ransom' but also an 'offering for atonement'.[44] Mark's Jesus, then, spoke of himself as the Servant who gave himself as the atonement offering *for many* (cf. 1 Tim. 2:6).

Eighth, it enables us to see the Book of Revelation as central to the New Testament. The Lamb of the visions is the Servant and his enthronement is the moment when the great judgement begins.[45] The plagues are the outpouring of wrath from the Holy of Holies and the name of the LORD on their foreheads protects the new royal priesthood. In the restored creation, the leaves of the tree of life are for the healing of the nations, and nothing is outside the covenant bond, nothing is accursed. All the servants of the LORD enter the Holy of Holies to see his face and all have the sacred name on their foreheads.

---

[44] LXX Exodus 30:12 renders *kopher* by *lutra*; the exact nuances of *kopher* still elude us, but if one possible rendering was *lutron*, this can be considered at Mark 10:45, given the context.
[45] See Chapter 5.

Finally, there are the words spoken at the Last Supper. No two versions are exactly the same but all agree that Jesus spoke of eating the bread as his body and drinking the cup of covenant blood. Matthew's version of the words over the cup immediately gives the context: 'This is my blood of the new covenant which is poured out for many for the forgiveness of sins.'[46] This is the Servant on the Day of Atonement, removing sins and renewing the covenant with his own blood.

In the fourth chapter I offer some suggestions as to how this paradigm might alter our reading of the New Testament and its relevance to some recurring problems of interpretation.

---

[46] Or 'the blood of my new covenant', Jeremias, *Words*, pp. 193–6, but in a high-priestly context, the meaning would have been the same. But see also Emerton, 'Aramaic'.

4

Re-reading

I was like one who gleans after the grape gatherers . . .

Ben Sira 33:16

THE distinction between the Jesus of history and the Christ of faith
has long been the major concern of historical criticism and its quest
for the original Jesus. If, however, Jesus' baptism was his resurrection
experience, there is a new paradigm by which to read the gospel
evidence. Pre- and post-resurrection are no longer the same as pre- and
post-crucifixion. Post-resurrection no longer means the period of the
early church, and the resurrected Christ is no longer just the figure of
the church's faith.

There had originally been two ascents known to the disciples, corresponding to the two ascents recorded in 2 *Enoch*. The first had been the
baptism experience, which was the rebirth, the transformation, the
resurrection, the raising up of the high priest. The second had been the
crucifixion which was the sacrifice of the final atonement and the
exaltation to the throne in heaven. The heavenly high priest was to
emerge again from his holy place and bring the Day of the Lord, the
Parousia. At an early stage the two ascents were fused and confused, I
suspect by Paul, as his letters show just how much he opposed the
beliefs of the Jewish Christians. Thus we have failed to recognize the
real significance of that Philip logion: 'He rose up first and then he
died.' The gospels which we now read as a record of the young church's
beliefs about Jesus could well be an accurate description of beliefs held
by some of the disciples before the crucifixion and they almost certainly
record what Jesus believed about himself.[1] The reappraisal I am

---

[1] Charlesworth's title, 'From Messianology to Christology', in *The Messiah* indicates
a massive assumption! He says: 'The proclamations and teachings in the earliest Jesus
communities in Palestine may reflect the use of something like a list of testimonies
about the Messiah; but these do not prove that the Jews had a common Messianology.
They are evidence of what the earliest Christians created' (my emphases). This calls for
comment. Whether or not the Jews of first-century Palestine had a common expectation
of the Messiah is irrelevant to the quest for Christian origins. The relevant question is:
Was there any established expectation for a messianic figure which could explain the

proposing would be a massive task, but in this chapter I shall offer a few suggestions.

Jesus as Melchizedek

First, there is the sermon at Nazareth. Luke is the only gospel to record the detail of how and why Jesus was rejected by his home community. It has been suggested that the incident is one of Luke's fictions, that Jesus began his ministry by declaring he would bring relief to the suffering and go to the Gentiles. He had been anointed to fulfil the prophecy of Isaiah 61. Luke's emphasis on the Gentiles who had been helped by the prophets may be his own, but the claim to the prophecy of Isaiah 61 was, I suggest, an authentic recollection of Jesus.

It is not impossible that Jesus knew the Melchizedek text found at Qumran, or something similar, which described the priest-king Melchizedek returning at the end of days to fulfil the prophecy of Isaiah 61. He would appear at the start of the tenth jubilee which would end with the final Day of Atonement. He was a divine figure and what Isaiah 61:2 describes as the year of the LORD's favour and God's day of vengeance were Melchizedek's year of grace. The great year began when he took his place in heaven among the holy ones to inaugurate the judgement. The sons of light were to be forgiven, set free and rescued from the power of Satan. The prophecy of Isaiah 52:7 was to be fulfilled; someone proclaiming peace and good news (i.e. the gospel) would appear and announce salvation and the kingdom of God ('Your God reigns'). The messenger would be Isaiah's Anointed One, the one also

---

way Jesus was proclaimed and presented? And is it likely that the Christian communities *created* the messianic ideal which inspired them? Charlesworth continues: 'Jesus' earliest followers were obviously pressed to prove their claim that he was the expected Messiah. Their efforts are evident in the remnant of the old tradition that Jesus would fulfil the messianic prophecies in the future when he returns as the Christ (Acts 2:36; Rom. 1:4), in the pneumatic exegesis of originally non-messianic prophecies and psalms (viz. Pss. 22 and 110), and in the addition of messianic episodes to the story of Jesus.' It would be more sympathetic to ask: Was there any tradition which described a messianic figure who would come and then return again? See below n. 6(v). And can we be sure that Psalm 110 was originally non-messianic when it was clearly a royal and priestly psalm? What is his agenda here? How can one reasonably state, p. 35: 'The gospels and Paul must not be read as if they are reliable sources for pre-70 Jewish beliefs about the Messiah' when the New Testament is the largest body of evidence for such beliefs, coming from the greatest Messianic group in pre-70 Judaism, the only one to have made any real impact. Why should their evidence be dismissed? What is the real agenda here? Cf. Dunn, 'Messianic Ideas' in *Messiah*, p. 381: 'In every case we have to avoid any impression of a fixed category which Jesus filled (or fulfilled) or a sequence of clear cut 'messianic ideas' which provided an agenda for Jesus' mission.' Why? Such a presupposition has been used, without success, to explain the secrecy motifs in Mark. If Jesus was *rewriting* the description of the Messiah, why was the church's emphasis on the fulfilment of older expectations and prophecies?

prophesied by Daniel. The picture of Melchizedek in the Qumran fragments is composed entirely of texts from the Old Testament and this raises a crucial question: was it an original compilation or was such a heavenly high priest familiar to Jesus' contemporaries? Were those texts in Isaiah and Daniel usually understood in that way?[2]

[2] (i) The importance of the Melchizedek text for understanding Christian origins is increasingly recognized. The mysterious figure in the text was originally introduced in 1965 by Van der Woude as 'A Heavenly Redemption Figure' and identified as an archangel, Michael. His original insights have proved broadly correct, despite the scepticism and caution of other scholars. Fitzmyer, 'Further Light', p. 25, considered 11QMelch an example of 'isolated Old Testament texts taken from their original context and strung together with some theological intention'. Melchizedek 'is apparently given a special role in the execution of divine judgement which is related to a jubilee year . . . which involves atonement for iniquity and the Day of Atonement is somehow related to it.' He concluded that even though the Qumran Melchizedek was exalted above all others in the heavenly assembly and was associated with the Day of Atonement and the divine judgement, and comparisons could be made with the Letter to the Hebrews, the tradition was not the same. Its importance lay in the fact that it, like the New Testament, conflated many independent themes and titles from the Old Testament. This is a remarkable combination of caution and assumption. Much has been written on 11QMelch but the obvious has yet to be conceded: Anderson, 'Jewish Antecedents' in Messiah, p. 532, although still having serious reservations about the archangel hypothesis, did concede a 'certain correspondence' between the figure in 11Q Melch and Hebrews, but Schiffman, 'Messianic Figures' in Messiah, p. 126, found no mention of a Messiah in 11QMelch. I suggested, Older Testament, p. 257, that Melchizedek was central to the old royal cult, that the role of the ancient kings was that of Melchizedek in 11QMelch. The texts quoted were part of an association of ideas known to be rooted in the older cult and could only be appreciated in their original context. Melchizedek was the king in his embodiment of the Spirit of Yahweh, the Holy One of Israel. This is why the Christology of Hebrews has pre-existence and adoptionism side by side (1:2; cf. 1:5), a warning that the labels by which we identify early Christologies may obscure more than they illuminate. It has been suggested (Horton, Melchizedek, p. 170; Dunn, Christology, p. 20) that the Melchizedek tradition grew from the silence of Scripture about his origins, but the reverse may be nearer the truth: the silence is due to his origins!

(ii) We cannot lightly dismiss the evidence from the early Christian period, cited by de Jonge and van der Woude, 'Melchizedek', pp. 323–6, that Melchizedek was a heavenly power. Origen, who was in touch with authentic but embarrassing traditions, believed he was an angel, according to Jerome, Ep. ad Evangelum 73. Most references to Melchizedek in the early Christian period are in works opposing heretics who regarded Melchizedek as a heavenly power, but so-called heretics are often most interesting! Horton p. 97 summarizes the heretics' position thus: 'Melchizedek had the role of intercessor and advocate for the angels whereas Christ had the same role for men.' This looks remarkably like the heaven-and-earth correspondence which characterized the worship of Qumran and the temple, and confirms what I am proposing; that the Messiah was the earthly aspect of the heavenly Melchizedek.

(iii) His description of Melchizedek in the gnostic texts Pistis Sophia and the Books of Jeu bears an uncanny resemblance to the high priest as I have reconstructed his role as the absorber of evil and renewer of the created order. In Pistis Sophia Melchizedek periodically descends among the archons, removes their strength and returns them to their appointed place in the universe. 'Melchizedek takes the strength or power which he has received from the archons and purifies it', taking it into the treasury of light, Horton, p. 139. (The images of purification and dross resemble Malachi 3:2–3, where the angel of the covenant comes to refine the sons of Levi.) Older material in Pistis

The prophecy of Daniel 9:24–7, which appears in the Qumran Melchizedek text, is notorious for its obscurity; Gabriel speaks to Daniel and says:

> Seventy weeks of years are decreed for your people and your holy city to finish the transgression, to put an end to sin, to atone iniquity, to bring the Righteous One of ancient times, to seal both vision and prophet and to anoint a most Holy One. Know therefore and understand that from the going forth of the word to restore and build Jerusalem to the coming of an anointed one, a prince, there shall be seven weeks . . .[3]

Sophia and the *Books of Jeu* describes how the curtain is drawn back and Melchizedek looks down onto the lower world. The souls captured by the evil one (here named Hecate) are brought back within the 'sphere', Horton, p. 144. (This is recognizable as the LORD, the royal high priest bringing his people back within the covenant bond, Ezekiel 20:33, 37.) The prayer of 'Jesus', p. 146, clearly originated in an atonement ritual: 'May you remit their sins and cause their unlawful acts to be cleansed . . . may you wipe them all away and cleanse them all . . .' What are we reading? Coincidence cannot account for so many similarities. This gnostic Melchizedek is directly descended from the Jerusalem high priest of the same name who appears in the Melchizedek text as the heavenly redeemer figure.

(iv) Cf. also Philo, *Allegorical Interpretation* III.82, where Philo explains that Melchizedek, whom he identified as the Logos, i.e. as the LORD (see my *The Great Angel*, pp. 114–33), offered 'wine instead of water', which, as John 2:11 observed, was the first manifestation of Jesus' Glory.

[3] (i) The history of attempts to reconstruct the original and then make some sense of it led Montgomery, *Daniel*, p. 400, to describe this passage as the 'Dismal Swamp of Old Testament criticism'. Verse 24 gives the context for the passage and shows how it relates to 11QMelch. Most of the words are obscure or difficult, but 'seventy weeks' and 'to atone iniquity' are beyond dispute. If this seventy weeks refers, as is usually assumed, to seventy weeks of years, then we have both here and in 11QMelch a period of 490 years after which there would be the great Day of Atonement. Given that 11QMelch refers to Daniel, they must be working with similar schemes. Daniel 9:24 therefore describes the Day of Atonement. The first three terms all describe one aspect of the rite: to confine or restrain iniquity (reading *lkl'* with MT), to seal sin (reading *lhtm* with MT) and to atone iniquity (undisputed words). Confining iniquity and sealing sin are both aspects of the Day of Atonement as I have reconstructed it: a rite for imprisoning Azazel, renewing the cosmic covenant and sealing the broken bonds with the Name. The other three terms (to bring in, to seal, to anoint) can also be understood in this setting; the Day of Atonement was the time when the LORD came forth from his holy place to atone the land (Deut. 32:43). The LORD coming forth from his holy place is a recurring theme elsewhere in the Old Testament (Pss. 18:7ff.; Isa. 26:21; 66:6; Mic. 1:3; and implied in Hab. 2:20ff.) and so the presence of 'to bring forth' in Daniel 9:24c could indicate the one who made atonement as he came forth. The words translated 'everlasting righteousness', *şdk 'lmym*, probably conceal Melchizedek. Psalm 110:4 describes a *khn l'wlm*, usually rendered 'a priest for ever', which characterized the priesthood of Melchizedek. The last term, 'to anoint a Holy of Holies' has traditionally been understood as a reference to the Messiah. The Greek of the LXX and Theodotion is ambiguous as *hagion* is in the accusative and could therefore be masculine or neuter. The Syriac and Vulgate assume a person, the Messiah. The titles Righteous and Holy One, as designations for the one who was to come on the Day of Atonement, are found also in Acts 2:14; Jesus is the Holy and Righteous One. Peter's sermon continues with Day of Atonement themes calling for repentance so that 'times of refreshing may come from the presence of the LORD'. Hippolytus, *On Daniel* xvii, PG x 653, read 'Holy of

The original circumstances of the Daniel prophecy need not concern us here; our task is to guess, we can do no more, what it might have meant in the time of Jesus.[4] The Qumran text shows that the anointed prince of Daniel 9 was Melchizedek, the anointed one of Isaiah 61. The themes of the Qumran text and Daniel 9 are also similar: the Qumran text speaks of the Day of Atonement at the end of the tenth jubilee (490 years) and Daniel 9 of the Day of Atonement at the end of seventy weeks of years (also 490 years). The one who brings atonement in the Qumran text is Melchizedek; in Daniel it is an

---

Holies' as a reference to the Son of God and linked it to Isaiah 61:1 and Luke 4:18. Later Jewish exegesis understood both 'Holy of Holies' and Eternal Righteousness' to refer to the Messiah, Montgomery, p. 376. The remaining term in Daniel 9:24, the fifth, is 'to fulfil or complete the vision'. Here the original *lhtm*, complete, has been confused with the earlier *lḥtm*, seal. 'Completing the vision and ?prophet' has to be understood in the same way as Hebrews 9 understands the fulfilling of the ancient cult in the coming of Melchizedek. Daniel 9:24, then, gives a glimpse of how the Day of Atonement was understood and 'Gabriel' is re-using established themes to predict the immediate future of Jerusalem. The Day of Atonement ritual was the pattern by which the future was predicted. If the emergence of the high priest was the Day of the LORD, events leading up to the Day would have been described or calculated in terms of the preceding events on the Day of Atonement, notably the death of an anointed one.

(ii) The Teacher of Righteousness was to know the secrets of the end times (1QpHab VII); '. . . all the mysteries of the words of his servants the prophets. He would learn them 'from the mouth of God', and he is described as the Priest (1QpHab II). The speaker in the *Hymns* makes a similar claim; 1QH I.21; VIII.16ff.; and especially XII.12ff. 'I, the Master, know Thee O my God, by the spirit which thou hast given me, and by Thy Holy Spirit I have faithfully hearkened to Thy marvellous council. In the mystery of Thy wisdom Thou hast opened knowledge to me, and in Thy mercies [. . .] the fountain of Thy might.'

(iii) 4Q541, possibly a part of the *Testament of Levi*, describes the wise man who will make atonement and arouse much hostility.

[4] Collins, *Daniel*, p. 354; a Messianic interpretation of Daniel 9:24-7 'is now abandoned by all but the most conservative interpreters'. This in itself suggests a curiously conservative attitude to prophecy, as though it had only one meaning, and that the original. Our concern, however, is not what these words meant in the second century BCE when they were being applied to the contemporary situation. The sequence suggests that even then 'Gabriel's' composition was not original. To understand what the words might have meant in the first century CE we have to take seriously the early Christian interpretation, that the prophecy referred to the Messiah. As later Jewish exegesis also found the Messiah here, Montgomery, p. 376, this suggests that the messianic application was traditional and not post-Christian. The same mistakes could be made with these verses as scholars have made with the Son of Man figure, namely assuming that we know as much as the first Christians knew, and that they had only Daniel 7 as their source. Whatever tradition underlies Daniel 9 could have been known in the first century CE; the fact that it has been possible to reconstruct the meaning of the Day of Atonement without reference to this text which clearly refers to it, shows that the component parts of the tradition were current in the first century CE. It is quite possible that the words 'To anoint the Most Holy ***', were thought to refer to the Messiah. 11QMelch seems to understand them in that way and it is quite possible that Jesus did too. There is also the person addressed in 4Q416; consecrated, made a Holy of Holies, *lqdwš qwdš(ym)*, increased in glory, and made as a first-born.

unnamed anointed prince (*nagid*). The Hebrew text of Daniel gives no indication of who this prince might have been, but the LXX translator thought he was the LORD, exactly what is implied by the Melchizedek text.[5] Anyone who knew these texts or the tradition they represented would have known that Isaiah's Anointed One was the heavenly high priest come for the great Day of Atonement. *This was the claim which Jesus made at the start of his ministry*, and Luke sets it in the synagogue at Nazareth.

Gabriel's words to Daniel describe the final atonement at the end of the seventy weeks of years; a time to imprison the rebel, a clear reference to the binding of Satan, to seal sin, a reference to renewing the bonds of the covenant which were sealed to exclude cosmic disorder, and to atone iniquity. The Righteous One of ancient times would come, the Holiest One would be anointed, fulfilling the vision and the prophecy. Gabriel prophesies that Jerusalem will be destroyed: first an Anointed One will be cut off (tradition reads this of Jesus), a prince will come and make a strong covenant with many, there will be an abomination, wars and desolations, and finally the destruction of the city and sanctuary. The text is impenetrable but the great atonement sacrifice seems to be the final act before the destruction of the city, which presumably would have been the judgement brought by the re-emerging high priest, here described as the prince to come.[6] Older themes are being re-used in Daniel 9; wars and desolations, the destruction of Jerusalem and the coming of the Anointed One indicate an origin among

[5] The anointed prince: LXX Daniel 9:25 has *polin kyrio*, i.e. 'build Jerusalem the city of the LORD', having read '*d* as '*yr* and understood *ngyd* as the LORD. Since there is no separate word translating *mšyḥ*, Montgomery, p. 401, suggests that the translator thought 'the anointed prince' was the LORD.

[6] The same sequence underlies the Book of Revelation and the Synoptic Apocalypse which is a summary of parts of Revelation. Each describes the events leading up to the Day of the LORD in terms of the Day of Atonement.

(i) The abomination of Daniel 9:27 is given by Jesus as a sign of end, Mark 13:14; this links the two sequences. Afterwards there would be heavenly portents and the appearance of the Son of Man.

(ii) Luke 21:20 specifically mentions the destruction of Jerusalem and this has been explained as his addition to the tradition, but is it? Revelation 18 describes the destruction of Jerusalem (not Rome originally) after an angel with great authority, who made the earth bright with his splendour, had come down from heaven. Was he the Son of Man figure? Daniel 9:26 seems to describe a future prince who will destroy the city, after the anointed prince has been 'cut off'. Cf. the disputed text in 4Q285 which could be read: the leader of the community, the Branch [i.e. the messiah] is put to death.... *Were the two figures of Daniel's prophecy, the anointed one and the one to come, in fact one and the same?* This would explain the *Letter of Barnabas* 7: '... when they see him coming on the Day they are going to be struck with terror at the manifest parallel between Him and the (scape)goat.' The Day of Atonement figure would return on the Day of the LORD.

(iii) Jesus warns in Mark 13:6 that there will be many false messiahs who say, 'I am he' (i.e. the Name), people claiming to be the LORD who was expected to come bringing the last judgement. Jesus' warning is evidence for a belief that the Messiah, the LORD,

those who opposed the cult of the second temple and its city and looked forward to its destruction. The hope for a new Jerusalem did not originate with John on Patmos.[7]

---

would come (and die in Jerusalem, although Jesus does not mention this in the Synoptic Apocalypse) and then return to bring the judgement, exactly what Peter says in Acts 3:19–20, and what is implied by the ritual of the high priest emerging on the Day of Atonement. Cf. also n. 6 (v) below.

(iv) Revelation 6 describes the woes which accompany the opening of the seven seals, after the slain lamb/Messiah has been enthroned in heaven. The Synoptic Apocalypse summarizes these woes (Mark 13:7–8 and similar but not identical sequences in Matthew and Luke). These are the desolations of Daniel 9:26.

(v) Revelation describes the LORD on the throne as the one who 'was and is and is to come', *ho erchomenos* (Rev. 4:8), presumably the one who was expected to come and bring the last judgement, the final act of the great Day of Atonement. Daniel 9:26 has a prince, *ngyd*, who is to come and the Synoptic Apocalypse has the coming of the Son of Man with clouds and angels for the last judgement. The details of the coming are like those of Isaiah 13:10; Joel 2:10 and Zephaniah 1:15, the Day of the LORD. This was not a transferral of imagery from the LORD to Jesus/the Son of Man as is usually suggested. The Son of Man figure was the LORD, who was manifested on earth as the Messiah. This is quite clear in *Asc.Isa.* 3:26; 4:14, where the Parousia is the return of the LORD, i.e. of Yahweh.

(vi) Daniel 9:27 probably means 'he shall make strong a covenant for many', another aspect of the Day of Atonement, when the eternal covenant was renewed and with it, the creation. The angel of the covenant, presumably the same figure, was expected to appear in the temple to bring judgement (Mal. 3:1). In the gospel sequence, this appears as the Last Supper, 'the blood of the covenant . . . for many, Matthew 26:28.

(vii) In Daniel 9:24–7 the Day of Atonement sequence is re-used and applied to the contemporary situation, calculating the time of the Day of the LORD. In the Synoptic Apocalypse the same thing happens: the sequence is re-used and applied, in the form we now read, to the persecution of the young churches waiting for the Day of the LORD as described in Revelation. The original underlying Daniel is probably lost beyond recovery, but was almost certainly a framework for determining future events based on the Day of Atonement.

[7] There are several indications of the older themes. First, the seventy weeks of years. The fashion has been to read this in the light of Jeremiah's prophecy of seventy years exile, lengthened by understanding that seventy sabbatical years, i.e. seventy times seven, was the true meaning of the prophecy. It is more likely that seventy was already a significant figure in Jeremiah's time, to describe a period of distress which would end with God's intervention. The Second Isaiah, without mentioning the seventy years, declares that the exile has ended with the judgement upon the angels who had ruled the old order; that period had ended with what we understood as the judgement and the new creation. There were others who believed that the time of exile had not ended; the material underlying Daniel 9 originated with them. In the period of the second temple there were several versions of the seven and seventy based scheme. There were also different ideas as to when the period of evil began. In the earliest parts of *1 Enoch*, the time of evil began with the fall of the angels and would end after seventy generations; cf. Luke 3 where the genealogy of Jesus has seventy generations from the time of Enoch, the fall of the angels, to the time of Jesus. These chapters in *1 Enoch* also have no place for a renewed temple in the future kingdom, envisage an earthly resurrection and the period of evil ending with divine intervention to judge the fallen angels. Later parts of *1 Enoch*, however, reckon the time of evil from the destruction of the first temple, the end of the royal cult. They predict an earthly struggle to bring in the kingdom, not just divine intervention. The struggle has become politicized rather than just a judgement

The themes of this prophecy account for several clusters of ideas in the New Testament. Peter's temple sermon in Acts 4 mentions the Anointed One and the fulfilment of prophecy and the atonement, but not the destruction of the city: Peter calls Jesus the Righteous One and the Holy One, exactly the names given to the Anointed One in Daniel. The prophecy has been fulfilled, he says, the Anointed One has suffered and atonement is possible (Acts 3:14–21). In the so-called Synoptic Apocalypse the disciples ask Jesus when the temple is to be destroyed, and he replies using the same imagery: the wars and desolations, and then the final act of the atonement, then the Parousia. False claimants would come claiming to be the LORD; 'I am He.'

The coming of the Anointed One and the destruction of Jerusalem appear in several places in Luke and also in Revelation where the Anointed One is the Servant Lamb approaching the throne (Rev. 5) and then emerging again from heaven wearing the Name and a robe sprinkled with blood (Rev. 19), the wars and desolations are the plagues brought by the angels, and the destruction of Jerusalem is the destruction of the great harlot. These themes in the Book of Revelation are at least as old as the material underlying Daniel 9 and perhaps account for Psalm 73:17, seeing the judgement on the wicked 'in the sanctuary of God'. Just as Daniel 7 re-used material from the first temple in the vision of the Man figure ascending, so too Daniel 9 reveals an older sequence. It is the tradition underlying Daniel that appears in the Melchizedek text and the New Testament, and this is why a sequence of themes can be discerned but no direct quotations.

Luke's account of what happened at Nazareth is accurate. Jesus declared himself to be the Melchizedek figure as the result of his baptism experience of ascent and transformation. Like the Qumran Melchizedek, he had taken his place among the angels.[8] Jesus came into Galilee

---

on the fallen angels. A new temple is part of the new age and resurrection is eternal life for the righteous, shining among the stars. This suggests that those who had an ongoing interest in a seventy based scheme, as yet unfulfilled, were those who believed that the troubles which began with the destruction of the first temple were not yet ended. These were the people who considered the restored Jerusalem a harlot (Isa. 57:7–10; cf. Rev. 17, originally of Jerusalem but reinterpreted as Rome); who preserved, and no doubt developed, the hopes of the ancient royal cult, and from whom, ultimately, came the prophecies of Daniel 9:24–7, 11QMelch and Jesus. For detail see my *The Older Testament passim*, but esp. pp. 56–63.

[8] The enthronement text, 4Q491, formerly thought to be part of the *War Scroll* but now classed as a *Hymn*, is the first person account of someone who had been enthroned among the angels. This is consistent with the Essene belief that they worshipped with the host of heaven, but the exalted status of the figure suggests a high priest as implied by 1Q Sb III: '. . . May he set you as a splendid jewel in the midst of the congregation of the saints. May he [renew] for you the covenant of the [everlasting] priesthood . . . 1Q Sb IV: 'May you be as an Angel of the presence in the abode of holiness . . . May you attend upon the service in the temple of the kingdom . . .' Hengel, *Studies*, p. 203, emphasizes the significance of this text for the early Christian use of Psalm 110 and suggests that Jesus may have made such a claim himself.

proclaiming that the time was fulfilled (that is the seventy weeks of years or the ten jubilees) and the reign of God had begun. The first miracle was the exorcism in Capernaum, fulfilling the hope that Melchizedek would rescue from the power of Satan and his spirits. The second miracle recorded in Capernaum was forgiving the sins of the paralytic; Mark says it was to show that Jesus had authority on earth to forgive sins. Had we more of the Melchizedek text we should doubtless discover why the cleansing of a leper was so important in establishing his identity. Jesus as Melchizedek is the major theme of the Letter to the Hebrews, and Psalm 110, the Melchizedek psalm, is the most frequently used text in the New Testament.

The Transfiguration

Then there is the Transfiguration, linked to the baptism because the voice from the cloud is like the voice at the Jordan and linked to the resurrection because the transfigured Jesus resembles the heavenly Jesus of Revelation. The Transfiguration appears in the same position in all three synoptic gospels as part of an established sequence of events: the confession at Caesarea Philippi, then the sayings about suffering and discipleship and then the Transfiguration. There is, however, unusual attention to the timing of these events; whereas synoptic pericopae tend to begin with a vague indication of time except when it was a Sabbath, here the time reference is quite precise; Matthew and Mark say it was six days after Peter's confession that disciples saw him transfigured.[9] This has prompted speculation that the events were linked to the autumn festivals; the Transfiguration was associated with Tabernacles, the ancient festival of enthronement, and the confession, six days previously, had coincided with the Day of Atonement.[10] Once Peter had recognized Jesus as the Anointed One, rather than just a prophet, Jesus was able to teach about the nature of this Messiahship, that he had to die.[11] This, as we have seen in Chapter 3, was the contemporary belief about the anointed high priest on the Day of Atonement; he was symbolically sacrificed, using the goat as a substitute. Jesus began at this point to

[9] Luke 9:28: 'After about eight days. . . .' But perhaps it points to the later tradition that the light of the Transfiguration was the 'mystery of the eighth day', the perfect vision of deity, Lossky, *Mystical Theology*, p. 220.

[10] Riesenfeld, *Jésus, passim*, shows how the traditions of enthronement associated with Tabernacles account for the imagery of the Transfiguration and thus events six days previously should be read in the context of the Day of Atonement. Burrows, 'Cosmological Patterns', pp. 57–8, suggested the connection lay in the saying about Peter the rock, the *'eben shetiyah* of the new creation. The link is more likely to lie in the belief about the sacrifice of the high priest on the Day of Atonement which Jesus was then able to reveal to his inner group of disciples, hence the teaching about his necessary suffering which follows the Confession.

[11] (i) Lindars, *Jesus*, pp. 60–84, argues that the prediction of the suffering did not originally include the prediction of resurrection.

teach his disciples about his role as the high priest, destined to be the sacrifice for the final Day of Atonement.[12] This is what he taught his disciples when he warned them they could expect a similar fate.[13] Those who were ashamed of Jesus would encounter the Son of Man when he came in glory as the judge but some of those present would see the kingdom of God[14] before they died. The next incident was the Transfiguration when three disciples saw Jesus in glory; *this is what Jesus had meant when he said they would see the kingdom before they tasted death*. Three of the disciples had been given the secret of the kingdom of God and Jesus forbade them to speak of what they had seen.[15] He then set his face, says Luke, to go to Jerusalem.

The pattern in the synoptic gospels suggests that Jesus' initial attempt to declare who he was provoked such a reaction in his home town that he adopted a different approach. Only a few were to know who

---

(ii) Peter's reaction and Jesus' response (Mark 8:33 and parallels) suggest that the 'battle with Satan' at the start of the ministry had been over this issue of suffering. The anointed high priest had to suffer and the temptation had been to find another way. Cf. Luke 24:26: 'Was it not necessary that the Anointed One should suffer and enter his glory?'

(iii) The addition in Matthew 16:17 suggests contact with the merkavah tradition; a master could not teach his disciples certain things but could confirm them when the disciple had discovered them for himself. Cf. *m.Hag* 2:1: the merkavah may not be expounded to a pupil unless he is wise and understands of his own knowledge.

[12] Matthew adds, 16:21: Jesus taught that he had to go to Jerusalem to suffer. The location of the sacrifice was significant.

[13] This is why the souls of the martyrs are under the altar, Revelation 6:9. The blood 'was' the soul, and after the atonement rituals, the remaining blood was poured under the great altar of sacrifice, *m.Yoma* 5:6. Those whose blood was to be a part of the great atonement would be envisaged as under the altar.

[14] Matthew 16:28 has 'Son of Man coming in his kingdom'; Mark 9:1 has 'That the kingdom of God has come with power'; Luke 9:27 has 'Kingdom of God'. Mark is probably the original saying. The meaning of seeing the kingdom before death was not that the Day of Judgement would arrive in their lifetimes (as can be seen from the problem implied in John 21:23), even though that is how it was understood by Matthew; it meant that, given that all would see the kingdom after they died, the three who saw the Transfiguration would see it before they died. This is the understanding of the Orthodox Church, Lossky, *Mystical Theology*, p. 220: 'But those who are worthy attain to the vision of "the Kingdom of God come with power" even in this life, a vision such as the three apostles saw on Mount Tabor.'

[15] According to Matthew 17:9 Jesus described the experience as a vision; Luke 9:32 says the disciples were 'heavy with sleep'. Hooke, *Resurrection*, p. 120, suggested this was the *trdmh*, 'a divinely caused state, a supernatural sleep' which falls on someone who is to receive a divine revelation as in Genesis 2:21; 15:12; Job 4:13; 33:15; Isaiah 29:10; Daniel 8:18; 10:9. Luke 9:32 implies that the disciples were asleep at the time of the Transfiguration. Whose words, then, described it? Is this a record of Jesus' own experience, like that of 2 *Enoch* 22:10 where the seer describes his own transformation as he is anointed: 'And I looked at myself and had become like one of his glorious ones.'

(ii) If the three had 'seen' the kingdom, then according to John 3:3 they had been born from above, they had been 'resurrected'. Having seen the vision the three disciples became a part of it and were transformed by it.

he was and what this meant. This appears in Revelation 10 as the mighty angel, the LORD, coming from heaven with an open scroll and telling his disciple to eat it, a sign that its contents were to be kept secret.[16] Only a few were to know who he was and what this meant. Jesus' own experience at the Jordan was communicated to just three of the disciples when he judged they were ready to receive it. The evangelists indicate this by describing the Baptism and the Transfiguration in a similar way; both had experiences of the heavenly throne. Jesus' failure to communicate to the larger group is recorded in the parable of the wedding garment; only those who had achieved the robe of glory, the ascent, were able to attend the wedding of the Lamb. The enigmatic saying

---

(iii) They had entered the cloud, an experience which Paul reinterprets of baptism, but which originally meant the experience of ascent as in Daniel 7 and 1 *Enoch* 14. John 1:14 records this as an experience of the Glory, something which had been denied to Moses, Exodus 33:18–20 and, apparently, to Philip, John 14:9. In 2 Peter 1:16 'Peter' claims to have seen the Majesty at the Transfiguration.

(iv) Hooke suggested that this experience for just three of the disciples was to prepare them for later events, cf. Acts 10:41, 'chosen beforehand' as witnesses . . . The post-crucifixion appearances thus confirmed what they had already learned from Jesus during the ministry; that he had been raised beyond physical death, that he had become the LORD.

(v) This would explain why the empty tomb traditions were not of primary importance to those who understood the original significance and context of 'being raised'. That there was an empty tomb did not in fact prove the resurrection to those who understood its real significance and the later emphasis on the empty tomb, the exoteric proclamation, served to distort and obscure the original proclamation. Paul knew only the exoteric tradition.

[16] Bauckham, *Climax*, pp. 243–57, rightly follows Mazzaferri in identifying the scroll of Revelation 5:1–9 and the scroll of Revelation 10:1–11. He also shows, p. 254, that the transmission of the revelation corresponds to the sequence in Revelation 1:1: 'The revelation of Jesus Christ, which God gave him to show his servants . . . and he made it known by sending his angel to his servant John.' But are the details of this transmission as he supposes? Is it not saying that this is the revelation which Jesus received from God, and which he, his angel, passed on to John. A comparison with the similar passage in Ezekiel suggests that the one who receives the scroll and eats it is the prophet, (Ezek. 3:3; cf. Rev. 10:10). The one who hands him the open scroll is the LORD (Ezek. 1:28ff.; cf. Rev. 10:1). In Revelation 5 the Lamb has received and opened the scroll, suggesting that the Lamb is the LORD (see below, Chapter 5). Eating the scroll does not indicate absorbing the message in order to reveal it; Origen commented that these eaten scrolls were a sign of the secret tradition. '. . . Our prophets knew of greater things than any of the scriptures which they did not commit to writing. Ezekiel, for example, received a roll written within and without . . . but at the command of the Logos (note it is the Logos, the second God!), he swallowed the book in order that its contents might not be written and so made known to unworthy persons. John also is recorded to have seen and done a similar thing' (*Celsus* 6:6, PG xi 1297). He goes on to relate this to the secret tradition of Jesus' teachings. Revelation 10 emphasizes that John is not to write down what he hears from the seven thunders and that he is to eat the scroll. This is a passage about secrecy. Jesus, who, as the Lamb, took the scroll and learned its secrets, passed them on to John. Cf. Daniélou's conclusion, 'Tradition', p. 208: 'Ainsi nous parait l'existence d'une succession des maîtres gnostiques ou maîtres spirituels, distincte de la succession des évêques, qui transmettent la foi des Apôtres . . .'

with which Matthew ends the parable: 'Many are called but few chosen' (Matt. 22:14) reflects the small number who were able to ascend and become the Chosen Ones, like Jesus (cf. John 1:34). The evangelists note, however, that the disciples still did not fully understand, which may be a literary fiction or it may be another accurate recollection, admitting *post eventum* that the disciples had not fully understood what Jesus was trying to communicate at the time. Jesus enabled three of the disciples to share his ascent experience and to become observers of the heavenly vision ('called') rather than full participants ('chosen'). The writer of Daniel 7 would have been in a similar position, seeing the ascent but not participating, whereas the Enochic ascent visions imply that Enoch was actually involved in the process. Seeing himself transfigured was what Jesus meant by the disciples seeing the kingdom before they died.

The experience of the Transfiguration was linked to the Passion; the text implies that the disciples were being prepared in some way for the events in Jerusalem. They were to tell nobody of the vision until after Easter. Peter's speech to Cornelius in Acts 10 says that the Easter Jesus was not manifest to all but only to those who had been *appointed beforehand* as witnesses, that is, prepared for the events (Acts 10:41), suggesting that some of the disciples had been given teaching about resurrection which was not available to everyone. Far from being a misplaced resurrection experience, the Transfiguration could prove to be important evidence for what I am proposing. The experience of the transfigured LORD was given to some of the disciples before the crucifixion; they had not fully understood what was happening, but the memory of these experiences later enabled them to proclaim that Jesus had been raised beyond physical death. This raising had originally taken place at the start of the ministry. Jesus had spoken of it and how he had become the Messiah. The post-crucifixion appearances proved to the disciples that what he had claimed was true: he had been raised up and he was the Messiah.[17]

[17] (i) Wellhausen, cited by Hengel, *Studies*, p. 19, said that Jesus had been crucified as the Messiah, but he then went on to make an unnecessary distinction: the crucifixion and resurrection had transformed Jesus into the Christian Messiah, but he had been held to be the Jewish Messiah by Peter and others before the crucifixion. This distinction is also implicit in Charlesworth's title 'From Messianology to Christology', see n. 1 above. Such a distinction implies a disjunction between Jewish expectation and Christian proclamation, a disjunction which cannot be assumed, but which is necessary for any theory that the Christian communities created their own theology.

(ii) Moule's 'Introduction' to *Significance* is still the best summary of the issues. There are some scholars who hold that resurrection was 'the expression of a faith already reached by the first Christians, rather than its cause', and others who hold that the resurrection was 'the cause of a faith which did not previously exist'. What I propose is a third possibility: that the post-crucifixion appearances confirmed an existing faith in the identity of Jesus, confirmed the messianic claim made before the crucifixion that he was the risen LORD. I find it hard to give serious consideration to the view that the Jesus traditions were 'swept forward by Jews who fervently claimed that he was the Messiah

The traditions of the empty tomb were originally distinct from those of the risen LORD and, apparently, not a part of the earliest proclamation.[18] The variety and discrepancy in the present gospel accounts of the post-Easter appearances is due to confusion between pre- and post-crucifixion experiences, the best known example being the incident of the great draught of fishes. Luke incorporates it in the initial call of the disciples and suggests that for Peter it was a moment of recognition whereas in John it is part of the second ending of the gospel but again it is a moment of special significance for Peter. This hypothesis would also account for the appearances in both Jerusalem and Galilee and would ease the problems created by Paul's list of appearances in 1 Corinthians 15.

There are several places where the pre- and post-crucifixion experiences seem to have seeped into one another. In Matthew's account of Jesus' last meeting with the disciples he says he has been given all authority in heaven and on earth; the implication is that this is the result of his death and resurrection. The disciples were divided among themselves; some worshipped, says Matthew, but some doubted. *A similar claim to authority is presupposed from the start of the ministry.* The healing of the paralytic demonstrated that Jesus had *authority* on earth, a claim condemned immediately as blasphemy (Mark 2:1–12). When Matthew and Luke collect together the teaching about the turn of the era they record that it was teaching not everyone could understand ('He who has ears let him hear'): Elijah had come in the person of John

---

but had to struggle against a Jewish background which did not specify what such a declaration meant, and also, more importantly, did not allow for a crucified Messiah and cautioned against any human declaration that a man was, or had been, the Messiah', Charlesworth, *Messiah*, p. 33.

(iii) Hengel, *Studies*, pp. 2–3, perhaps said more than he realized when he made these points: '. . . at the centre of the primitive Christian message – at once offensive and salvific – was this: it was the sinless Messiah the eschatological emissary and saviour . . . who sacrificed his life "for the many", that is, for all. Hence Paul's recurring protestation that the substance of his proclamation is "[the] Christ crucified". This can be balanced with the resurrection formula, which occurs almost as frequently in Paul and later authors, "God raised Jesus from the dead", that is, the man Jesus, not some ethereal, semi-divine figure'. The original sequence must have been that the man was raised before the Christ was crucified.

(iv) Morton Smith, *Clement*, p. 244: 'These experiences which Jesus's disciples had during his lifetime probably shaped and produced their visions of him after his death. Thus the resurrection and ascension stories are reflections of the transfiguration experiences which were produced in the "kingdom of God".' The recollection of their initiation almost certainly does lie behind the three disciples' account of the transfiguration, but I am not happy with Morton Smith's description of what these experiences were; I suspect that they were in fact a part of the otherwise secret traditions of the Jerusalem priesthood and that is why it was the temple hierarchy who had Jesus put to death. See Elior, n. 22(ii) below.

[18] A good summary in Brown, *Conception*, pp. 117–29, or Pannenberg, *Jesus*, pp. 88–106.

the Baptist, mighty works had been performed and a great judgement was prophesied for the town of Galilee. Only a few had understood; hidden things had been revealed to babes and 'all things' had been given over to Jesus. Luke adds that the seventy returned having discovered their power over demons and Jesus saw this as the fall of Satan, the heavenly battle realized on earth (cf. John 12:31). John 3:35 is similar but the context is very significant; the Father has given all things to the Son, the one who has come down from heaven bearing witness to what he has seen.

One possible construction on the evidence is this: Jesus' transformation experience enabled him to claim, and to exercise, authority over evil in all its forms. The tradition in John suggests that the authority was the result of an ascent experience. This authority was then given to some of the disciples when they joined him in his Melchizedek task of driving back the power of Satan. The authority was given to Jesus at the start of the ministry; the whole tradition of the miracles presupposes such an authority which our present reading of the gospels would assign to the post-crucifixion period. It is possible that the gospels were written entirely with the wisdom of hindsight and that the post-crucifixion gift of authority was read back into the ministry. It is just as possible, however, that the tradition of authority was an authentic recollection of Jesus' claims and style, and that the problem has arisen over when the 'resurrection' authority was given, when Jesus was exalted, when he became the LORD.

The Teaching of the Risen LORD

Had we only the canonical gospels our story might end there, but the existence of a number of non-canonical texts adds a whole new dimension to the problem. The characteristic form of these texts is a post-resurrection discourse between Jesus and a select group of disciples, usually assembled on a mountain top, who are given secret teaching about the heavenly places, the garments of light which they would be given, and their own ascent. Certain themes invite speculation: the appearances of the risen LORD are theophanies; Jesus ascends in a chariot of the spirit (*Apocryphon of James* CG I.2:14; cf. *Odes of Solomon* 38) and he is described as the great high priest (*Epistle of the Apostles* 42; cf. Ignatius, *Philadelphians* 9). Most curious of all, perhaps, is the length of the post-resurrection period; the *Pistis Sophia* says that Jesus was with his disciples for eleven years, but other texts say it was for eighteen months or a similar number of days.[19] *Eighteen months would correspond well enough to the traditional length of the ministry from baptism to crucifixion; was*

---

[19] *Apocryphon of James*, CG I.2:2 says 550 days; Irenaeus, *Against Heresies* I.3.2, PG vii 469 and I.30.14, PG vii 703 says eighteen months. *Ascension of Isaiah* 9:16 (OTP 2) says 545 days.

this the origin of the post-resurrection discourses with the disciples?
Were they in fact distant memories of secret teachings given by Jesus
to the disciples before his crucifixion? And what of the ascents of
the disciples themselves? In the *Apocryphon of James* and in the
Dialogue of the Saviour named disciples ascend and have visions of
the heavens and the abyss. These texts are notoriously difficult to
date, but the *Apocryphon of James* and the *Dialogue of the Saviour*
could be from the first half of the second century. In other words,
they are among the earliest Christian writings outside the New
Testament.

The *Apocryphon of James* is in the form of a letter from James the
Righteous to an unnamed enquirer.

> You asked me to send you the secret teaching which was revealed to me
> and Peter by the LORD. . . . Be careful and take heed not to rehearse to
> many this writing which the Saviour did not wish to divulge even to all of
> us, his twelve disciples . . . (*Ap.J.* 1)

He goes on to describe how the LORD appeared to his assembled disciples
550 days after his resurrection; what he looked like, whether he was
man or angel, is not recorded. He drew aside Peter and James for special
instruction and when this was finished he ascended, borne up by a
chariot of the spirit. Peter and James ascended after him. In the first
place the two saw and heard wars and trumpets. Then they rose higher
and saw and heard the angelic hosts but they were not permitted to
ascend further into the presence of the majesty. The other disciples
summoned them back to earth and learned what they had seen of the
exalted Christ.

Irrespective of the pedigree of the actual teaching in this text, there
are several interesting details. The epistolary form is reminiscent of the
beginning of Revelation; the ascent of Peter and James is like the ascent
of John at the beginning of Revelation and the unnamed person
mentioned by Paul in 2 Corinthians 12:1–4. Jesus being carried up in
the chariot of the spirit is similar to *Odes of Solomon* 38. From this we
may conclude that the components of this post-resurrection discourse
genre were well attested in known Christian texts. Further, it is unlikely
that ascent would have been associated with a prominent figure such
as John if the practice had been totally alien to the teaching of Jesus
and the tradition of the churches.

The Epistle of the Apostles is another post-resurrection discourse,
but in no sense is it a gnostic text.[20] The disciples touch the risen LORD
who then speaks to them:

[20] Why choose the post-resurrection discourse? Schneemelcher, *Apocrypha* I, p. 229,
quoting Vielhauer, says, the 'gnostic' form of a text with no obviously gnostic
content was 'an attempt to combat gnostic opponents with their own weapons'.
Daniélou, *Tradition*, p. 203, suggested exactly the opposite: he thought the gnostics
chose a revelation discourse form in order to give an air of authenticity to their own
compositions!

Rise up and I will reveal to you what is above the heaven and what is in heaven and your rest that is in the kingdom of heaven. For my Father has given me the power to take up you and those who believe in me (*Ep.Ap.* 12).

After they have recognized him, Jesus tells his disciples how he descended to become incarnate; he reveals the time and manner of his second coming and shows how he fulfils the prophecies. The text ends with a description of the ascension; there is thunder, lightning and an earthquake, the heavens open and a cloud takes Jesus away. The voice of many angels is heard, welcoming Jesus and saying, 'Gather us, O Priest, unto the light of the majesty.' *Jesus is the priest of the angels.*

In the *Sophia of Jesus Christ* the risen LORD appears 'like a great angel of light' whose likeness cannot be described. In the *Apocryphon of John* the appearance of the risen LORD is a classic description of a theophany. A light shines and the earth shakes, and a figure with three forms appears in the light.[21] The *Pistis Sophia* describes a blaze of light, an earthquake and a commotion in the heavens. The *Letter of Peter to Philip* describes a great light and a voice when the disciples were gathered together on the top of the Mount of Olives.

Later orthodoxy strove to condemn this material as heretical, but its very quantity and consistency must raise questions as to its origin. It was Daniélou who wisely observed that if the later gnostics presented their strange teachings in the form of post-resurrection secret teachings, it must have been because they wanted them accepted as genuine. If a forgery does not resemble the original it has little chance of being accepted and so the gnostic fiction of post-resurrection secret teachings indicates that there had been genuine secret teachings in this form.

Such a belief in secret teaching persisted in the church for centuries. Eusebius, quoting a lost writing of Clement of Alexandria, wrote this: 'James the Righteous, John and Peter were entrusted by the LORD after his resurrection with the higher knowledge. They imparted it to the other apostles and the other apostles to the seventy, one of whom was Barnabas'. (*History* 2:1 quoting the lost *Hypotyposes*, PG xx 136). Clement chose to call the teaching gnosis,[22] and this has raised suspicions

---

[21] The text is not clear about the first form but the second and third were an old man and a servant. For plurality in theophany see Ezekiel 1 and Genesis 18. Also Segal, *Two Powers*, pp. 33–59.

[22] (i) Daniélou, *Gospel Message*, p. 447, thought this 'gnosis' was the key to understanding Clement's thought. It is clear that Clement knew the temple traditions of ascent as I have reconstructed them, 'Secret Tradition', pp. 33–8. He also knew more of the apocalyptic writings and more about them than we do: he knows 1 *Enoch* (*Inst* 3:2, PG viii 576; *Misc* v.1, PG ix 24) and *The Assumption of Moses* (*Misc* vi.15, PG ix 356) but also the *Apocalypse of Zephaniah*, a work now lost. He also knew the *Gospel of the Egyptians* (*Misc* iii 9, PG viii 1165) of which Epiphanius, *Against Heresies* II.1.62.2, PG xli 1052, said: '. . . many strange things were handed down (in it) as having come secretly from the Saviour . . .'; and the *Gospel according to the Hebrews* (*Misc* ii.9, PG viii 981).

in the minds of those who are certain that Jesus had no dealing with gnosis. There are, however, several passages in the New Testament which speak of heavenly powers, cosmic struggles and mysteries. Either these were an unauthorized addition to the teaching of Jesus or there was more to that teaching than appears in the gospels. Morton Smith suspected that the Pauline letters, read literally, give a far clearer picture of the teaching of Jesus than do the gospels. There may, he said, have been a 'seepage of secret material into originally exoteric texts. . . . More of the esoteric teaching is found in the epistles of Paul, the oldest Christian documents, and those most surely written for reading within the closed circles of the churches . . . Paul enables us to glimpse the true beliefs of the congregation to which he writes, and he is to be preferred, as a source for early Christian thought to the later, comparatively exoteric, gospels.'[23]

Recent work by M. D. Goulder has drawn the lines rather differently. He suggests that some of the original beliefs of the Palestinian Christians can be recovered from Paul's descriptions of his enemies. The accounts of the church in the New Testament show that there were two different 'missions', two different versions of the faith which 'agreed about the significance of Jesus' but were divided on most other issues. The original Palestinian Christians 'lost the great battle'[24] and because the New Testament was largely written by the followers of Paul, the details of the earliest years have been lost. A characteristic of the Palestinian Christians was their belief in visions and the 'knowledge' which they gave. The envoys of the Palestinian Christians were the group at Colossae who insisted on the Jewish calendar, food laws and the cult of angels, and who claimed to have had visions (Col. 2:16–18) which gave gnosis, knowledge. Knowledge and vision are also linked in 1 Corinthians 1–2 where Paul is opposing those who crucified Jesus; although he calls them 'the rulers of this age' he must be referring to Jews.[25] If Goulder is correct in identifying knowledge and visions as characteristic of the Jerusalem Christians rather than as evidence for pagan mysteries or

---

(ii) *Contra* Elior, 'Mysticism', p. 47, the 'knowledge' of priests and angels was not parallel in the sense of separate; it was identical. This is why the fallen angels were depicted in some traditions, e.g. *1 Enoch*, as betraying their knowledge. They were 'fallen' priests. Suter, 'Fallen Angel', pp. 122–4, suggests that the version of the fallen angels myth in *1 Enoch* 6–16 reflects the problems of priestly marriages at the beginning of the second Temple period. This may indicate 'when' the knowledge was 'betrayed', cf. *Jubilees* 4:15 – the angels came to earth to teach their knowledge as in Malachi 2:6–7, the duty of a priest who was an angel of the LORD of Hosts. Also, perhaps, Hosea 3:6.
[23] Morton Smith, *Clement*, p. 251. The alternative, Hengel, *Son*, p. 2, is that the epistles record an immediate decline from the original teaching of Jesus into an acutely hellenized mystery cult.
[24] Goulder, *Tale*, p. x and p. 188.
[25] See Goulder 'Vision and Knowledge'; there are details in this reconstruction with which I cannot agree, but it serves as a working hypothesis. See also Goulder 'Sophia', 'Visionaries' and Fossum, 'Colossians'; Attridge, 'Angel'.

gnosticism in the young churches, this is important additional evidence for identifying what Clement calls 'gnosis, knowledge'.

The gnosis which Clement knew was, I suggest, the unwritten tradition of the teaching of Jesus, whom he regarded as identical with the LORD of the Old Testament.

> If then we assert that Christ himself is Wisdom, and that it was his working which showed itself in the prophets, by which the gnostic tradition may be learned, as he himself taught the apostles during his presence; then it follows that the gnosis which the knowledge and apprehension of things present, future and past which is sure and reliable, as being imparted and revealed by the Son of God, is wisdom (*Misc* vi.7, PG ix 281, 4).

Revealed is an important word since this immediately places his gnosis in the realm of visionary experience rather than of intellectual inquiry. Those who have this truth, he said, enter in through the tradition of the LORD *by drawing aside the curtain* (*Misc* vii.17, PG ix 548). This is temple imagery. What was beyond the curtain in the temple was the heavenly world, the subject of the apocalyptists' visions. Second, Clement's mysteries had their roots in the Old Testament; 'On the one hand then are the mysteries which were hid until the time of the apostles and were delivered by them as they received them from the LORD and, concealed in the Old Testament, were manifested to the saints' (*Misc* v.10, PG ix 93). In other words, the roots of his secret tradition were pre-Christian. Paul, he says, 'clearly reveals that knowledge belongs not to all . . . for there were certainly among the Hebrews some things delivered unwritten . . .' (*Misc* v.10, PG ix 96). Third, the goal of his gnostic was *theoria*, contemplation, and what he says about the effect of this contemplation shows that it was identical to the ascent which transformed the merkavah mystics into angelic beings. 'The gnosis itself is that which has descended by transmission to a few, having been imparted unwritten by the apostles. Hence knowledge or wisdom ought to be exercised up to the eternal and unchangeable habit of contemplation (*Misc* vi.7, PG ix 284). The gnostic, says Clement, is transformed by his contemplation and becomes divine;

> (Gnosis) leads us to the endless and perfect end, teaching us beforehand the future life we shall lead, according to God and with gods. . . . Then become pure in heart and near to the LORD, there awaits them restoration to everlasting contemplation; and they are called by the appellation of gods, being destined to sit on other thrones with the other gods that have first been put in their places by the Saviour (*Misc* vii.10, PG ix 480).

> He also prays in the company of angels, as if being already of angelic rank . . . (*Misc* vii.12, PG ix 508).

Note the resurrection imagery here and that worshipping with angels was exactly the claim of the Qumran community! Note also: 'On this wise it is possible for the gnostic already to have become God; "I said ye are gods and sons of the Highest"' (*Misc* iv.23, PG viii 1359).

Gnostic souls . . . reckoned holy among the holy . . . embracing the divine vision not in mirrors or by means of mirrors, but in the transcendently clear and absolutely pure insatiable vision which is the privilege of intensely loving souls. . . . Such is the vision attainable by the pure in heart. This is the function of the gnostic who has been perfected: to have converse with God *through the great High Priest* (*Misc* vii.3, PG ix 417).

Clement was not unique. Ignatius of Antioch claimed to know 'celestial secrets and angelic hierarchies and the dispositions of the heavenly powers and much else both seen and unseen' (*Trallians* 5, PG v 680). Since he also warned against 'the teachings and time-worn fables of another people' (*Magnesians* 8, PG v 669) we can only conclude that the bishop was summarizing sound Christian teaching early in the second century. 'To Jesus alone *as our high priest* were the secret things of God committed,' he wrote to the Philadelphians. (*Philadelphians* 9, PG v 703–4.) Thus he agrees with Clement and with the writer of the *Epistle of the Apostles*; there were secret teachings given to *Jesus the high priest*.[26]

Origen also knew of a secret tradition which was given to the disciples after the resurrection which he understands as the Easter event. Explaining 'I have yet many things to say to you but you cannot hear them now' (John 16:12), he says that Jesus found it impossible to take his disciples beyond the surface meaning of the Jewish law and 'postponed such a task to a future season, to that namely which followed his passion and resurrection' (*Celsus* 2:2, PG xi 797). He claimed that both Old and New Testament were sources of the secret or ineffable tradition. There can be little doubt that what he described in this way was the tradition which, in another context and at an earlier period, we should have called apocalyptic. It is clear that he knew *1 Enoch* although he recognized that it was not scripture.[27] Nevertheless, he had no doubt that the secret tradition of the apocalypses was rooted in the Bible and he dismissed Celsus' claim that it had come from Persia.

. . . our prophets did know of greater things than any in the Scriptures which they did not commit to writing. Ezekiel, for example, received a scroll written within and without but at the command of the Logos he

[26] (i) Irenaeus, *Demonstration*, gave an account of the essential teachings of Christianity. The first topic was knowledge of the seven heavens with their powers and archangels, and the relationship of Word and Wisdom. He knew that this teaching was enshrined in temple traditions about the menorah.
(ii) Compare 1QH I.11 – like *1 Enoch* 17–36; 72–82: also 1QH XIII; 1QM XIV.14.
(iii) Stone, 'Lists', for details of what was revealed.
[27] His knowledge of *1 Enoch* is clear from *First Principles* I.3.3, PG xi 148; *Homily on Numbers* 28:2, PG xii 802; *Celsus* 5:54, PG xi 1265. The traditions were rooted in Scripture, *Celsus* 6:23, PG xi 1325. The extent to which he understood the tradition of the apocalypses can be seen in his speculations about angels: discussing Matthew 22:23 he wonders whether some people do become angels before the general resurrection.

swallowed it in order that its contents might not be written and so made known to unworthy persons. . . . And it was related of Jesus, who was greater than all these, that he conversed with his disciples in private and especially in their secret retreats concerning the gospel of God; but the words which he uttered have not been preserved because it appeared to the evangelists that they could not be adequately conveyed to the multitude in writing or speech (*Celsus* 6.6, PG xi 1297).

Jesus 'who beheld weighty secrets and made them known to a few' (*Celsus* 3.37, PG xi 969) had had knowledge of angels and demons. This emphasis on secret teaching appears time and again in Origen's writings. In the preface to *First Principles* we read :

The following fact should be understood. The holy apostles . . . took certain doctrines . . . and delivered them in the plainest terms to all believers. . . . There were other doctrines, however, about which the apostles simply said that things were so, keeping silence as to how or why . . . (*Preface* 3, PG xi 116).

Like Clement, he knew that the tradition did not originate with Jesus:

The Jews used to tell of many things in accordance with secret traditions reserved to a few, for they had other knowledge than that which was common and made public (*On John* XIX.31, PG xiv 552–3).

Daniélou suggested that this knowledge might have been the names of the angels which were part of the secret teaching of the Essenes. It is more likely that it was the secret teachings of the priests. Even in the New Testament Jesus was described as the revealer and as the high priest who had passed beyond the curtain. The secret traditions of the priests became the secret traditions of Christianity. The secret things of which Jesus spoke were, or became, forbidden.[28]

There is evidence of secrecy in the synoptic gospels but no agreement as to its significance. The references to private teaching (e.g. Mark 4:10; 7:17; 10:10) are not significant; the location is not a mountain top and the topics were such matters as the purity laws and divorce, hardly esoterica. The evidence for a secret teaching is to be found in the reference to the mystery of the Kingdom (Mark 4:11), not given to those outside (Matt. 13:11). The parable of the sower describes the

---

[28] (i) Many priests became Christian, Acts 6:7.

(ii) The traditions about James, the first leader of the Jerusalem church, suggest that he continued to act as a priest or even as high priest, Eusebius, *History* 2:23 (PG xx 197). See also my 'Secret Tradition', pp. 60–1.

(iii) Deuteronomy 29:29 and 30:11–14 suggest that there had been a secret tradition. Given the opposition of the Deuteronomists to so much of the cult of the first temple, it is not beyond possibility that what they were opposing here was the priestly ascent tradition. Compare CD V.5 which implies a secret tradition known to the Zadokite priests. Also Bockmuehl, *Revelation*, pp. 44–5; and pp. 117–23 on the 'mysteries of Israel', 'the keepers of mysteries' and 'the scrolls of secrets' b.*Shab* 6b, 96b; b.*BM* 92a.

(iv) 2 *Esdras* 4:8; m.*Ḥag* 2:1; *Mekhilta of R. Ishmael* on Exodus 19:20. See also Chapter 1, n. 26.

different responses even of those who were the good soil; only some of them 'yielded one hundredfold'; the rest were only thirtyfold or sixtyfold. Q implies that Jesus had revealed something to his disciples which kings and prophets had longed for but not achieved. (Matt. 13:16–17; Luke 10:23–4; cf. Rev. 5:3.) 1 Peter 1:10–12 speaks of things into which angels longed to look, things which were revealed to the prophets and have now been proclaimed as the gospel. John's Jesus says that only those born from above can see the kingdom (John 3:3). In his letter to Rome, Paul writes of 'the revelation of the mystery which was kept secret for long ages but is now disclosed and through the prophetic writings made known to all nations' (Rom. 16:25–6). The implication must be that the disciples had been enabled to see something, literally, which had been denied to the angels, prophets and kings of the past.

What they saw concerned the person of Jesus. The confession at Caesarea Philippi shows that many people had recognized Jesus as a prophet, but only Peter (and the disciples) knew he was the Messiah. This enabled some of them to see the transfigured Jesus six days later, seeing the kingdom of God before their death as Jesus had promised them. As the gospel stories are told, there is evidence for at least two attitudes towards Jesus on the part of those who followed him; there were those who saw him as a great prophet and a healer (presumably this is what is implied by the reaction in Luke 7:16) and there were those who saw him as more than just a prophet. These two levels of understanding co-existed throughout the ministry. The recognition of the risen LORD came to some before the crucifixion, to some afterwards and to some not at all; Jesus' Messiahship was not just written into the ministry as the result of the later church's hindsight.

The tradition of secret teaching was no doubt an opportunity for the creative minds of later generations to add what they thought Jesus ought to have taught. (The same has often been said about the composition of the gospels, but it has been phrased rather differently; the community adapted sayings, prophets gave new sayings and so forth, which were added to the original stock.) Nevertheless, the persistent belief that there had been a large body of teaching from the risen LORD cannot be ignored, especially when there are so many references to mysteries in the rest of the New Testament.

The Mind of the Messiah

It is time to look again at the hypothesis of the messianic secret. In its original form, Wrede explained the secrecy motifs in Mark's gospel by saying that they were evidence for two different stages in the understanding of Jesus. Jesus himself had not understood himself to be the Messiah; the messianic texts had been created by the young church in order to make it appear that its own claims about Jesus as the Messiah

had come from Jesus himself. The earlier belief had been that he became
Messiah at the resurrection whereas later it was accepted that he had
also been Messiah during his earthly life. The young church combined
the two positions by means of the secrecy motifs; Jesus had been Messiah
during the ministry but this was kept secret until after the resurrection.[29]
There have been many modifications to the thesis and many well-
founded criticisms, not least that Wrede used very few of the relevant
primary sources and that he offered no explanation of how the resurrection came to be seen as proof of Messiahship if this had not been part
of Jesus' teachings about himself. Nevertheless, it is possible that Jesus
did have difficulty in convincing people who he was, not because they
had a totally different expectation of what the Messiah would be like,
but because Jesus' claims were seen as bizarre and blasphemous. It is
possible, too, that the secrecy motif was not a later fiction to accom-
modate developing belief but an accurate recollection of what had
happened. Had there been different perceptions of Jesus during the
ministry, these could all have fed into the common stock of memories
about him. The inner group had known about the Messiahship before
the crucifixion but those followers who had seen Jesus as no more
than a prophet came to realize who he was after the crucifixion. Luke's
account of the two disciples going to Emmaus suggests this; they saw
Jesus as a great prophet but were subsequently convinced that he was
more than a prophet. Those who joined the church at Pentecost almost
certainly included people who had formerly held Jesus to be a prophet,
and would have told their stories about him in this way.

   The form critics too have attempted to reconstruct something of the
earliest communities from the traces of growth and development still
discernible in the gospel texts. Something similar should be possible
for the growth and development of Jesus' own consciousness of sonship
unless we adopt that 'reverent process of insulation'[30] which is such an
effective hindrance to any real understanding. There are certain parables,
for example, which seem to be autobiographical. The parables of the
growth of the kingdom could well describe Jesus' own awareness of
the kingship of God within himself in the earlier period of his life,
growing like the secret seed or the leaven. After the experience at his
baptism he could describe the discovery of the kingship as the pearl of
great price or the hidden treasure for which he had to give up everything.
The saying about putting one's hand to the plough and not turning

   [29] (i) Sanday, 'Injunctions', p. 324, put the contrary and prevailing view: the secrecy
was due to Jesus 'recasting' the current views of the Messiah in order to remove its
political overtones. More recently, Dunn, 'Messianic Secret', p. 127, reprinted in Tuckett,
Secret: 'The command to silence is given not so much because Jesus' Messiahship is
secret but because it is misunderstood.'
   (ii) The tradition that the messiahship dated from the resurrection is probably
authentic; what is not is the assertion that such teaching cannot have come from Jesus
himself!
   [30] Underhill, *Mystic Way*, p. 74.

back (Luke 9:62) was drawn from personal experience. The sayings where the Son of Man seems to be someone other than Jesus could have originated before his baptism, when he knew the traditions but had not experienced the transforming ascent.[31]

This hypothesis would also account for the accusation of blasphemy: the claim to forgive sins was linked to Jesus' authority as Son of Man (Mark 2:7–10).[32] The incident in John 10 where Jesus was stoned for blasphemy, 'making himself God', was probably drawn from life; Jesus justified his claim not only by his good works but also by referring to Psalm 82 which speaks unambiguously of beings in the heavenly council who are called sons of God Most High. At the trial he was accused of blasphemy when he agreed, apparently, that he was the Messiah, the Son of God and that as Son of Man he would be enthroned in heaven and come on the clouds. It is possible that all these incidents were the result of a sophisticated reworking of traditions by the young churches but the simpler explanation has also to be considered; that this is an accurate recollection of how the ministry was and that the accusations of blasphemy were just that. Jesus was conscious that he had become the divine figure, that he was the LORD, the Son of God Most High,

---

[31] (i) Underhill, *Mystic Way*, p. 103: 'Each successive redaction of those gospels removed them a little further from that shining world of wonder in which they had their origin, to deposit them at last in the anatomical museums where the dead fancies of faith are preserved.'

(ii) Hengel, *Studies*, pp. 75–6, summarizes the traditional position: the antiquity of (Q) is established by the fact that 'it contains neither of the titles most frequently used by the later church, *Christos* and *Kyrios*, nor a clear, unambiguous reference to the early Christian kerygma of the death and resurrection of Jesus ... the coming Son of Man is clearly distinguished from the contemporary teacher Jesus ... all this clearly indicates ... this source reflects the sayings of Jesus ... The foundations of this collection could ... partially derive from the pre-Easter period.'

Another interpretation could be put on these findings: that the Son of Man sayings came from the pre-baptism period, and the others from the public, exoteric teaching of the ministry. The recognition of Jesus as the Christ, the LORD, was what distinguished the esoteric from the exoteric teaching, and without this recognition any teaching about the death and resurrection (or rather, resurrection and death!) of the Christ would have been irrelevant.

(iii) It has also been suggested, Mack, *Lost Gospel*, pp. 203ff., that the growth of the early community can be detected in the three proposed strata of Q; the earliest stratum was proverbial sayings and teachings, the authentic words of Jesus; the second stage suggests a time of social conflict and the language of judgement comes into the sayings; the third stage shows Jesus as the Son of God whose kingdom would be revealed only at the end of time. Were this analysis correct, it could be showing not the growth of the early church but rather a development in the teaching of Jesus himself. What Mack calls Q1 would be an early stage of the teaching, before the baptism. Q2 would be from the early part of the ministry, reflecting the problem with his family and the rejection by his own people. Q3 would be sayings to the disciples.

[32] Lindars, *Jesus*, pp. 44–7, suggests that 'Son of Man has an indefinite quality', and that the saying means simply, 'a man may have authority to forgive sins'. Despite the evidence of 4Q242 which he cites, it seems more likely that Jesus was making a specific point about himself.

visiting his people. Thus he spoke of God Most High as his father, and all who received the Spirit in their turn became such sons of God (Luke 6:36; Rom. 8:15; Gal. 4:6)

Vestiges of Jesus' merkavah experience are to be found in the Book of Revelation and also in the synoptic apocalypses and the Son of Man sayings. It was suggested some time ago that the present form of the book of Revelation incorporated material from the circle of John the Baptist; in particular, it was suggested that the *Apocalypse of the Lamb* originated there.[33] In the years before his public ministry, I suggest, Jesus knew these traditions and was shaped by them. At first, he knew them as an observer, much as the seer of Daniel 7 observed the ascent of the Son of Man, but after the baptism experience he participated in the vision, as Enoch had done, and knew he had been transformed. He identified himself as the Lamb of the vision with all that that entailed. He must have revealed this to his inner group, and this is why John's gospel links the baptism of Jesus with his recognition as the Lamb of God who takes way the sin of the world. The cluster of titles in the first chapter of the gospel – Lamb of God, Son of God, Messiah, King of Israel and Son of Man – may be far more than a literary device to preface the gospel. The titles probably reflect the expectations of those who cherished the *Apocalypse of the Lamb*, those for whom the Lamb was the ancient Servant of the LORD. Many scholars have suggested that the Book of Revelation includes allusions to the gospels,[34] but an

---

[33] Ford, *Revelation*, pp. 30f., drew attention to the link between John and the Lamb texts in the gospels.

[34] (i) The similarities between the Book of Revelation and other parts of the New Testament were listed by Charles, *Revelation*, vol. 1, pp. lxxxiv-vi) He assumed that Revelation echoed the other texts, but the examples he gave could also have been used to show that Matthew, Luke, 1 Thessalonians, 1 and 2 Corinthians, Colossians, Ephesians, Galatians, 1 Peter and James (the parallels he identifies) all knew the traditions in Revelation. It seems more likely that such a diverse collection of writings all knew the one text (or rather, the tradition) than that the seer composed his vision using a desk full of early Christian writings. When discussing the seven seals of Revelation 6, Charles virtually concedes that the tradition in Revelation antedates that of the gospels, but does not make the obvious connection, vol. 1, p. 158–9: 'It is remarkable that neither in Luke on the one hand nor in Matthew and Mark on the other can we find the full list of woes that appears in Revelation. . . .' The question naturally arises therefore: Did our author make use of two of the Gospels, Luke, together with Matthew or Mark; or did he use the document behind the Gospels, the Little Apocalypse, the existence of which so many scholars have felt themselves obliged to assume; or thirdly, was he simply dependent on oral tradition for his material? The tradition behind the Gospels was the earliest form of Revelation, the form in which Jesus delivered it to his inner group of disciples.

(ii) Bauckham, *Climax*, pp. 92–117, discussed the relationship between Revelation 3:3, 20; 16:15 and the Parousia parables. He suggested that the sayings, both in Revelation and elsewhere, were dependent on the parables and were evidence of a process of deparabolization(!) into simile or metaphor. The same evidence would also be compatible with another model: that the underlying stratum of Revelation came from Jesus himself and that John supplemented the prophecies at a later date, adding allusions

exactly opposite position is also possible; that some of the visions of Revelation, because they were known to Jesus and developed by him, find echoes in the gospel record of his ministry. The sequence of woes in the Little Apocalypse is an obvious example of this, as are the angel reapers, the sheep and the goats, the thief in the night, and the great wedding feast. The identification of Jesus as Son of Man, destined to return and bring the last judgement, did not originate in the creative theologising of the young church; it was part of an existing hope which also involved the sacrificial death of the central figure. Jesus may originally have seen the Man figure as someone other than himself, but after the experience of his baptism he grew to accept that this was his role, with all that it entailed by way of death in Jerusalem as the great atonement sacrifice. Jesus expected that he would return and bring the judgement.

The paradigm I am proposing answers several questions. It shows the link between Christology and Soteriology and roots both in first-century Palestine, interpreting what is there within the resources of available tradition. The resurrection was reported and interpreted only by Jews and the original meaning of resurrection may well have been the secret of Christian origins which died with the Palestinian church. The paradigm I am proposing also shows that what Jesus believed about himself was identical with what the young church preached about him, even though he had been imperfectly understood at times. It makes Jesus himself the author and finisher of the faith, rather than the early communities, a supposition which has been fashionable for some time. The great message of atonement was not just a damage limitation exercise on the part of a traumatized group of disciples who could find no other way of coming to terms with the death of their leader.[35] The sources do enable us to see how Jesus understood his own death, if only we listen to what they are saying and do not sit in judgement upon them with preconceived notions of what could and could not

---

to the exoteric teaching of Jesus. The parables were for those who had not been given the secrets of the kingdom, Mark 4:11. It is possible that allusions to known parables would have served to establish the connection between the esoteric teaching and that which was more widely known. The wedding feast of the Lamb, Revelation 19:9, appears in exoteric form as the parables in Matthew 22:1–14 and Matthew 25:1–13. There are also allusions to Jesus' mystical experiences in the synoptic sayings, e.g. Matthew 7:9, is reminiscent of Matthew 4:3, turning stones into bread, and Luke 10:18 cannot be explained in any other way.

(iii) The only conclusion to be drawn from these investigations is the need to examine one's premises before one examines a text! Both the priority of Revelation and its originating with Jesus are inherently more probable. How else can one explain its presence in the canon, the allusions to its contents elsewhere in early Christian writings and the evidence for a secret tradition going back to Jesus?

[35] (i) This view has been around since the work of Reimarus (1694–1768).

(ii) Hengel, *Studies*, p. 14: Does the Christian faith then not rest on a grandiose self-deception?

have been the case. The predictions of the Passion were made by Jesus, even though the details may have been added later.

The paradigm I am proposing also raises enormous questions and I hope to be able to pursue these at some time in the future. I have become dissatisfied with the many contemporary approaches to the New Testament and find myself in complete agreement with Martin Hengel who wrote recently of some New Testament scholarship which has become 'confused with some sort of historical science fiction'.[36] So many approaches, whilst proclaiming their own sophistication, are in fact naive. Christian source texts cannot be read with twentieth-century eyes; we need to stand where they stood, look where they looked and then we may be granted a glimpse of what they saw. Vladimir Lossky wrote this of the Transfiguration; it applies equally to those who would seek to understand the New Testament:

> To see the divine light with bodily sight, as the disciples saw it on Mount Tabor, we must participate in and be transformed by it, according to our capacity.[37]

Jesus believed himself to be the LORD manifested on earth. From the few fragments of material that survive we can begin to reconstruct the secret tradition of the temple priesthood, the world within which he lived and died. He had known the traditions of the mystics for some time before his own experience of ascent and profound illumination. This is why the Book of Revelation is a part of our New Testament. He achieved at his baptism that sense of complete identification with God which the mystics so often call the resurrection life. The gospels tell us almost nothing about the interior journey that ended in Gethsemane, when he finally accepted his death, but sufficient has survived for us to deduce that it was shaped by a profound conviction that he was the High Priest who had been chosen to make the great atonement. He had been raised up at his baptism and become the LORD, the Son of God Most High, and his ministry was a conscious expression of that conviction. He was the risen LORD before his death, the LORD who had to give his life to his people. Thus the Gospel of Philip had preserved for us an extraordinary fragment of the earliest faith:

> The Nazarene is he who reveals what is hidden. . . . Those who say that the LORD died first and then rose up are in error for he rose up first and then died. If one does not first attain the resurrection, will he not die? Jesus did not reveal himself in the manner in which he was, but it was in the manner in which they would be able to see him that he revealed himself. . . . He revealed himself to the angels as an angel and to men as a man. . . . He became great but he made his disciples great that they might be able to see him in his greatness.

---

[36] Ibid. p. 68.
[37] Lossky, *Mystical Theology*, p. 224.

5

Revelation

The preoccupation with minutiae is so complete that the larger issues often seem to be obscured. Nobody would argue that the many volumes of hermetic textual analysis so characteristic of our discipline cannot contribute anything; but is it not obvious that the specialist argument can work quite effectively to block the larger, the more interesting and, perhaps, the more intellectually serious perspective?

BERNHARD LANG
Monotheism, p. 10

THE central figure in the Book of Revelation is the Lamb and yet this title continues to defy explanation. The Lamb has been identified as the lamb of Isaiah 53:7,[1] as the warrior ram of the Enochic *Animal Apocalypse*,[2] as the Passover lamb[3] and as the Akedah ram or the atoning sacrifice.[4] The problem with these suggestions is that none explains the most powerful image; the Lamb on the throne. This Lamb is not a meek and gentle figure, despite all the sermons to that effect; this is a warrior, a conqueror who controls and reveals the destiny of the creation and is worshipped by the hosts of heaven and the redeemed of the earth.

A theory now generally discredited is one I should like to explore again; that the Lamb was the Servant. This was first suggested as an explanation of the Lamb of God in John 1:29, 35; the one who takes away the sin of the world was seen as a reference to Isaiah 53:12, the Servant who bore the sin of many.[5] The Lamb/Servant was then transferred to the Book of Revelation as a possible explanation for the title there.[6] The suggestion was not well received on the grounds that

[1] By e.g. Swete, *Apocalypse*; Charles, *Revelation*.
[2] Dodd, *Interpretation*; Ford, *Revelation*. As a symbol of power, Kiddle, *Revelation*.
[3] Barrett, 'Lamb'; Schüssler-Fiorenza, *Justice and Judgement*; who, however, includes sacrificial lambs in *Vision of a Just World*; Roloff, *Revelation*.
[4] Farrer, *Revelation*; Hayward, 'Present State'; also Beckwith, *Apocalypse*, p. 315, who suggests the Lamb as an atoning sacrifice.
[5] Burney, *Aramaic Origin*, p. 107, building on Ball, 'Aramaic Archetype', suggesting word play on Aramaic which could also include the meaning 'child'; Jeremias, *Servant*, p. 82.
[6] Lohmeyer, *Die Offenbarung*, pp. 54-5.

there were problems with the words used for 'lamb'[7] and that there was no obvious Servant Christology in Revelation.[8] Further 'in the numerous references in Revelation to the Lamb there is no unity or coherent scheme . . .' we see an author making various attempts to broaden the use of the lamb image by combining it with other apocalyptic formulas'.[9] I want to explore the possibility that *the Lamb is the key to a highly developed Servant Christology in Revelation*, but that this has not been recognized because the Servant Christology has itself been wrongly defined. The enquiry has been too narrowly based.[10]

It is beyond doubt that the earliest descriptions of Jesus say or imply that he was the Servant.[11] Although there are only a few direct quotations from Isaiah in the New Testament[12] there are many allusions in the pre-Pauline tradition which seem to be liturgical formulae.[13] Jeremias concluded: 'The christological interpretation of the Deutero-Isaiah servant belongs to the earliest period of the Christian community and at a very early stage became fixed in form . . . of the *'ebed* texts of Deut Isa. only Isaiah 42:1–4, 6; 49:6; and Isaiah 52:13–53:12 were interpreted messianically in the New Testament. But those are the precise texts which Palestinian Judaism – as opposed to Hellenistic – interpreted messianically'.[14] The gospels imply that Jesus identified himself as the Servant, but the absence of Servant material from 'Q' indicates that this was not part of his public teaching; 'Jesus only allowed himself to be known as the Servant in his esoteric and not in his public preaching.' It would be strange indeed if there were no place for the Servant figure in Revelation, the most esoteric of all the early Christian texts.[15]

The problem is to establish what was believed about the Servant in the first century CE. Clearly, we cannot simply take the Masoretic Hebrew, read it with twentieth-century eyes and then move directly to the New Testament. Nor must we slip into the circularity of illuminating

---

[7] Dodd, *Interpretation*, pp. 235–6; Hooker, *Servant*, p. 104.

[8] Hooker, *Servant*, p. 126, and Fekkes, *Prophetic Traditions*, p. 154.

[9] Barrett, 'Lamb', p. 216. Also Aune, *Cultic Setting*, p. 72.

[10] E.g. Barrett, p. 214, 'The words of the heavenly voice (at the baptism) may be based in part upon Isaiah 42:1; but they do not contain the word "servant"; in the oldest tradition they are addressed to Jesus only, and there is no reason for thinking that a reference to the first Servant Song implies also a further reference to the last.' Hooker, *Servant*, devoted less than one page to Revelation.

[11] I find Jeremias, *Servant*, more convincing than Hooker, *Servant*, as I shall show later.

[12] Matthew 8:17; 12:18–21; Luke 22:37; John 12:38; Acts 8:32ff.; Romans 15:21.

[13] Matthew 12:18–21; Mark 1:11; 9:12; 10:45; 14:24 and parallels; Luke 2:32; 22:37; John 1:29, 36; 3:14; 10:11, 15, 17, 18; 12:34, 38; Romans 4:25; 8:32, 34; 1 Corinthians 11:23–5; 15:3–4; Philippians 2:6–11; 1 Timothy 2:6; Hebrews 9:28.

Also Acts 3:13–4; 4:30; 7:52; 22:14; 1 Peter 1:11; 2:21–5; 3:18; 1 John 2:1, 29; 3:5, 7; 4:10. See Jeremias, *Servant*, pp. 88–93.

[14] Jeremias, *Servant*, p. 93.

[15] Ibid. p. 104; it is significant that 'secret teaching' emerges again as a context, see Chapter 4.

Christian material with other Christian material. Early Christian texts show that the Servant was important for Christology; other material must be used to establish who that Servant might have been.

We have already seen that traces survive from the first temple which suggest that the Servant had been associated with human sacrifice or a ritual which represented it.[16] Isaiah 53 had been used to interpret Genesis 22 independently of Christian influence and thus some Servant traditions may have survived in the Akedah texts. Genesis 22 has a ram offered as a substitute for the son who had been demanded by the LORD and the sacrifice was regarded as an atonement which was recalled in all subsequent offerings. Hebrews 9:12 implies that the animals were regarded as substitutes as late as the first century and the text implies they were substitutes for the high priest. This suggests a link between Isaac, the Servant and the high priest. More curious still are the traditions that Isaac was not redeemed but sacrificed and then restored to life. Were they known in the first century? It was also said that Isaac saw a vision of angels or the Shekinah when he was bound on the altar.[17] Was this also Servant tradition? The temple tradition which breaks the surface in the *Similitudes of Enoch* shows that the one granted the vision of the throne became a holy one, a son of man and it is only a short step from this to giving the Servant the Name when he had been exalted after his suffering (Phil. 2:9) or making the crucified Jesus LORD and Christ (Acts 2:36). *It is this apotheosis, I suggest, that is described in Revelation as the enthronement of the Lamb. In other words, the Lamb of Revelation is the Servant.*

The Servant in the Targum and the Similitudes

In the first century, the Servant was a triumphant ruling figure not unlike the Lamb in Revelation. The *Targum* and the *Similitudes of Enoch* agree on this, and even if it could be proved that both were post-Christian, it is unlikely, as I shall show later, that the tradition itself is post-Christian. When Nickelsburg studied the so-called inter-testamental texts on this exaltation theme, he demonstrated the importance of the fourth Servant Song but reached the surprising conclusion that the Servant motifs in Wisdom 4–5 and *1 Enoch* 62–3 were a *reinterpretation* of Isaiah 52–3 as 'a scene anticipating the judgement and punishment of its audience' and *contrary to the original intent of the poem.*[18]

---

[16] See above Chapter 3, n. 20.

[17] (i) First found in *F.T.* and *T.N.* and may have developed from relating Genesis 22:14 to Isaiah 53:11. 1QIsᵃ 53:11 supports this: '. . . he shall see light'. There is nothing in *T.Isa.* which represents 'the light'. See below n. 34.

(ii) *T.Job* 3:18 interprets 'the slave, free from his master' as 'Isaac, the Servant of the LORD was delivered from bonds by his master . . .'

[18] (i) The relationship between the Christian and targumic interpretations of Isaiah 53 is 'much debated' Syrén, 'Targum', pp. 208–10. Several scholars advocate a pre-Christian origin for the ideas in the *Targum*, but none supports a pre-Christian date for

Significantly, the Servant material was found to carry the *resurrection* tradition and accounted for the hope expressed in 2 Maccabees 6–7. He found, however, no literary dependence between Wisdom, *1 Enoch* and 2 Maccabees, but rather 'three separate witnesses to a common (oral) tradition each, no doubt, adding details perhaps from Isaiah itself, not found in their common *Vorlage*'. These details would almost certainly have determined the way in which the Servant Songs were read and understood in the first century.[19]

The Servant in the *Targum* is so strikingly different from the Servant we usually discover for ourselves in Isaiah 53 that some explanation is demanded, especially as the reading of the *Targum* in the synagogue would have been preceded by the reading of the original Hebrew text. The most obvious would be that the Targum reflects the Jewish/Christian conflict over its meaning, but this cannot be demonstrated with any degree of certainty. The central figure of the song is identified as 'my Servant the Messiah' (*T.Isa.* 52:13) and the suffering of the original figure has been transferred to that of the nations whom he will judge. Thus Isaiah 53:7 becomes: 'The mighty ones of the peoples he shall deliver up like a lamb to the slaughter' and Isaiah 53:9 becomes: 'He shall deliver the wicked into Gehinnam and those that are rich in possessions which they have obtained by violence unto the death of destruction.' The Servant himself will scatter many nations (*T.Isa.* 52:13) and will pray on behalf of the people's transgressions (*T.Isa.* 53:4) and transfer their sins to their enemies (*T.Isa.* 53:8). Since there is nothing in the Masoretic text to suggest that the Servant is a messianic figure, it would be remarkable if such an interpretation had been introduced into the *Targum* after the advent of Christianity. Even though the *Targum* cannot be dated, this must be a strong argument for a messianic understanding of the passage before the Christian era, an argument strengthened by the reading of 1QIs[a] 52:14 which has *mšḥty* for MT *mšḥt*. What has altered in the *Targum* is not the belief that the passage describes the messiah but rather the nature of that Messiah and his work. The Servant in the *Targum* is a conqueror and judge, as is the central figure in Revelation. The Servant of the *Targum* is a priestly figure who makes intercession as does Jesus in Hebrews. The difference lies in the fact that the Servant of the *Targum* does not suffer; it may have been this which was intended to counter the Christian usage and that the manner of the Servant's atonement was the point at issue.[20]

---

the present text. Chilton, *Glory*, p. 94, favours a post-70 date but does not find any clearly anti-Christian tendencies.

(ii) Nickelsburg, *Resurrection*, p. 76.

[19] That the meaning of the Servant texts altered has to be demonstrated not assumed.

[20] (i) 'Even allowing for the Targumic translation technique, the section *T.Isa.* 52:13–53:12 stands out by the unusual freedom of its paraphrase in the context of *T.Isa.* 40–66 which elsewhere keeps more closely to the Hebrew text', Jeremias, *Servant*, p. 71.

The *Targum* Servant has other significant characteristics. After his exaltation his face is not marred, the usual rendering of Isaiah 52:14, but holy (*T.Isa.* 53:2). The Servant makes intercession and builds up the sanctuary which has been polluted by their transgressions (*T.Isa.* 53:5), brings judgement on Israel's enemies and gathers in the exiles (*T.Isa.* 53:8–9), purifies and cleanses the remnant and has a kingdom (*T.Isa.* 53:10). It is possible that the *Targum* Servant has been assembled from other Servant texts in the Old Testament. The radiant face of the *Targum* Servant could have been drawn from the shining face of Moses the Servant of the LORD, and the hope that he would rebuild the sanctuary could have come from Zechariah's oracle of the Servant called the Branch (Zech. 6:12; or, by implication, from Ezek. 37:24–8). The Servant as the judge of Israel's enemies could have come from David the Servant (2 Sam. 3:18) and the ingathering of the exiles from Ezekiel 34:4. Purifying and cleansing was, by implication, the role of the Servant in Isaiah 53. It is, then, *possible* that the *Targum* Servant was created from usable material in the tradition long after the 'original' figure had been forgotten.[21]

On the other hand, the *Targum* Servant could have been an accurate recollection of something older, since all the 'Servant' texts elsewhere in the Old Testament which could have contributed to the *Targum* figure could equally well have been independent witnesses to an ancient Servant tradition more like that of the Targum than that of our usual understanding of Isaiah. The *Targum* Servant, I suggest, did derive from such a figure, who had been the royal high priest (who was also the Qumran Melchizedek and the Christian Messiah). He was no longer a human figure but had been transformed by his ascent; he made intercession and purified the temple (the rebuilding was a post-exilic addition); he was enthroned and established the divine law throughout the creation; his atoning acts absorbed the evil which threatened to fragment the people and thus he enabled those who had been cut off to be restored. Finally, he transferred the sins of Israel to the head of Azazel or whoever preceded him in the atonement rituals.

There is nothing in the text of Isaiah 53 as now read to associate it directly with the ritual of atonement, apart from the reference to making a sin offering. How then could such a broadly based set of allusions 'reappear' in the *Targum* after several centuries unless there had been an unbroken tradition of understanding the figure in that way? Such apparent additions to the text must have been acceptable to a large number of people, since a *Targum* shows how the text was actually

---

(ii) Grelot, *Poèmes*, pp. 220–4, thought it a 'recomposition'.
(iii) Syrén, 'Targum', p. 205, quotes H. S. Nyberg: '. . . a rewrite which has preserved nothing of the idea and architecture of the original edifice; instead it used only the building stones to erect something completely new.'
[21] Much as the Qumran Melchizedek and the Christian Messiah are thought to have originated.

understood. Since we cannot assume that the understanding of the figure changed, the *Targum* Servant could well preserve important features of the original and he is certainly the figure we should bring to any reading of the New Testament.

Second, there is the evidence of the *Similitudes of Enoch*, undateable texts since none has yet been identified among the Qumran *Enoch* material. The ideas in them, however, are easily identified; the visions of the *Similitudes* are three parallel accounts of the triumph of the Chosen One when he is enthroned as judge. This enthroned Messiah is not sufficiently Christian to have been the original creation of a Christian author but much of what is said about him identifies him immediately as the Servant. The visions of Enoch describe the enthronement of the Chosen One and his Day of Judgement. They could be an elaborate, original composition from a later period, a series of visions designed to create an entirely new view of the Messiah for which there was no precedent. Or there could be a simpler explanation; that the *Similitudes* were fragments of an ancient tradition preserved only by Christian hands because that was the tradition on which Christian claims were based.[22]

The context of the Chosen One's enthronement can be deduced from *1 Enoch* 47. Since *1 Enoch* 46 resembles Daniel 7,[23] there can be little doubt that the Righteous One (a title of the Servant), whose blood is brought to the throne, is the Man figure who has ascended. The Ancient of Days, seated on the throne, opens the books for the judgement.[24] The similarities between Daniel 7, the Day of Atonement ritual and the fourth Servant Song might indicate that *1 Enoch* 46–7 is an original

[22] Charlesworth, 'Seminar', p. 323, reporting on the conclusions of the 1978 SNTS Pseudepigrapha Seminar in Paris: '. . . no one agreed with Milik's late date (AD 270) for the Parables; these date from the early or later part of the first century AD'. This conclusion is significant; yet the real issue remains open. Are these Jewish Parables pre-Christian . . .? Also Knibb, 'Date'.

[23] Hartmann, *Prophecy*, pp. 118–26.

[24] There are many problems with this chapter, not least the relationship between the blood of the righteous (singular) in v. 1 and the blood of the righteous (plural) in v. 2, but there is a strong possibility that it refers to Isaiah 53:11 (Black, *Enoch*, p. 209), and that the Righteous One is the figure who appears in *1 Enoch* 38:2 and 53:6. If so, then the obscurities of *1 Enoch* 47:4 may be those of the fourth Servant Song. 'And the hearts of the holy were filled with joy, Because the number of the righteous had been offered, And the prayer of the righteous had been heard, And the blood of the righteous had been required before the Lord of Spirits.' The number of the righteous (other MSS have number of righteousness) makes no sense. It may derive from Isaiah 53:12 where the Hebrew also makes little sense ('was numbered with transgressors') but where the preceding clause says the Servant poured out his soul. *1 Enoch* 47:4a might then describe something which had been brought near/offered (other MSS read 'had come'); 47:4b 'The prayer of the righteous had been heard'; and 47:4c 'the blood of the righteous one (singular) had been avenged by, been required by, or been admitted before, the Lord of Spirits'. (*bqš*, thought to be the underlying verb, has many meanings, the most significant of which must be 'to seek (the face of the LORD)', in the sense of going into the divine presence.)

composition based on these texts; or the chapters could be an independent witness to the matrix of all three. The setting of the *Similitudes* is the heavenly temple; the Elect One of Righteousness dwells under the wings of the Lord of Spirits (*1 En.* 39:7) which must be a reference to the cherub throne in the first temple; the heavenly beings sing the trisagion (*1 En.* 39:12) which Isaiah had also heard in his temple vision; and the Elect One sits on the throne of glory as did the Man figure in Ezekiel's vision of the chariot (Ezek. 1:26; cf. *1 En.* 44:3; 61:8).[25]

The questions raised by the figure in the *Similitudes* are made more complex by the composite and fragmentary state of the text but the Messiah sits on the throne of God (*1 En.* 51:3) as the ruler and judge of all (*1 En.* 62:6; 69:27) just as Solomon sat on the throne of the LORD as king (1 Chron. 29:23) and the Lamb occupied the heavenly throne in Revelation. This must be a memory of the royal cult. The debate about the enthronement psalms has not yet reached any conclusion and we do not yet know who was the God and King who went in procession into the sanctuary as described in Psalm 68. The king extolled in Psalm 45 has a divine throne or is addressed as 'God'.[26] The *Similitudes* and Revelation, I suggest, are in this tradition. The Chosen One, the Righteous One, the Man, the Anointed One, were all royal titles and the Servant figure of the Songs was the king as high priest, his Melchizedek role, offering his blood before his enthronement as ruler and judge. The atoning and triumphant Servant was, however, the one whom we have already identified as the LORD, emerging from his holy place to atone the land. This identification, even if it cannot be explained or understood, must not be ignored as it is the key to understanding the Lamb of Revelation.[27]

[25] (i) He can easily be identified as the Servant, triumphant after he has effected the great atonement which precedes the enthronement. He is the Anointed One (*1 En.* 48:10; 52:4). He is the Chosen One (Isa. 42:1; cf. *1 En.* 40:5; 45:3, 4; 49:2, 4; 51:3, 5; 52:6, 9; 53:6; 55:4; 61:5, 8, 10; 62:1). He is the Righteous One (Isa. 53:11; cf. *1 En.* 38:2; 47:1, but there are problems here; 47:4; 53:6; also 46.3 the son of man who has righteousness). He has the LORD's spirit upon him (Isa. 42:1; cf. *1 En.* 62:6). He establishes justice (Isa. 42:4; cf. *1 En.* 41:9; 45:3; 49:4; 55:4; 61:9; 62:2ff.; 69:27). He is the light of the peoples (Isa. 42:6; 49:6; cf. *1 En.* 48:4). He is hidden in the shadow of the LORD's hand (Isa. 49:2; cf. *1 En.* 39:7; 48:6; 62:7). Kings are amazed and humbled before him (Isa. 49:7; 52:15; cf. *1 En.* 48:5–10; 55:4; 62:1–9). Apart from the obvious similarities to the Servant, he is also designated son of man (*1 En.* 46:2–6; 48:2; 62:5, 7, 9; 63:11; 69:26–9; 70:1; 71:14, 17, though the last two contain problems). These examples of son of man translate three different expressions which may be significant.

(ii) See also Schäfer, *Hidden and Manifest*, pp. 40–3. *The Hekhalot Rabbati*, which he holds to be the macroform of earliest Merkavah traditions, depicts the *yored merkavah* as the Chosen One who has messianic qualities.

[26] LXX *ho thronos sou ho theos*. Harris, 'Translation', argues for the vocative. See below n. 75.

[27] How, for example, are we to understand Jeremiah 30:9? 'They shall serve the LORD their God and David their king whom I will *raise* up for them.'

We have thus in the *Targum* and the *Similitudes* two independent witnesses to a tradition which associates the Servant with judgement; the *Targum* paraphrases the fourth Song so as to make it a description of the Messiah bringing judgement and restoration to his people; the *Similitudes* describe the heavenly enthronement of the Messiah and his time of judgement in terms strongly reminiscent of the Servant without actually quoting from Isaiah. The *Targum* is thought to be excluding Christian interpretations of the Servant, perhaps concerning the manner of the atonement and yet the *Similitudes* were preserved only by Christian hands and some have even suggested they were a Christian composition. This must indicate that the judgement tradition common to both antedates the advent of Christianity and thus could be the setting of Revelation.

The Servant in the Old Testament

If we examine the 'Servant' in the Old Testament as a whole, the figure of the *Similitudes* and the translation of the *Targum* seems closer to the original than has been supposed. Several characters in the Old Testament had been given the title: Abraham was the Servant (Gen. 26:24) as was Moses who has the title some forty times, the most interesting being Numbers 12:7–8 where Moses the Servant is distinguished from the prophets; they only receive revelations in visions and dreams whereas Moses speaks with the LORD 'mouth to mouth, clearly and not in dark speech, and *he beholds the form of the* LORD'. It was his 'vision of the LORD' which gave Moses his authority and distinguished him from other prophets.

David was also a Servant of the LORD. He was the LORD's agent when his people were in distress; 'By the hand of my Servant David I will save my people from the hand of the Philistines and from the hand of all their enemies' (2 Sam. 3:18). The LORD made a covenant with his Servant, his Chosen One, to establish his dynasty for ever. He had exalted him and anointed him and would be his strength (Ps. 89:4, 20–1). The promise to David the Servant of the LORD was part of the natural order, the covenant with the day and the night; as long as the one endured, so would the other (Jer. 33:21–6). Ezekiel also knew the role of the Servant King. After the LORD's judgement he would set over his people one shepherd, his Servant David; 'I the LORD will be their God and my Servant David shall be prince among them.' The covenant of peace would be established and prosperity and freedom would return to the land (Ezek. 34:24–31). In chapter 37 the Servant has a similar role; after the dry bones have been restored to life, the divided and scattered people were to be reunited under one ruler. 'My Servant David shall be king over them and they shall all have one Shepherd' (Ezek. 37:24). The covenant of peace would be established and the temple restored to their midst.

In the post-exilic prophets the Servant has another title: the Branch (Zech. 3:8). The text at this point is far from clear[28] but the context is significant; the Day of Atonement. The guilt of the high priest is taken away and he is given the right of access to the presence of the LORD. A stone with seven eyes engraved by the LORD is set before (or is it literally 'before the face of'?) Joshua. The LORD then removes the guilt of the land. The mysterious stone with seven eyes must have been part of the Day of Atonement ritual. All this, however, is a vision of heaven which would have had a counterpart in the temple rituals and vestments. The stone must have been the engraved seal worn by the high priest on the front of his turban; 'It shall be upon Aaron's forehead and Aaron shall take upon himself any guilt incurred in the holy offering' (Exod. 28:38).[29] It is into this setting that the LORD brings his Servant the Branch. The other Branch oracle, which does not use the title Servant, is equally opaque. The Branch is Joshua and he is to grow up in the place of another and to build the temple of the LORD (Zech. 6:12). The implication is that Joshua was the Branch in the earlier oracle; if so, then we have there a vision of the high priest vested in heaven and then brought forth as the 'Branch' to make atonement. Haggai, in this as in so much else, differs from Zechariah; he names Zerubbabel as the Servant of the LORD but the titles are significant: his Servant is the Chosen One and the Seal (Hag. 2:23).[30]

[28] The LXX says that the LORD speaks to him 'in person and not in riddles' and for the Hebrew 'form of the LORD' it has 'Glory of the LORD', as does *T.O.* What Moses could and did see of the LORD was hotly debated; the LXX and *Targum* reflect this sensitivity and say that he saw the Glory, a point made also by Exodus 33:20–3. Others thought differently; Moses had seen the God of Israel (Exod. 24:10) just as Isaiah had done (Isa. 6:1). It was the Deuteronomists who were adamant that no form, *tmnh*, the same word, had been seen.

[29] (i) *3 Enoch* 4:6–10 (Schäfer #887) is similar, presumably based on the same tradition. The exalted Enoch has been taken up to the heavenly height and appointed as prince and ruler among the angels. Three of them, 'Uzzah, 'Azzah and 'Aza'el object to Enoch's place of honour and the Holy One says, 'I have chosen this one in preference to all of you . . .' Enoch/Metatron is then given the title *Na'ar*, the Youth, because Enoch was the youngest of the angels. 'Originally it meant *servant*' Alexander, *3 Enoch ad loc.* The sequence in Zechariah 3 is identical; Satan objects without success to Joshua's installation as high priest. He is then presented as the Servant, the Branch, with the right of access to the heavenly court.

(ii) *3 Enoch* 11–13 (#895–7) describes how Enoch/Metatron is taught all the mysteries of the world and then robed and crowned and named 'the lesser Yahweh', 'as it is written, "My Name is in him"'. What was the underlying temple tradition? The high priest wore the Name but there is no suggestion that he was thought of as 'the Lesser LORD'. *3 Enoch* 16 (#856) records how Metatron was dethroned because he had caused Aḥer to think there were two powers in heaven. The enthroned high priest, I suggest, had originally been the Servant, the one who was given the Name and thus became the LORD, not the lesser LORD. *3 Enoch* reflects both the ancient belief and the problems it later created.

[30] (i) The high priest 'was' the Seal, Ezekiel 28:12, reading *ḥwtm* with LXX as 'the seal' either 'of the pattern', *tbnyt*, or, less likely, 'of measurement', *tknyt*. There are many difficulties in Ezekiel's Tyre oracles, but much suggests a link to both the high

Even so brief a survey as this reveals certain patterns. The Servant in these texts was Chosen, raised up and anointed. He had seen the LORD and spoken with him face to face. He was part of the covenant of peace and was known as the Seal. He had a role in the Day of Atonement and was also the Branch (perhaps better translated 'the Shoot'). All these associations appear in Isaiah's Servant Songs and raise the question: were all these other texts written with the Isaiah material in mind or are they independent evidence for a Servant figure?[31] The former possibility suggests that Isaiah's Servant was a major figure in the tradition if such worthies as Moses, David and the future Messiah acquired his characteristics; the latter that Isaiah's songs were inspired by a significant figure in the pre-exilic tradition. The description of Moses in Numbers 12:7–8 could have been influenced by Isaiah's composition[32] but it would be very interesting indeed if the aspect of Moses drawn from the Servant figure was that he had spoken with God face to face and thus seen the transforming glory (Exod. 34:29) since these are the elements of the fourth Servant Song which have become obscured in the Masoretic text. The Qumran Hebrew knew that the Servant was anointed rather than marred (52:14) implying that his transformation made him different from ordinary mortals[33] and only the Greek and the Qumran Hebrew reveal that the Servant saw the light (53:11) after his time of suffering.[34] The other glimpses of

---

priest and the Servant. LXX 28:13 has a gemstone list which corresponds to that of the high priest's breastplate. Until the relationship between the Hebrew and Greek texts can be established, we cannot know whether the oracle changed to or from its present Hebrew form. There must have been someone who saw expulsion from the mountain of God as a possible fate for the high priest. There are interesting similarities to the 'negative' reading of Isaiah 52–3. Onlookers were appalled at his fate (Ezek. 28:17–19; cf. Isa. 52:14). The King corrupted, *šḥt*, his wisdom (Ezek. 28:17), the Servant is marred, *mšḥt* (Isa. 52:14). The Servant was *ḥll* (Isa. 53:5) and also the King (Ezek. 28:8, 9, 16, 18). It is impossible to translate *ḥll*, but 'defile, make mortal, deprive of divinity' would be fairly close. Cf. also Isaiah 41:9: '. . . You are my Servant. I have chosen you and not cast you off.' Why say that?

(ii) Sealing with the Name was part of the covenant terminology; Job 9:7; *Prayer of Manasseh* 3. The seal of the Name on the foreheads of the faithful kept them safe from the wrath, Ezekiel 9:4; Revelation 7:2; 14:1. Nehemiah 'sealed' the covenant, Nehemiah 10:1–2.

[31] 'Seen the Lord' and 'spoken face to face', cf. Isaiah 49:3 'Israel . . .' and perhaps Isaiah 50:4 '. . . the tongue of those who are taught . . .'; Covenant of peace, cf. Isaiah 42:6; the Seal, cf. Isaiah 53:5 (see below); Day of Atonement, cf. Isaiah 53:10; the Branch/Shoot, cf. Isaiah 53:2.

[32] Assuming that the present form of Numbers is exilic or post-exilic.

[33] The *Targum* description fits here more naturally than the alternative that he was disfigured by leprosy. 'The Messiah, what is his name? . . . The Rabbis say, "The leprous one" . . . as it is said, "Surely he hath borne our sicknesses . . ."', *b.San* 98b.

[34] There is debate as to whether 'the light' was original: some regard it as an insertion to clarify the original Hebrew text but most modern commentators accept it, e.g. Whybray, Herbert. Syrén, 'Targum', p. 203, n. 5. See Chapter 3, n. 22(i), also n. 66(iii) below.

the Servant in Psalm 89, Jeremiah, Ezekiel, Haggai and Zechariah are unlikely to have drawn directly on the text of Isaiah and so must be independent evidence for the Servant figure who inspired him.

Many attempts have been made to identify Isaiah's Servant.[35] The structure of his text suggests that a comparison is being made; the sufferings are being interpreted as well as described, and this suggests a paradigm. The prior question has to be: Who or what did the prophet have in mind when he described the sufferer in this way? I suggest that his inspiration was the central figure in the atonement ritual and that this was still known in the first century CE. There is insufficient evidence to determine whether the immediate inspiration of Isaiah's Songs was a particular individual and his sufferings, interpreted in the light of the cult figure or the suffering of the people as a whole. For our purposes this is of secondary importance, since what matters is to reconstruct the underlying paradigm.

There is no agreement as to the extent of the four so-called Servant Songs and their text is often far from clear. 'No passage in the Old Testament, certainly none of comparable importance, presents more problems than this,' wrote C. R. North of the fourth Song. 'How should a passage which, by hypothesis, was originally intelligible, even though difficult, have been scrambled into something which is intelligible no longer? It contains no sentence upon which some cardinal doctrine depends.'[36] Perhaps his judgement was premature; a text in such an uncertain state does arouse the suspicion that it has been scrambled and is it therefore unwise to be too certain that it contains nothing of great importance.

The subject of the fourth Song is atonement; this much at least is clear. What is not clear is the exact process by which this atonement was effected and it is these disputes which led to distortions in the

---

[35] For survey see North, *Servant*; Whybray, *Thanksgiving*; Mettinger, *Farewell*. Most significant is the evidence of Origen, *Celsus* 1:55, PG xi 763, where he tells of his debate with Jewish scholars about the identity of the Servant of Isaiah 52–3. The Jews of that time regarded the Servant as a personification of the whole Jewish people and not as an individual figure. The *Targum* interpretation has no hint of this collective view, suggesting that the *Targum* Servant, a Messianic figure, was the earlier view and that the Servant as Messiah could have been known to Jesus, Aytoun, 'Servant', p. 174, a view confirmed later by the readings of 1QIs[a].

[36] (i) North, *Second Isaiah*, pp. 168, 226.

(ii) Hengel, *Atonement*, p. 8; regards the ideas of Isaiah 53 as 'at best on the periphery of the Old Testament'.

(iii) McLean, 'Absence', p. 549, also regards the ideas of Isaiah 53 as 'foreign to anything else in the Old Testament' and proceeds to cite the later texts such as Exodus 32:30–3 as evidence for the only possible attitude to atonement. A less monolithic view of the Old Testament invites other conclusions!

(iv) What is certain is that the fourth song (if they are songs) has forty-six words or expressions not found elsewhere in the Second Isaiah (ibid. p. 168) and the ancient translations only add to the problem since they seem to have incorporated an element of interpretation into their renderings.

Hebrew text and the wide variety of renderings in the versions. Since the Qumran Hebrew is substantially the same as the Masoretic,[37] the problems in the Hebrew text must have arisen before the major text families became distinct. This takes us back to the exile or to the earliest years of the second temple, to the period when Israel was adjusting her cult to the new situation of having no monarchy. Moses was taking over the role of the king as lawgiver and intercessor.[38] Whoever wrote Exodus 32:30–4 had the issue of atonement in mind. After the sin of the golden calf, Moses returned to the LORD to ask if he would forgive (*ns'*) the sin. He offered his own life, presumably as a substitute, and was told by the LORD that neither atonement nor substitution was possible. Whoever had sinned would be blotted from the LORD's book and judgement would follow. The LORD then sent a plague. This is a familiar pattern: sin, atonement (i.e. the LORD bearing the sin), and then plague if there is no atonement. What is new is that the LORD did not bear the sin nor did he accept the life of the leader as atonement. Each sinner took responsibility for his own sin, as taught by Jeremiah and Ezekiel. The implication is that former generations had expected their leader to offer himself as the atonement sacrifice and had expected the LORD to bear their sins.

Whatever happened to the text of the fourth Song happened at this time, when the heirs of the Deuteronomists were intent upon establishing the era of the law. The myth of the Garden of Eden, which had originally told of the pride of the priest kings and their angel counterparts (Ezek. 28) became the tale of Everyman and his disobedience.[39] Eden was no longer the temple and wisdom no longer made humans divine; it had become a sin. Small wonder, then, that the text of the fourth Song has become opaque. Even the most superficial reading of what has survived shows that it describes someone who is exalted, becomes wise and by his wisdom/knowledge and self-giving effects atonement, the greatest of the temple rituals.[40]

The key to understanding the fourth Song and the atonement it describes must lie in the term Servant of the LORD, a term of special significance even in the early Christian communities, who used it of Jesus (e.g. Acts 3:13; 4:30). Again, we cannot assume that they did not

[37] I shall deal with the significant differences later.
[38] See my *The Older Testament*, p. 150.
[39] Ibid. pp. 233–45.
[40] Echoes of this original setting could well account for some of the readings both in the *Targum* and the versions. Jeremias, *Servant*, p. 67, lists examples which could indicate the age of the *Targum* tradition but several of them also suggest its matrix: e.g. T.Isa. 6:10 shows that Heb *rp'*, heal, was read *rph*, remit, (cf. Mark 4:12 *aphethe autois*, a similar understanding) which Jeremias suggests was 'mistaken'. The Atonement rite as I have reconstructed it would have made remission of sin and healing synonymous. Also Isaiah 53:4 *hlynw*, infirmities becomes T.Isai *hwbn'*, our sins; Isaiah 53:7 *ngš* read by LXX as *ngs,*, abused, but T.Isa. read *ngš*, he approached; Isaiah 53:10 has *dk'w*, crush with sickness but LXX understood it as an Aramaism and translated *katharisai*, cleanse him. Sickness as sin, 'approaching', 'cleansing' all indicate the old rites.

know the meaning of the term or that their meaning of 'Servant' could not be located on the trajectory which connected the Servant Songs to the *Targum* and the *Similitudes*. Jeremias' conclusions are significant: the home and origin of the title, he said, was in the first Palestinian community. In the gentile churches it lived on as a liturgical formula which 'became fixed at an early date and which was anchored in the Eucharistic prayer'.[41] One explanation of this could be that the Servant title was associated with liturgy because the early churches were aware of its original context in liturgy.

Contemporary with the Palestinian community who described Jesus as the Servant was Philo, who gave many of the 'Servant' titles to his Logos. He was 'judge and mediator' (*Questions on Exodus* II.13; cf. Isa. 53:12); 'Israel', meaning 'the man who sees God' (*Confusion of Tongues* 41, 146; cf. Isa. 49:3); 'the Bond of all things' (*On Flight* 112; *On Planting* 8–9; cf. Isa. 42:19b; 49:7; 53:5); 'the Covenant' (*On Dreams* II.237; cf. Isa. 42:6; 49:8); 'the Seal' (*On Flight* 12; cf. Hag. 2:23); 'the Branch' (*Confusion of Tongues* 62; cf. Zech. 3:8). The Logos is also described in terms of the menorah (*Heir* 215; cf. Isa. 42:3). Above all he is described as the high priest, the first-born and as the LORD.[42] Here is first-century evidence for the Servant figure, although not by that name, which can easily be located on a trajectory between Isaiah 53 and its *Targum*.

The description of Isaiah's original Servant both confirms and supplements the picture elsewhere, suggesting that there had been an unbroken tradition of the Servant's role and function. There are also echoes of the royal psalms. The first Servant Song is Isaiah 42:1–4 or 1–9 and the speaker is the LORD, vv. 1, 6–9. The hearers are not named nor is the Servant but he is introduced as though present, being proclaimed, perhaps confirmed in his role. He is simply 'my Servant whom I uphold, my Chosen in whom my soul delights', cf. Psalms 2:7; 18:20; 89:4, 21. He has been given the Spirit of the Lord to bring forth *mšpṭ*, cf. Psalm 51:13. He is described in menorah imagery as a stem of the lamp who, despite appearances, will not be extinguished, cf. Psalms 18:29; 132:17.[43] Thus he is the visible sign of the LORD's presence with his people. When the LORD speaks, he says to his Servant: 'I have called you in righteousness, I have taken you by the hand and kept you, *'srk*.' The words are reminiscent of the call of Jeremiah, but there *'srk* is translated 'I formed you' giving 'Before I formed you in the womb I knew you and before you were born I consecrated you; I appointed you a prophet to the nations' (Jer. 1:5). Perhaps something similar would be appropriate for Isaiah 42:6; '. . . I have formed you and appointed you as a Covenant for the

[41] Jeremias, *Servant*, pp. 85, 84.
[42] See my *The Great Angel*, pp. 114–33.
[43] See my *The Older Testament*, p. 229.

people, a Light to the nations'. The main theme of this Servant text is his role in bringing forth *mšpṭ*, vv. 1, 3, 4, a word whose meaning is uncertain. It is perhaps best understood together with *ṣdqh* as the two characteristics of the ideal king. The *mšpṭ* of the king brings *mšpṭ* to the desert and his *ṣdqh* brings *ṣdqh* to the land. The pattern is clear in Isaiah 32:

> Behold a king will reign in righteousness, *ṣdq*
> and princes will rule in justice, *mšpṭ* (v. 1).
> Then justice *mšpṭ* will dwell in the wilderness
> and righteousness *ṣdqh* abide in the fruitful field (v. 16).

This transformation of the natural order is because the Spirit has been poured out from in high, v. 15, and the effect of righteousness will be peace, v. 17.[44]

If the Servant's *mšpṭ* is understood in this way, the first text describes him as the king, renewing the natural and moral order of the creation. As in Isaiah 32:15, the gift of the Spirit to the Servant precedes the coming of *mšpṭ*. The Servant is to bring forth *mšpṭ* to the nations, 42:1, and he will succeed in this despite appearances 42:3.[45] He will establish *mšpt* on the earth; in other words he will establish what we recognize from other sources as the covenant of peace or the covenant of eternity, the *bryt 'lm*. This is probably the *bryt 'm* of 42:6, a term which is unknown outside the Servant passages.[46]

The second Servant Song is Isaiah 49:1–4, or 1–12. The Servant himself speaks and knows that he was chosen even before his birth, vv. 1, 5; cf. Isaiah 44:2; Psalm 22:10–11. His mouth has been made like a sharp sword. The Servant recounts his experience of being commissioned: 'You are my servant, Israel in whom I will be glorified.' The phrase is obscure but seems to mean that the Glory will be shown by means of the Servant.[47] The Servant for his part feels that he has

---

[44] Thus Murray, *Covenant*, pp. 42ff., 56ff. Also Psalm 72:1–4; when the king has *mšpṭ* and *ṣdqh* righteousness and peace flourish. Psalm 85 begins with the assurance that the LORD has forgiven (*nś'*) iniquity and withdrawn his wrath and it ends with the proclamation that *ṣdq* and *šlm* have embraced and the land will prosper. Cf. also Psalm 101:1; Isaiah 51:4–5. There has been much dispute as to the meaning of *mšpṭ*; ethic, judgement, religion, truth and revelation have all been suggested, North, *Second Isaiah*, p. 108, but these ideas are too modern. The Servant bringing forth probably indicates the high priest emerging from the Holy of Holies.

[45] Cf. Isaiah 49:8 where there is a similar sequence of ideas.

[46] (i) Cf. Isaiah 11:4 where the messianic figure, endowed with the Spirit of the Lord, brings judgement to the earth and restores harmony to the creation.

(ii) Also 4Q252 5.2 where someone named the Staff, *mḥqq*, is the Covenant of the Kingdom.

[47] (i) Mowinckel, *He That Cometh*, pp. 462ff., and Westermann, *Isaiah ad loc.* argued that Israel was not part of the original poem.

(ii) The address resembles Psalms 2:7 and 110:4. Eaton, *Deutero Isaiah*, p. 64 suggests that Israel could be an enthronement title like Immanuel, derived from (*śrh*) to be king, cf. Isaiah 9:6,7; *mśrh* the rule of the messianic child.

exhausted himself in vain, v. 4, and yet knows that his *mšpt* and *p'lh* are with the LORD.[48] The remainder of the passage is three oracles to the Servant; he has to bring back God's people and be a light to the nations, v. 6; though despised and abhorred he will be acknowledged by rulers and princes because he is the Chosen One and he is assured of help and support in his role as the Covenant.[49]

The third text is Isaiah 50:4–6 or 4–9 and it is different from the others insofar as the Servant is not named but assumed to be the speaker. There are four sections: in the first the speaker claims he has been inspired by the LORD to speak, but the exact meaning of v. 4 is unclear.[50] He then describes his suffering at the hands of tormentors.[51] The third

---

(iii) Is this the earliest evidence for 'the man who sees God'? This is certainly how it would have been understood in the first century CE. There are numerous examples in Philo, e.g. *Allegorical Interpretation* II.34; III.186, 212; *Confusion of Tongues* 56, 72, 146, 148. For detailed discussion see J. Smith, 'Prayer', p. 266. Origen, *On John* II.189, PG xiv 169 quotes from an otherwise lost work, '*The Prayer of Joseph*', which describes Jacob's heavenly counterpart as the angel Israel, 'the man who sees God'. Also CG II.5.105 where the being at the right hand of the heavenly throne is identified as Jesus the Christ but also named as the first-born, Israel, the man who sees God. Borgen, *Bread*, pp. 115–18, 175–9 suggested a link between 'the man who sees God' and merkavah mystics.

(iv) Did these traditions originate with the Servant who 'saw the light' 1QIs^a?

(v) Burrows, *Gospel*, p. 67, compared this second song to Micah 5:1–3; both speak of the return of the scattered people and of a ruling figure with divine power and glory.

[48] (i) *lryq*, in vain, literally 'emptiness', cf. Psalm 73:13 where the purpose of suffering is made clear when he sees the end of the wicked in the sanctuary.

(ii) The primary meaning of *p'l* is do make, and *mšpt* seems to mean the work of establishing right order; the line possibly means 'I know I am establishing right order with the LORD and working with God'.

[49] (i) v. 7 'the servant of rulers' perhaps better, 'my servant Meshullam', cf. Isaiah 42:19b where Meshullam and the Servant stand in parallel. Meshullam could mean 'the one who is bound by the covenant of peace', *pu'al*, but perhaps read as *pi'el* 'the one who makes the covenant of peace'. See below n. 63.

(ii) This is consistent with the third oracle, v. 8b . . . I have appointed you as *bryt 'm* (*bryt 'lm*) to establish the land . . .

(iii) Note that the later 'version' of the Servant was Isaac whose time of trial was his 'binding' when he saw angels or the Glory. This would be consistent with 49:8a; ' In a time of favour I have answered you, in a day of salvation I have helped you (cf. Ps. 69:15). See also my *Older Testament*, p. 255–7, for evidence that Psalm 91:11 and esp. 110:3–4 describe angels helping the king in his time of trial before being declared the Melchizedek priest.

[50] '. . . the tongue of those who are taught' is hardly sense. The purpose of the inspiration is to know how to *** but this key word is opaque; answer, sustain, speak a timely word have been suggested. Perhaps Psalm 2:7 and 2 Samuel 23:2 are relevant.

[51] (i) This could be a literal description of his suffering or, as has been observed, it could describe the New Year ritual of the *Akitu* rites in Babylon in which the king was the key figure. There is no proof of any such ritual in Jerusalem but its existence must be borne in mind when weighing possibilities.

(ii) In the first century CE this was associated with the scapegoat; see Chapter 3, n. 35 on *Barnabas*.

section declares his confidence in the LORD[52] and the fourth that none can declare him guilty.[53]

The fourth Song gives the fullest description of the Servant and his role and should be read in the light of the later texts. This would have been the way it was understood in the first century CE by those who used 'Servant' texts to describe Jesus and, in view of the considerable correspondence between the 'later' figure and the priest king reconstructed from other sources, is likely to be fairly close to Isaiah's original 'Servant'. Some of the fourth Song (53:7–9 but not 8d) describes the bearing of Isaiah's sufferer but most reveals the Servant figure to whom he is compared.

The Servant becomes wise (52:13) and exalted. Note that the wisdom is something positive,[54] and that the exaltation occurs at the beginning of the sequence. The next two verses are obscure but, if we follow the Qumran text, the LORD anoints him and his appearance and 'form' alter. This is a familiar sequence; Enoch was also taken up and anointed and then his appearance changed. He learned the secrets of heavenly knowledge.[55] 3 Enoch shows clearly that Enoch became the Servant (3 En. 10, Schäfer #894).[56] The transformation in the fourth Song is accompanied by astonished recognition on the part of the kings, another theme found in the Similitudes, where the kings and the mighty have to recognize and acknowledge the Chosen One when he has been

[52] (i) The lawcourt imagery in v. 8 resembles Isaiah 41:21–2 and 43:8–10.

(ii) The confidence in 'One who makes me ṣdq', is reminiscent of Job 19:25–7, but since most of this text is opaque, we do not know what Job's go'el was expected to do. Job expresses confidence that he will see God and then, like the Servant of the second song, says, 'My heart faints within me', klw klyty bḥqy, Job 19:27; cf. Isaiah 49:4 kḥy klyty, I have spent my strength for nothing . . . yet my mšpt is with the LORD'.

[53] There are several echoes of the Servant in Job; both deal with the reason for human suffering. The fourth section of the third song reaffirms confidence in the LORD's help; none can declare him guilty. Again, there is an echo of Job; the three friends who tried to explain Job's suffering by saying that he must have done some wrong to deserve it were condemned for having spoken falsely about the ways of God (Job 42:7).

[54] (i) In Genesis 3:6 the fruit of the tree makes one wise like the 'elohim; cf. 2 Samuel 14:20 where David is wise as the 'elohim but this is no sin.

(ii) 'Exalted and lifted up'; like the LORD in Isaiah 6:1 and the king in Psalm 89:20.

(iii) The usual translation of śkl, hiph, Isaiah 52:13 is 'prosper', but LXX has sunesei, understand.

[55] This is clear in 3 Enoch 11 but also in 1 Enoch 41ff. and is implicit in 1 Enoch 17–36 and Daniel 12:3a. This must also be the context for the enigmatic 4Q534–6, which describes someone who is the Elect, bḥyr, of God; cf. Isaiah 42:1, 'my Chosen', bḥyry. Lights (?) would be revealed to the mysterious figure and the holy ones (?) would teach him everything. He would then reveal mysteries like the highest angels and would himself know the mysteries of all mankind. In his youth he would not be remarkable but would receive a vision and then acquire wisdom. The description of this 'Elect One' fits the Servant as well as any of the other figures such as Noah who have been proposed.

[56] It is possible that 1 Enoch 71 also describes his transformation.

revealed (*1 En.* 48, 62).[57] Isaiah's Servant was to sprinkle many nations, another indication of a priestly theme.[58] This first section of the fourth Song, I suggest, describes the first ascent of the priest king, when he was anointed, the occasion when he first 'became' divine with the gift of wisdom. Perhaps this is how we should understand Psalm 89:20–1, 27–8;

> Of old thou didst speak in a vision to thy faithful one and say:
> I have set the crown/consecration* upon one who is mighty,
> I have exalted one chosen from the people.
> I have found David, my Servant;
> With my holy oil I have anointed him . . .
> He shall cry to me, 'Thou art my Father,
> My God and the Rock of my salvation.'
> And I will make him the first-born,
> The highest of the kings of the earth . . .
> * with BHS but LXX has 'help'

The fourth Servant Song then describes how the divine royal son was revealed but not immediately recognized. The question asked in 53:1b is perhaps better read, 'To whom has the seed/son of the LORD been revealed?', a question answered in 53:10: '. . . when he makes himself an offering for sin, he shall be revealed as the seed/offspring and shall "prolong days" . . .'[59] Again, the revealing of the Chosen One is a

[57] (i) Perhaps the reaction of the kings in Isaiah 52:14–5 was horror at their own fate as in *1 Enoch.*

(ii) Cf. the account of the Akedah in LAB 32:4; 'You shall not slay your son, nor shall you destroy the fruit of your body. For now I have appeared so as to reveal you to those who do not know you and have shut the mouths of those who are always speaking evil against you.'

[58] 'Sprinkle', *yzh*, many nations; thus Hebrew, Aquila and Theodotion. But *yzh* elsewhere has as its object the liquid sprinkled, not the person or place. Other suggestions include: 'many nations shall sprinkle the Servant' (thus North, *Second Isaiah*, p. 228 following Nyberg); or assume a second verb not found elsewhere, *nzh*, leap, as Arabic; or assume from *rgz*, quake, and emend to *yrgzw* to approximate to LXX *thaumasontai*. Our main concern is how the text was understood in the first century AD; Wordsworth, *En-Roeh*, proposed *khn yzh* for *kn yzh'*, thus giving 'a priest he shall sprinkle . . .' which is implicit in the Vulgate *Iste asperget gentes* . . . and in the literal rendering of both Aquila and Theodotion. Even if the 'later' 'priestly' appearance of the servant figure in the *Targum* could be shown beyond doubt to be post-Christian, this does not exclude the possibility of a tradition connecting the original figure with the later one, in other words, a point on the trajectory of development would have been located in the first century and relevant to our understanding of the figure in early Christian material.

[59] Not 'arm' *zrw'*, but 'seed/son' *zr'* (despite gender of verb), in view of 2a 'he grew up like a *ywnq* . . .' literally sucking child, as in LXX *paidion*. LXX Isaiah 48:14 read *zr'* not as 'arm' but 'seed'. 'Arm of the LORD' is found elsewhere in Isa. only at 51:9, although 'arm' with LORD implied occurs six times. The imagery suggests, 'To whom has the LORD's son been revealed?', royal imagery as in Psalm 2. There is wordplay on the familar tree imagery for the royal house, cf. Isaiah 11:1, the root, and *smh*, branch, Jeremiah 23:5; Zechariah 3:8, or *nsr* shoot Isaiah 11:1, 14:9. The question: 'To whom has the LORD's son been revealed?' is answered in 53:10, *yr'h zr'*, not 'he shall see seed', but niph'al *yera'eh*, 'he shall be revealed as the son'; cf. Genesis 22:14, after the trial of Isaac 'the LORD will be seen'.

recurring theme in the *Similitudes* (48:7; 62:7; also 69:26) and he too brings 'length of days' (*1 En.* 71:17).

'A man of pains and knowing sickness'[60] could describe any suffering figure, but 'we esteemed him stricken, smitten by God and afflicted' is explicable if the original context of the fourth Song was the Deuteronomic belief that suffering was the punishment for wrong-doing.[61] The poem rejects this in favour of the priestly explanation of his suffering and here we see the 'Servant' behind Isaiah's suffering figure. He 'carried *nś*' our sicknesses' and was 'pierced through for our rebellions'.[62] There follows the mid-point of the poem, 53:5b: 'The covenant bond of our peace was upon him and by his joining us together we are healed.'[63]

[60] 'Knowing' reading 1QIs^a *ywd'*.

[61] This is the debate in Job, which also rejects the Deuteronomists' view of suffering.

[62] Carried, *nś'* is also 'forgive'. 53:5 gives the real meaning of the suffering; he was pierced/wounded, *mḥll*, for our rebellions, *pš ym* the sins particularly associated with the Day of Atonement. Wounded, *etraumatisthe*, thus LXX, but Aquila has 'profaned, defiled', *bebelomenos*. Pierced, *ḥll*, cf. Zechariah 12:10, 'They shall look on me whom they have pierced', even though the verb here is *dqr*. Other possibilities for *ḥll* may be found in Ezekiel 28, where the many facets of the punishment/humiliation of the angel 'king' are all *ḥll*. Strangers *ḥll* his splendour, 28:8; he would die the death of *ḥll*, 28:8; and would realize his mortality at the hands of those who *ḥll* him 28:9; he was *ḥll* from the mountain of God and from his sanctuary 28:16, 18. The one meaning which would encompass all these would be 'defile, make mortal, deprive of divinity'. In the case of the 'king' his fate was caused by his own pride and greed; in the case of the Servant, the poet had originally thought the affliction a punishment from God, presumably for his wickedness. He then recognized another explanation; the sufferer was the sin offering. What the Ezekiel and Isaiah texts have in common is the theme of the high priest. It is possible that they were both inspired by the same events; Ezekiel described the high priest thrown from his sanctuary with the destruction of the temple, and Isaiah, having originally thought this, realized that it was in fact the realization of the Day of Atonement ritual in the events of history. The overall theme of the prophecy is that the time of renewal and re-creation has begun; were he working with the Day of Atonement paradigm, the renewal after the trauma of the exile would presuppose an atonement offering. 'Crush', cf. 53:10, see above n. 40.

[63] (i) *mwsr šlwmnw* (1QIs^b *šlmnw*) is not found elsewhere. This is the key to understanding the Servant's atonement and I propose a different reading which accords better with an atonement and covenant context. *mwsr* is usually thought to be from ysr, discipline, hence chastisement; another possibility is from '*sr*, tie, bind, which also gives *mwsr*, bond. Thus Psalm 2:3, *mwsrwtymw* 'bonds (of the cosmic covenant)'; 'Let us burst asunder their bonds', say the kings and rulers who want to rebel against the authority of the LORD and his anointed. Cf. Jeremiah 2:20; 'You burst your bonds and said "I will not be a servant" and Jeremiah 5:5.' When the LORD becomes king over his people, said Ezekiel, a priest from the first temple, he will bring them to judgement, purge out rebels and transgressors and then cause them to pass under the rod or sceptre 'into the bonds of the covenant' (Ezek. 20:33ff., esp. v. 37). Isaiah 53:5b would then be read; 'The covenant bond of our peace (*šlm*) was upon him.' The parallel would not be; 'By his stripes we are healed' but rather; 'By his joining us together we are healed.' In a context of punishments, *ḥbrwt* is read 'stripes, blows', but the more common meaning of *ḥbr* is unite, join together, sometimes in a ritual or magical context. Identical consonants in Exodus 26:4, 10 mean 'something to join the tabernacle curtains'! Thus the parallel to the covenant bond would be a ritual of unification which the servant

53:6 repeats the recognition of why the Servant suffers; the LORD has caused the iniquity of all the people to * * * on him.[64] The Servant 'theology' returns in v. 10; he is recognized as the atonement sacrifice[65] and after his time of trial he will see (or, with 1QIs^a be saturated with)

---

performed to effect 'healing'. That both words have two significant and appropriate meanings is probably not coincidence.

(ii) The Ugaritic text KTU 1.14, apparently an expiation ritual, has the repeated line *mšr, mšr, bn/bt 'ugrt* and several possibilities have been proposed for *mšr*. De Moor and Sanders, 'Expiation', opted for 'drag off', following Montgomery. He emends Numbers 31:16 to *lmsr m'l yhwh*, 'to detract from the LORD', but MT has *lmsr m'l byhwh*, 'to * * * unfaithfulness against the LORD'. Given that *m'l* is a priestly word associated particularly with breach of the covenant, Milgrom, *Leviticus*, *msr* must have a technical meaning within this context, and presumably in the Ugaritic text also. LXX has 'turn away and ignore the word of the LORD', clearly a paraphrase. De Moor and Sanders also cite Mari letter A2677 which mentions 'conjurors, *wasipe* (see (iii) below) ... and *mu-ús-si-re* to expiate the Haneans, *li-ka-ap-pí-ru-šu-nu-ti*'. Here, following Durand, *Archives*, they opt for 'purificators' as the meaning for *mšr*. 'In view of the prominent place of *mšr, mšr* in the Ugaritic expiation ritual, it is at least remarkable that in Mari a *mussiru* was a cultic official capable to [sic] expiate sins', p. 290. This increases the possibility that *mwsr* in Isaiah 53:5b should not be read as 'chastisement' but rather as some ritual process within the covenant making/atonement.

(iii) Cf. Murray, *Covenant*, p. 79, on '*sp*, citing McLaurin; "*sp* ... most often used to be rendered "gather" ... In some passages (for example, 2 Kgs 5:6, where the king of Syria asked the king of Israel to do it for Naaman) '*sp* must have the sense of "heal or exorcize". This Hebrew word, at least, seems to be borrowed from the Akkadian word (itself borrowed from Sumerian) meaning to practise exorcistic healing.'

(iv) The Logos was the Bond of Creation and the Covenant; this is where the titles originate.

(v) Bringing into the covenant bond is the key to understanding Jesus' ministry and in Paul it appears as 'justification', see above Chapter 3.

[64] (i) The meaning of *pg'* is a problem. Here *hiph'il* 'the LORD caused * * * *the iniquity of us all*', *hpgy'*, but also in v. 12, *ypgy'* '*he * * * for transgressors*' or, *with LXX hamartias* and BHS based on 1QIs^a, 'he * * * for transgressions'. The meaning of *pg'* here must be similar to the role of Aaron in Wisdom 18:23, the Servant was placed to intercept, or placed himself to intercept, the wrath, the result of transgression. A similar sequence of ideas occurs in Isaiah 59:15–21, where there is no man to 'intervene' and then the revelation of the victorious 'arm' *zr'* of the LORD, his *ṣdqh*, righteousness, who brings salvation and vengeance and comes as 'Redeemer' to Zion. The concluding prose describes the covenant.

(ii) 1QH VI looks forward to the heavenly worship when there will be no need of a mediator or 'messenger' to make reply.

[65] (i) The imagery of atonement sacrifice shows the Servant to be the inspiration of the hymn in Philippians 2 and its kenotic theology. The Servant makes himself an '*šm*, the offering to redress *m'l* which, as Milgrom, *Leviticus*, p. 347, has shown, is sacrilege or violation of the covenant. The offering was the blood/life, Leviticus 17:11, which was first sprinkled and smeared to cleanse and consecrate, Leviticus 16:19, and then poured under the great altar, *m.Yoma* 5:6. Hence 'he emptied himself', Philippians 2:7. It is significant that the accompanying image, 'crush him with sickness', was understood by LXX as 'to cleanse him', see above n. 40.

(ii) Jeremias, *Servant*, p. 97 and notes. Not the LXX but the Hebrew text underlies Philippians 2:6–11: *doulos* is a direct rendering of '*bd* (Isa. 52:13); *heauton ekenosen* (Phil. 2:7) renders *h'rh npšw* (Isa. 53:12); *morphe* (Phil. 2:6, 7) renders *t'r* (Isa. 52:14) as in Aquila; *etapeinosen heauton* (Phil. 2:8) renders *m'nh* as in Aquila, Symmachus,

light and be satisfied with knowledge.[66] The Servant makes many righteous, i.e. restores them to the covenant bond because he bears their iniquities.[67] The triumph in 53:12 is a reference to the Servant's role as the judge, which is so clear in the later texts.

What Servant figure, then, are we looking for in the Book of Revelation? In the first century CE the Servant was still remembered under various titles; he was Philo's Logos, Israel, the man who sees God. He was the Man, the Chosen One, the Anointed of the *Similitudes*. He was the royal high priest who performed the great atonement and entered the Holy of Holies, the place of the heavenly throne. This atonement was a blood rite to protect his people from the wrath which would otherwise have destroyed them, to restore the covenant and to renew the creation. The Servant interposed himself between the people and the wrath and absorbed into himself the consequences of their sins, thus keeping the community together. The temple ritual mirrored

---

and Theodotion; *hupekoos* renders *n'nh* (Isa. 53:7), cf. *hupekousen* in Symmachus (in Eusebius); *dio* (Phil. 2:9), *lkn* (Isa. 53:12) and *huperupsosen* (Phil. 2:9) renders *yrwm wns' wgbh m'd*.

(iii) Hooker, *Servant*, pp. 120–3, found 'no connection whatever' between the Servant of the fourth Servant Song and the figure in Philippians 2. She denied that there was any linguistic evidence for linking 'emptied himself ... unto death' with Isaiah 53:11 but did not refute in detail the evidence of Jeremias cited above. She suggested that the passage in Philippians 2 was not an interpretation but 'a summary of what actually happened'. Such statements as 'God has highly exalted him' however, cannot have been made simply as a result of observing events in human history; they presuppose a myth and none fits better than that of the Servant and his role on the Day of Atonement as I have described it. Adam, the alternative figure most frequently proposed, gives no obvious explanation of the *kenosis* which is the key to the passage, although the Adam figure did have similarities to the high priest/Servant insofar as Adam replaced the heavenly high priest as the one thrown from the garden of God when the story of Eden was rewritten after the exile, see my *Older Testament*, pp. 240–3. This accounts for such similarities as there are. Cf. 2 *Enoch* 30:11; 'And on earth I assigned him to be a second angel, honoured and great and glorious. And I assigned him to be a king, to reign on the earth and to have my wisdom ...'

(iv) Vermes' conclusion, *Scripture*, p. 204 is relevant; 'The two main targumic themes of the Akedah story, namely, Isaac's willingness to be offered in sacrifice and the atoning virtue of his sacrifice, were already traditional in the first century AD.'

[66] (i) 1QIs^a 'saturated'.

(ii) 'see light': thus LXX and 1QIs^a, which radio carbon dating indicated could be as old as the late fourth century BCE, Bonani, 'Dating', p. 845, thus its absence from 'later' version has to be explained, cf. n. 34 above; '... and be satisfied, filled with, knowledge', cf. Ezekiel 28:12 where the heavenly 'king' was 'full of wisdom' *ml' ḥkmh*, a sign of divinity, and Enoch was given knowledge before he became an angel, see above n. 55.

(iii) The Akedah tradition is that Isaac saw the light of the Shekinah and this vision expressed the true meaning of the experience. See Vermes, *Scripture*, pp. 194–5.

[67] 'The Righteous One my Servant shall make many righteous and bear their iniquities.' The *Targum* here suggests the original setting; 'to bring many into subjection to the law'. The Righteous One is the one who brings people back into the covenant bond, what Paul was later to describe as justification, see n. 63(i). He does this as the high priest who absorbs and bears away the iniquities which had breached the covenant bond.

the heavenly reality of the LORD's dealing with his people; the Servant figure 'was' the LORD. Lost beyond recovery are the original temple rituals although traces remain in such traditions as substituting an animal for the central figure, the atoning efficacy of the Akedah and the heavenly vision. As a result of the suffering, whatever that may have been, the Servant was granted a vision of heaven (cf. 2 Sam. 23:1) and 'entered into his glory' (Luke 24:26; Heb. 2:9; Rev. 5 *passim*). He was then the heavenly judge, enthroned and triumphant. Deuteronomy 32:43 and the *Assumption of Moses* 10 both show that the LORD coming forth from the Holy of Holies with the atoning blood was also the LORD coming as judge.[68]

The Servant as the Lamb

The Servant figure in the Book of Revelation is the Lamb. Jeremias concluded that the titles 'Lamb' and 'Servant' both derived from the Aramaic *ṭly'*, and thus from the Palestinian church. He began with the 'Lamb who takes away the sin of the world' in John 1:29, explaining it in the light of Isaiah 53:12, and concluded: 'Also the description of Jesus in Revelation (twenty-eight times) as *arnion* must on account of the lack of an analogy in late Judaism go back to the same ambiguous *ṭly'*.[69] Hooker was sceptical and thought the case rested on supposition and lacked any supporting evidence. She thought the Apocalypse of St. John far removed from the Servant concept.[70] More recently, Fekkes wrote of the Servant/Lamb theory: '. . . there is little to commend its adoption in Revelation.' He too wrote that in John's 'very broad and highly developed presentation of Christ there is no clear trace of Servant theology . . . if John is here primarily dependent on a Servant Christology, one would expect to find further traces of it in his many descriptions of Christ'. Barrett had found 'no unity or coherent scheme'.[71]

I should like to offer these traces, the unity and coherent scheme in the theology of Revelation, considering first the 'Lamb' texts. The Lamb is enthroned after it has been sacrificed (Rev. 5:6); this is the exalted Servant of Isaiah 53 but also of the *Similitudes*, the *Targum* and Philippians 2:9. When the Lamb opens the Book of Judgement it is the scene in *1 Enoch* 46–7, where the blood of the Righteous One is brought

---

[68] *Contra* Bauckham, *Climax*, p. 184: 'The *novelty* of John's symbol (of the Lamb) lies in its representation of the sacrificial death of Christ as the fulfilment of Jewish hopes of the Messianic conqueror' (my emphases).

[69] Jeremias, *Servant*, p. 83. Also Malina, *Revelation*, pp. 101–2, who cites Epiphanius, *Against Heresies* I.1.16.2, PG xli 252 that *ṭl'* was used in the second temple period as the name for the constellation of Aries, the Ram. The Ram was the first in the zodiac, the 'head of the cosmos'.

[70] Hooker, *Servant*, pp. 104, 126.

[71] J. Fekkes, *Isaiah*, p. 154; Barrrett, 'Lamb', p. 216.

before the throne and judgement can begin. The elements of the Enochic vision are all present in Revelation 5–6: in addition to the blood of the slain Lamb, there is the prayer and praise of the holy ones in heaven (Rev. 5:8–10; cf. *1 En.* 47:2) and the prayers of the righteous which ascend to heaven as do the prayers of the saints offered with the incense (*1 En.* 47:1; cf. Rev. 5:8). The cry of the martyrs for justice (Rev. 6:9–10) is exactly the cry of *1 Enoch* 47:2, 'that the prayer of the righteous may not be in vain before the Lord of Spirits, that judgement may be done unto them, and that they may not have to suffer for ever'. The Head of Days is seated on the throne in glory (Rev. 5:1; cf. *1 En.* 47:3) and the books are opened before him (Rev. 5:6ff.; cf. *1 En.* 47:3), cf. the distinction between the elders and the angels (Rev. 5:11). Later, the Lamb is itself enthroned. Texts such as Revelation 7:9 are ambiguous but Revelation 7:17 and 22:1–3 show clearly that the throne of God is the throne of the Lamb. The Lamb presides over the judgement of the followers of the beast (Rev. 14:10) just as the Elect One sits on the throne to judge Azazel and his hosts (*1 En.* 55:4; cf. 45:3; 61:8) or the Servant Messiah delivers the wicked to destruction (*T.Isa.* 53:9).

The blood of the Lamb is a major theme of the Book of Revelation. The Lamb stands 'as though it had been slain' (Rev. 5:6), a curious image which invites investigation. The standing one could be a description of one who had been resurrected;[72] 'as though he had been slain' should perhaps be 'although he had been slain'. The resurrection hope was, as Nickelsburg has shown, a part of the Servant tradition.[73] The standing one (cf. Acts 7:56) later occupies the divine throne (Rev. 22:3), an image drawn from the Day of Atonement ritual which shows what one part of the blood rite had symbolized. Leviticus prescribes that the blood be first taken and sprinkled upon the *kprt*, which was above the ark and between the cherubim. Leviticus describes rites in the second temple period which were already using substitutes but even so the antecedent of the *kprt* can be discerned. It was the place from which the LORD spoke to Moses (Exod. 25:22), and was more than just a lid for the ark; it was probably a sacred object which represented the throne and it was here that the blood was placed.[74] The blood of the goat 'as the LORD' was a substitute for the life of the high priest, the LORD, who had passed into the Holy of Holies, into heaven. When it was placed on the *kprt* the LORD

[72] Aune, *Cultic Setting*, p. 116, n. 4, suggested that the title of Simon Magus, 'the standing one', could have been the 'Semitic way of claiming to be "the resurrected one" (cf. *m.Sanhedrin* 10:1; Gaster, *Samaritan Eschatology*, p. 107)'.

[73] Nickelsburg, *Resurrection*. The 'shortest' version of the Servant Songs, i.e. the verses accepted by most scholars, are cited some seventy times in his index.

[74] Kasher, Appendix to *DJD* vi. Hall, 'Living Creatures', p. 613: 'A proper background for interpreting (Rev. 4:6 and 5:6) is the 'mercy seat' described in Exodus and the first-century tradition applying 'mercy seat' imagery to the heavenly throne of God.'

was enthroned.[75] The Epistle to the Hebrews makes this clear: 'For Christ has entered . . . to appear in the presence of God on our behalf. . . . Not to offer himself repeatedly as the High Priest enters the holy place yearly with blood not his own . . .' (Heb. 9:24–5). Thus the blood on the *kprt* had been the enthroning of the One who had offered himself, the slain Lamb/Servant upon the throne. The tradition of 'substitution' appeared in Christianity as the body/bread of the Last Supper and the blood/wine which re-established the cosmic covenant and, in Matthew's account, dealt with sin.

When the High Priest emerged from the Holy of Holies with the blood it was the time of atonement for the land and judgement for those who had shed the blood of the LORD's servants (Deut. 32:43, the Song of Moses; cf. Rev. 15:3). This pattern is clear in the New Testament; the LORD entered heaven with the blood of the great atonement and was enthroned. Then there was a period of waiting until the LORD re-emerged from the Holy of Holies bringing judgement for his enemies and atonement for the land (i.e. the new creation). Peter's sermon speaks of killing the Author of life, blotting out sins, times of refreshment coming from the presence of the LORD, and Christ returning at the appointed time (Acts 3:15–20). The Epistle to the Hebrews knew of the time of waiting as the great Day of Atonement was realized: Christ offered the sacrifice, sat enthroned and then waited for the time of judgement (Heb. 10:12–13). Clearest of all is the judgement on Babylon for 'the blood of his servants' (Rev. 19:2; cf. Deut. 32:43), when the mighty angel with great authority comes down from heaven, making the earth bright with his splendour (Rev. 18:1). The day of the LORD in the Old Testament, which became the Parousia of the New, was the logical outworking of the belief in the great atonement, the time when the LORD would re-emerge from the heavenly sanctuary to bring judgement and healing. This was the revelation of the Servant as the Son.

The blood which made white the robes of the multitude in heaven (Rev. 7:14) is another element of the Day of Atonement. There may be allusion here to the belief recorded in the *Mishnah*: 'A thread of crimson wool was tied to the door of the sanctuary and when the he-goat reached the wilderness the thread turned white, for it is written, 'Though your sins be as scarlet they shall be as white as snow' (Isa. 1:18; *m.Yoma* 6:8). The primary reference, however, seems to be to the priests who served in the sanctuary and wore white linen on the Day of Atonement (Lev. 16:4), the dress of the angels who served the heavenly sanctuary (1Q Sb IV). The angel state of all the faithful was shown by their white

---

[75] Frankfort, *Kingship*, pp. 43–4, describes an ancient Egyptian custom, current as late as the time of King David, that the royal insignia were believed to carry the divine power, especially the throne which was believed to be the source of the king's divinity. The throne was Isis and the king was described as her son. Cf. Schäfer, *Hidden and Manifest*, pp. 12–14; the throne in *Hekhalot Rabbati* is personified.

robes in the heavenly sanctuary; the blood of Christ had made them all priests to his God and Father (Rev. 1:6), but the martyrs had themselves been a part of the great atonement sacrifice. The blood which remained after the sprinkling ritual of the Day of Atonement was poured out at the base of the altar of sacrifice and ran away beneath it (*m. Yoma* 5:6); in the vision, this is the souls of the martyrs beneath the altar, the martyrs whose blood had been part of the great atonement. They were given white robes (Rev. 6:9–11). What had formerly been the unique privilege of the high priest on the Day of Atonement was open to all: after the great sacrifice, all stood before the throne in the temple to serve God day and night (Rev. 7:15), all were his servants and all saw his face (Rev. 22:3–4; cf. Heb. 4:16; 10:19–22).[76]

The Servant Lamb as the LORD

Once the Servant had been enthroned and given the Name (*1 En.* 69:26) he became the LORD and the other 'Lamb' texts do identify the Lamb and the LORD. Even the song of the elders before the throne (Rev. 5:9–10), which resembles the Passover liturgy recorded in *m.Pesaḥim* 10:5–6, implies that the Lamb was the LORD. The Passover liturgy praises the LORD for redeeming his people whereas the song in Revelation praises the Lamb.[77] A comparison of the hymns in Revelation 4 and 5 shows that what is sung to God in the first hymn is sung to the Lamb in the second: 'The effect of this is to align God's initial act of creation with the creative work of the Lamb in redemption.'[78] Now restoring the creation was the *raison d'être* of the autumn festivals, the blood being the life of the LORD to heal and recreate. It is possible that underlying the *egorasas* of Revelation 5:9 there lies the Hebrew *qnh* which most frequently means buy, but can also mean either create (as in Gen. 14:19, 22; Deut. 32:6) or redeem (as in Exod. 15:16; Ps. 74:2). The Lamb creating/redeeming would be appropriate in such a temple setting, especially if the Lamb was the LORD.

The wrath is the wrath of the Lamb (Rev. 6:17) but it is also the wrath of God, brought from the temple by the angels who carry the seven bowls of wrath, the seven plagues (Rev. 15:5–8). Numbers 17:9ff. (Eng. 16:43ff.) has a similar picture; wrath goes forth from the LORD in the form of a plague which can be halted by Aaron's act of atonement. The Levites' role is to make atonement and thus prevent plague breaking forth from the sanctuary (Num. 8:19). A blood ritual very similar to that of atonement was prescribed for the Israelites in Egypt; the LORD

---

[76] Cf. Schäfer, *Hidden and Manifest*, p. 59; 'God revealed himself to Akiva as the prototype of the *yored merkavah* and Akiva is authorised to transmit this revelation to man.'

[77] Fekkes, *Isaiah*, p. 156, n. 52, draws attention to the similarity of *m.Pesaḥim* 10:5–6 and Revelation 5:9–12 as evidence for Passover motifs in Revelation.

[78] Carnegie, 'Worthy', p. 249; the whole question of the *worship* of the Lamb is central to any understanding of Revelation.

brought plague which did not strike the houses where the blood was smeared on the doorposts (Exod. 12:13). The plagues in the Book of Revelation are similar to those of Exodus, and this has been part of the case for identifying the Lamb and the Passover Lamb. This list, however, has as much in common with the list in Deuteronomy 28 as it does with the Exodus plagues. Only water turned to blood is distinctive of the plagues of Egypt. There is Passover imagery in Revelation, but it is not the major theme.[79]

Ezekiel 9–10 also described the wrath coming out of the sanctuary, but brought by six angels, not seven. Only those marked with the old letter *tau*, the diagonal cross, were saved from the wrath. This *tau* was the ancient sign of the LORD, signed on the forehead of the high priests when they were anointed (*b.Horayoth* 12a). It was this same majesty, the Name on Aaron's high priestly diadem, which defeated the wrath (Wisd. 18:24–5) and in Revelation it was the 'seal of the living God', marked on their foreheads, which protected the servants of God from the wrath (Rev. 7:2–3). Elsewhere this seal is described as the name of the Lamb and of his father (Rev. 14:1). What this means has to be deduced from juxtaposing Psalm 2:4–7, where the LORD names his son as the one who has been set on the holy hill (cf. Ps. 89:27–8), and Philippians 2:9 where the exaltation of the Servant is described as giving him the Name. The Servant King became the LORD at his enthronement/ exaltation and had the same name as his 'Father'. Thus the name of the Lamb must have been the LORD.

The Lamb has a book of life (Rev. 13:8; 21:27; also in 17:8; 20:12, 15; 22:19, and Phil. 4:3 as simply 'the book of life'). The one who has the seven spirits of God has the power to blot out a name from this book (Rev. 3:1–5). In earlier tradition this had been the LORD's book (Ps. 69:29), Moses had asked the LORD to accept his life as atonement for the sins of Israel, to be blotted out of the LORD's book (Exod. 32:32). The LORD had said that such atonement was not possible, that each sinner bore the consequences of his own sin (Exod. 32:33). Again, the Lamb in Revelation is the LORD. There is also more than a hint in Exodus 32 of how the 'atonement' issue became so obscured. The belief that the leader could offer his own life for the sins of the people had been rejected in favour of individual responsibility, an idea developed by the prophets of the exile, the very period in which the cult of the monarchy had been transformed into that of the second temple, so aptly described by Robertson Smith as 'an antiquarian resuscitation of forms which has lost their intimate

---

[79] It does not, for example, explain the enthronement of the Lamb. The Servant/ Atonement model which I propose explains more of the imagery than does the Passover. Barrett, 'Lamb', wrote: 'But those passages which most plainly speak of the death of Christ as expiation do not speak of it in terms of the Passover. . .' p. 217. He went on to suggest that it was the Eucharist which prompted the fusion of the Passover and Atonement themes.

connection with the national life and therefore lost the greater part of their original significance'.[80]

The Lamb is a warrior (Rev. 17:14) conquering the followers of the beast. There is no further description at this point, apart from the names Lord of Lords and King of Kings. Elsewhere this warrior figure is described as Lord of Lords and King of Kings but also as the Word of God riding out from heaven on a white horse (Rev. 19:11–16). He has eyes of fire (cf. Rev. 1:14 and 2:18 where the one with eyes of fire is the Son of God) and a secret name; he wears a robe sprinkled with, or dipped in, blood and from his mouth there comes a sharp sword (cf. Rev. 1:16); he judges and he makes war. Much of this description is drawn from the Old Testament: the one who wore a robe sprinkled with blood as he came to bring salvation and judgement was the LORD (Isa. 63:3 but also the high priest emerging from the sanctuary). The winepress imagery of that vision also appears in Revelation 14:19–20. The angel with eyes of fire who appears in Daniel 10:5–6 is unnamed but was identified by Hippolytus in his commentary on Daniel as 'the Lord not yet indeed as perfect man but with the appearance and form of man' (*On Daniel* iv, PG x 645). The one who came forth from heaven to bring judgement and atonement was the LORD (Deut. 32:43). The Word of God was also a way of describing the LORD; in Wisdom 18:15 it is the Word who comes down from the throne in heaven to destroy the first-born of Egypt. The other descriptions of the warrior suggest the Servant (Isa. 49:2, the sword in the mouth) and the king (Ps. 2:9, ruling with a rod of iron). The warrior Lamb is LORD, Servant and King.

The rest of the Lamb texts confirm that it was the LORD. The bride of the Lamb is the new Jerusalem, just as the restored Jerusalem had been the bride of the LORD (Isa. 54:5); both were cities set with jewels (Isa. 54:11–12; cf. Rev. 21:10–21). The Lamp is the Lamb (Rev. 21:23); the temple menorah had formerly been the symbol both of the presence of the LORD with his people and of the king. The Servant had been described as a broken lamp which would not be extinguished (Isa. 42:3–4)[81] and the seven lamps of the menorah were the seven eyes of the LORD in Zechariah's temple vision (Zech. 4:2, 10).[82] The menorah theme also occurs in Revelation 5, where the Lamb has the seven horns and the seven eyes. Farrer suggested that the seven eyes could also be a reference to the stone with seven eyes given to Joshua the high priest (Zech. 3:9; Eng. 'facets');[83] the LORD then removed the guilt of the land, he atoned it. The Lamb who had 'the seven eyes which were the seven spirits of God' (Rev. 5:6) was the royal figure of Isaiah 11 upon whom was the sevenfold spirit to judge the earth, destroy the wicked and

---

[80] Smith, *Lectures*, p. 216.
[81] See my *The Older Testament*, p. 229.
[82] *Numbers R.* 15:10.
[83] Farrer, *Revelation*, p. 95.

restore the creation. It was also the Servant of Isaiah 42:1, who had been given the spirit of the LORD to bring forth justice. *Bring forth* must allude to the atonement ritual when the high priest carried blood out from the Holy of Holies to bring judgement and healing.

Two observations from *1 Enoch* may explain how the Servant came to be the Lamb. First, there are three types of giants in the *Animal Apocalypse*; elephants, camels and asses (*1 En.* 89:6). These represent the three types of giant; the mighty ones, the fallen ones and the Elioud (*Jub.* 7:22). Milik suggests that word play and assonance influenced the choice of animal here.[84] If this is so, word play on *ṭly'* would have made a Lamb the obvious choice to represent the human aspect of the Servant. Second, the apocalypses depict humans as animals but when they become angels they are said to change into 'men'. (Cf. Rev. 21:17 where 'man' is explained as meaning angel.) The *Animal Apocalypse* says Noah was born a bull but became a man (*1 En.* 89:1); Moses was a sheep who became a man (*1 En.* 89:36). This was one of their ways of describing apotheosis. Another appears at the end of the *Similitudes*; Enoch was raised upon the chariot of the spirit and took his place among the sons of God (*1 En.* 70–1). *2 Enoch* has a similar description; Enoch stood before the throne and was transformed into one of the glorious ones (*2 En.* 22). Similar again is one of the *Odes of Solomon*; the one who speaks as Christ has been taken up by the spirit into the presence of the throne to be named as Son of God (*Ode* 36). In *3 Enoch* 4 the exalted Enoch has been taken to heaven as Metatron, the greatest of the angels. One of his many titles is *n'r*, not, surely 'Youth' as verse 10 suggests, but rather 'Servant' as he is described in *3 Enoch* 10:3.

Revelation is the only true apocalypse in the canon of the Western church, but there is nothing unusual about its form or content. It has a temple setting and it is clearly composite, with duplication and repetition, interpretation and additions. Like other apocalypses, Revelation has a curious relationship to the texts which became canonical; there are many similarities yet little by way of direct quotation. This suggests that the apocalypses represent another aspect of the culture which produced the Hebrew Bible, a culture which retained the forms and images of the older cult.[85] It is unlikely that the visionaries picked over the scriptures for a phrase here and a word there to compile their vivid descriptions of heaven, even though comments on Revelation often

---

[84] Milik, *Enoch*, p. 240, suggests that the elephants, the camels and the asses 'are the three categories of giants which Syncellus enumerates in his quotation of *Enoch* 7 . . . our writer of the sacred history makes an unmistakable reference to it which is based on a play on words and assonances: *'rdy'* = elioud; *gbry'* = gml'y; *npyly'* = pyly''.

[85] Perhaps the culture of those who did not accept the 'reforms' of the Deuteronomists. See my *The Older Testament*.

assume this is how it was compiled.[86] A mystic steeped in the temple tradition would probably have described his experiences in this way without any conscious 'borrowing' from say Ezekiel or Daniel. The question which has to be asked is: 'Who introduced these temple traditions into Christianity?' Where did Revelation originate?

Revelation is a collection of Palestinian material used and re-used by those who came to be called Christians. John on Patmos gave it the form we know today but he was not the master mystic. Revelation itself begins: 'The Revelation of Jesus Christ which God gave him to show to his servants. . . .' Why should these not be the visions of Jesus, the visions which inspired him and with which he in turn inspired an inner group of disciples? The synoptic gospels imply such visionary experiences in the account of the temptations, in the Little Apocalypse and the vision of Satan falling from heaven. The fourth gospel presents Jesus as one who has been in heaven and come to earth as the revealer, just as in Revelation he passes on the secrets of the sealed scroll. After the baptism (and the earliest form of the tradition is that only Jesus heard the voice declaring that he was the Son, the Beloved) Jesus himself became part of that vision of which he had formerly been an observer. This was the moment which corresponded to Enoch's translation. The transfiguration was when the circle of initiates widened, and with the resurrection appearances it widened still further. Jesus' ministry worked out on earth the reality of the great judgement and atonement he was bringing. The Lamb was central to this vision and whatever the Lamb was, Jesus believed himself to be. The Servant Lamb is central not only to the understanding of Revelation, which is still far from being the open book and unsealed prophecy it was intended to be; the Servant Lamb is central to any understanding of Jesus, since it is what he believed himself to be.

> We shall not cease from our exploration,
> And the end of our exploring
> Will be to arrive where we started
> And to know the place for the first time.
>
> T. S. ELIOT
> *Little Gidding*

---

[86] What Schüssler-Fiorenza, 'Phenomenon', p. 302, so aptly described as relying on the Old Testament as a 'source and motif arsenal for . . . apocalyptic statements'. She also warned, p. 300, against a 'desk labors' model for the origin of scriptural allusions in apocalypses, reminding that 'enthusiastic groups steeped in scripture' even today communicate in this way.

Bibliography

Primary Sources and their Translations

COMPENDIA and SERIES

Ancient Near Eastern Texts Relating to the Old Testament, J. B. Pritchard, 3rd edn. (Princeton, 1969).

The Apocrypha and Pseudepigrapha of the Old Testament, ed. R. H. Charles, 2 vols (Oxford, 1913).

The Old Testament Pseudepigrapha, ed. J. H. Charlesworth, 2 vols (New York & London, 1983, 1985).

A Manual of Palestinian Aramaic Texts, J. A. Fitzmyer and D. J. Harrington (Rome, 1978).

The Dead Sea Scrolls in English, tr. G. Vermes, 4th edn. (London, 1995).

Discoveries in the Judaean Desert, M. Baillet, J. Milik and others (Oxford, 1955–68).

The Dead Sea Scrolls, tr. F. G. Martinez and W. Watson (Leiden, 1992).

The Dead Sea Scrolls Uncovered, R. Eisenman and M. Wise (Shaftesbury, 1992).

Josephus, ed. H. St. J. Thackeray and others, LCL (London, 1926–65).

Philo, ed. F. H. Colson and others, LCL (London, 1929–62).

Diodorus Siculus, ed. C. H. Oldfather and others, LCL (London, 1933–67).

The Nag Hammadi Library, ed. J. M. Robinson (Leiden, 1977).

The Gnostic Scriptures, tr. B. Layton (London, 1987).

The Ante-Nicene Christian Library, ed. A. Roberts and J. Donaldson (Edinburgh, 1868–72; Grand Rapids, 1950–2).

The Apocryphal New Testament, tr. M. R. James (Oxford, 1924, 1980).

New Testament Apocrypha, ed. E. Hennecke, rev. W. Schneemelcher, tr. R. McL. Wilson, 2 vols (Cambridge, 1991–2).

Patrologia Graeca, ed. J. P. Migne (Paris, 1857–66).

Corpus Christianorum, Series Latina (1954–65).

Early Christian Writings, tr. M. Staniforth (London, 1968).

The Mishnah, tr. H. Danby (Oxford, 1933, 1989).

The Babylonian Talmud, ed. I. Epstein, 35 vols (London, 1935–52).

Targum Neofiti, ed. A. Diez Macho (Madrid, 1970–8).

The Targum of Onkelos and Jonathan ben Uzziel on the Pentateuch with the Fragments of the Jerusalem Targum, tr. J. Etheridge (London, 1862; New York, 1968).

Midrash Rabbah, ed. H. Freedman and M. Simon, 10 vols (London, 1939, 1961).
Bet Ha Midrasch, ed. A. Jellinek (Jerusalem, 1938).
Synopse zur Hekhalot-Literatur, compiled by P. Schäfer (Tübingen, 1981).

SEPARATE TEXTS

The Book of Enoch, R. H. Charles (Oxford, 1912).
The Books of Enoch. Aramaic Fragments of Qumran Cave 4, J. T. Milik (Oxford, 1976).
The Ethiopic Book of Enoch, M. A. Knibb, 2 vols (Oxford, 1978).
The Book of Enoch, or 1 Enoch, M. Black (Leiden, 1985).
The Songs of the Sabbath Sacrifice, C. Newsom, HSS 27 (Cambridge, Mass., 1985).
The Targum of Isaiah, J. F. Stenning (Oxford, 1949).
The Mekhilta of Rabbi Ishmael, J. Z. Lauterbach (Philadelphia, 1933).
Eusebius, *The History of the Church*, tr. G. A. Williamson (London, 1965).
———, *The Proof of the Gospel*, W. G. Ferrar (London, 1920).
The Odes and Psalms of Solomon, J. Rendel Harris (Cambridge, 1909).
The Odes of Solomon, J. H. Bernard (Cambridge, 1912).
The Odes of Solomon, J. H. Charlesworth (Oxford, 1973).
The Excerpta ex Theodoto of Clement of Alexandria, R. P. Casey (London, 1934).
Hippolytus, *On Daniel*, M. Lefèvre, Sources Chrétiennes, vol. 14 (Paris, 1947).
———, *On the Holy Theophany* in The Ante-Nicene Fathers, ed. A. Roberts and J. Donaldson, vol. 5 (repr. Grand Rapids, 1981, pp. 234-7.
Irenaeus, *Demonstration of the Apostolic Preaching*, J. Armitage Robinson (London, 1920).
Novatian, *On the Trinity*, H. Moore (London, 1919).
Melito of Sardis, *On Pascha and Fragments*, S. G. Hall (Oxford, 1979).
The Apocryphal Acts of the Apostles, W. Wright, 2 vols (London, 1871).
Didascalia Apostolorum, R. H. Connolly (Oxford, 1929).
Rituale Armenorum, F. C. Conybeare (Oxford, 1895).
Ritus Orientalium, Coptorum, Syrorum et Armenorum in administrandis sacramentis, H. Denzinger, 2 vols (Würzburg, 1863-4).
The Gospel of Philip in 'Nag Hammadi Studies XX', ed. B. Layton (Leiden, 1989).
Pistis Sophia, tr. G. R. S. Mead (London, 1921).

Secondary Literature mentioned in the notes

Alexander, P. S., 'The Historical Setting of the Hebrew Book of Enoch', in *JJS* 28 (1977), pp. 156-79.
———, *3 Enoch* in OTP 1.
Alter, R., *The Art of Biblical Narrative* (London, 1981).
Anderson, H., 'The Jewish Antecedents of the Christology in Hebrews', in Charlesworth, *Messiah*, pp. 512-35.
Attridge, H. W., 'On Becoming an Angel', in Bormann, *Religious Propaganda*, pp. 481-98.

Aune, D. E., *The Cultic Setting of Realised Eschatology in Early Christianity* (Leiden, 1972).

Aytoun, R. A., 'The Servant of the Lord in the Targum', in *JTS* 23 (1922), pp. 172–80.

Ball, C. J., 'Had the Fourth Gospel an Aramaic Archetype?' in *ExpT* 21 (1909–10), pp. 91–3.

Bammel, E., 'Die Täufertraditionen bei Justin', in TU (1966), pp. 53–61.

Barker, M., *The Older Testament* (London, 1987).

——, *The Gate of Heaven* (London, 1991).

——, *The Great Angel* (London, 1992).

——, 'The Secret Tradition', in JHC 2 (1995), pp. 31–67.

——, 'Atonement. The Rite of Healing', in *SJT* 49.1 (1996), pp. 1–20.

Barr, J., *The Garden of Eden and the Hope of Immortality* (London, 1992).

Barrett, C. K., 'The Lamb of God', in *NTS* 1 (1954–5), pp. 210–18.

Barton, S. and Stanton, G. eds., *Resurrection. Essays in Honour of Leslie Holden* (London, 1994).

Bauckham, R., *The Climax of Prophecy* (Edinburgh, 1993).

Beckwith, I. T., *The Apocalypse of John* (Grand Rapids (1919) 1967).

Bentzen, A., *King and Messiah* (ET London 1955).

Benoit, A., *Le Baptême* (Paris, 1953).

Bertrand, D. A., *Le Baptême de Jésus* (Tübingen, 1973).

Bigg, C., *The Epistles of St Peter and St Jude*, ICC (Edinburgh, 1901).

Bockmuehl, M. N. A., *Revelation and Mystery in Ancient Judaism and Pauline Christianity* (Tübingen, 1990).

Boismard, M.-E., *Le Diatessaron de Tatian* (Paris, 1992).

Bonani, G. and others, 'Radio Carbon Dating of Fourteen Dead Sea Scrolls' in *Radio Carbon* 34.3 (1992), pp. 843–9.

Borgen, P., *Bread from Heaven* (Leiden, 1965).

Bormann, L., ed., *Religious Propaganda and Missionary Competition in the New Testament World: Essays Honoring Dieter Georgi*, SNT 74 (Leiden, 1994).

Brock, S. P., 'The Syrian Baptismal Ordines', in *Studia Liturgica* 12 (1977), pp. 177–83.

——, 'The Syrian Baptismal Rites', in *Concilium* 122 (1979), pp. 98–104.

Brown, R., *The Virginal Conception and Bodily Resurrection of Jesus* (London, 1974).

Burney, C. F., *The Aramaic Origin of the Fourth Gospel* (Oxford, 1922).

Burrows, E., 'Some Cosmological Patterns in Babylonian Religion', in Hooke, *Labyrinth*, pp. 43–70.

——, *The Gospel of the Infancy and other Biblical Essays* (London, 1940).

Carnegie, D. R., 'Worthy is the Lamb. The Hymns in Revelation', in Rowdon, H. H., ed., *Christ the Lord. Studies Presented to Donald Guthrie* (Leicester, 1982).

Charles, R. H., *A Critical and Exegetical Commentary on the Revelation of St John*, ICC (Edinburgh, 1920).

Charlesworth, J. H., *Jesus within Judaism* (London, 1988).

——, 'Seminar Report. The SNTS Pseudepigrapha Seminars at Tübingen and Paris on the Books of Enoch', in *NTS* 25 (1979), pp. 315–23.

Charlesworth, J. H., ed., *The Messiah* (Minneapolis, 1992).
——, and Collins, J. J., eds., *Mysteries and Revelations*, *JSP* Supplement 9 (Sheffield, 1991).
Chernus, I., *Mysticism in Rabbinic Judaism* (Berlin & New York, 1982).
Cheyne, T. K., 'The Date and Origin of the Ritual of the Scapegoat', in *ZAW* 15 (1895), pp. 153–6.
——, *Jewish Religious Life after the Exile* (New York & London, 1898).
Chilton, B. D., *The Glory of Israel* (Sheffield, 1983).
Collins, J. J., *A Commentary on the Book of Daniel* (Minneapolis, 1993).
Cross, F. M. and others, ed., *Magnalia Dei. The Mighty Acts of God. In Memory of G. E. Wright* (Garden City, NY, 1976).
Dahl, N. A. and Segal, A. F., 'Philo and the Rabbis on the Names of God', *JSJ* 9 (1978), pp. 1–28.
Daniélou, J., 'Les Traditions Secrètes des Apotres', in *Eranos-Jahrbuch* 31 (1962), pp. 199–217.
——, *The Development of Christian Doctrine before the Council of Nicaea*, vol. 1, *The Theology of Jewish Christianity* (London & Philadelphia, 1964); vol. 2, *Gospel Message and Hellenistic Culture* (London & Philadelphia, 1973).
Davies, W. D. and Allison, D. C., *The Gospel According to St Matthew*, vol. 1, ICC (Edinburgh, 1988).
Day, J., *God's Conflict with the Dragon and the Sea* (Cambridge, 1985).
De Jonge, M. and Van der Woude, A. S., '11Q Melchizedek and the New Testament', in *NTS* 12 (1966), pp. 301–26.
Delling, G., 'The Significance of the Resurrection of Jesus for Faith in Jesus Christ', in Moule, *Significance*, pp. 77–104.
De Moor J. C. and Sanders, P., 'An Ugaritic Expiation Ritual and its Old Testament Parallels' in *UF* 23 (1991), pp. 283–300.
De Vaux, R., *Ancient Israel. Its Life and Institutions* (1957 ET London, 1961, 1965).
Doctrine Commission of the Church of England, *The Mystery of Salvation* (London, 1995).
Dodd. C. H., *According to the Scriptures* (London, 1952).
——, *The Interpretation of the Fourth Gospel* (Cambridge, 1953).
Douglas, M., 'Atonement in Leviticus', in *JSQ* 2 (1993–4), pp. 109–30.
——, 'The Stranger in the Bible', in *AES* 35 (1994), pp. 283–98.
Dunn, J. D. G., *Christology in the Making* (London, 1980).
——, 'Messianic Ideas and their influence on the Jesus of History', in Charlesworth, *Messiah*.
——, 'The Messianic Secret in Mark', in Tuckett, *Secret*.
Eaton, J., *Festal Drama in Deutero-Isaiah* (London, 1979).
Edsman, C.-M., *Le Baptême de Feu* (Leipzig & Uppsala, 1940).
Edwards. M. J., 'The Epistle to Rheginos', in *NT* 37 (s), pp. 76–91.
Ehrman, B. D., *The Orthodox Corruption of Scripture* (Oxford, 1993).
Eliade, M., *Myths, Dreams and Mysteries* (London, 1960).
——, *Birth and Rebirth* (London, 1961a).
——, *Shamanism. Archaic Techniques of Ecstacy* (Revised ET London, 1964).
——, *The Sacred and the Profane* (New York, 1961b).

Elior, R., 'Mysticism, Magic and Angelology', *JSQ* 1 (1993–4), pp. 3–53.

Emerton, J. A., 'The Aramaic underlying *to haima mou tes diathekes* in Mk xiv. 24', in *JTS* 6 (1955), pp. 238–40.

——, 'The Origin of the Son of Man Imagery', in *JTS* 9 (1958), pp. 225–42.

Engnell, I., *Critical Essays on the Old Testament*, tr. J. T. Willis (London, 1970).

Farrer, A., *The Revelation of St John the Divine* (Oxford, 1964).

Fekkes, J., *Isaiah and Prophetic Traditions in the Book of Revelation* (Sheffield, 1994).

Fenwick, P. and E., *The Truth is the Light* (London, 1995).

Fishbane, M., 'The 'Measures of God's Glory in the Ancient Midrash', in Gruenwald, *Messiah*, pp. 53–74.

Fitzmyer, J. A., 'Further Light on Melchizedek from Qumran Cave 11', in *Essays on the Semitic Background of the New Testament* (Missoula, 1974).

——, *The Gospel According to Luke I–IX*. Anchor Bible (New York, 1981).

Ford, J. M., *Revelation*. Anchor Bible (New York, 1975).

Fossum, J., 'Colossians 1:15–18a in the Light of Jewish Mysticism and Gnosticism', in *NTS* 35 (1989), pp. 183–201.

Frankfort, H., *Kingship and the Gods* (London & Chicago (1948, 1962).

Garnet, P., *Salvation and Atonement in the Qumran Scrolls* (Tübingen, 1977).

Gaster, M., *Studies and Texts*, vol. 1 (London, 1925).

Ginzberg, L., *Legends of the Jews*, 7 vols (Philadelphia, 1909–38).

Goulder, M. J., *A Tale of Two Missions* (London, 1994a).

——, 'Visionaries of Laodicea', in *JSNT* 43 (1991a), pp. 15–39.

——, 'Sophia in 1 Corinthians', in *NTS* 37 (1991b), pp. 516–34.

——, 'Vision and Knowledge', in *JSNT* 56 (1994b), pp. 53–71.

Grabbe. L. L., 'The Scapegoat Tradition. A Study in Early Jewish Interpretation', in *JSJ* xviii (1987), pp. 152–67.

Gray, J., 'Ba'al's Atonement', in *UF* 3 (1971), pp. 61–70.

Grelot, P., *Les Poèmes du Serviteur. De la lecture critique à l'herméneutique* (Paris, 1981).

Gruenwald, I., *Apocalyptic and Merkabah Mysticism* (Leiden, 1980).

——, *From Apocalyptic to Gnosticism. Studies in Apocalypticism, Merkabah Mysticism and Gnosticism* (Frankfurt, 1988).

——, and others, eds., *Messiah and Christos. Studies in the Jewish Origins of Christianity. Presented to David Flusser* (Tübingen, 1992).

Halifax, J., *Shamanic Voices; A Survey of Visionary Narratives* (New York, 1979).

Hall, R. G., 'The Ascension of Isaiah. Contemporary Situation, Date and Place in Early Christianity', in *JBL* 109 (1990), pp. 289–306.

——, 'The Living Creatures in the Midst of the Throne. Another Look at Revelation 4:6', in *NTS* 36 (1990), pp. 609–13.

Halperin, D. J., *The Faces of the Chariot. Early Jewish Responses to Ezekiel's Vision* (Tübingen, 1988).

Harris, M. J., *Raised Immortal. Resurrection and Immortality in the New Testament* (London, 1983).

——, 'The Translation of 'elohim in Psalm 45:7–86', in *TynB* 35 (1984), pp. 65–89.

Hartmann, L., *Prophecy Interpreted* CB NT Series 1 (Uppsala, 1966).
Harvey, A., *A Journey in Ladakh* (London, 1983).
Hayward, C. T. R., 'The Present State of Research into the Targumic Accounts of the Sacrifice of Isaac', in *JJS* 32 (1981), pp. 127–50.
Hengel, M., *The Atonement. The Origins of the Doctrine in the New Testament* (ET London, 1981).
——, *Studies in Early Christology* (ET Edinburgh, 1995).
Herbert, A. S., *Isaiah 40–66* (Cambridge, 1975).
Himmelfarb, M., 'Revelation and Rapture. The Transformation of the Visionary in Ascent Apocalypses', in Charlesworth, *Mysteries*, pp. 79–90.
Hooke, S. H., ed., *The Labyrinth* (London, 1935).
——, *The Resurrection of Christ as History and Experience* (London, 1967).
Hooker, M. D., *Jesus and the Servant* (London, 1959).
Horbury, W., 'The Aaronic Priesthood in the Epistle to the Hebrews', in *JSNT* 19 (1983), pp. 43–71.
Horton, F. L., *The Melchizedek Tradition* (Cambridge, 1976).
Jansen, H. L., 'The Consecration in the eighth chapter of Testamentum Levi', in *The Sacral Kingship. Contributions to the central theme of the VIIIth International Congress for the History of Religions, Rome, April 1955* (Leiden, 1959), pp. 356–65.
Jenson, P. P., *Graded Holiness. A Key to the Priestly Conception of the World* (Sheffield, 1992).
Jeremias, J., *The Eucharistic Words of Jesus* (ET London, 1964).
——, and Zimmerli, W., *The Servant of God* (ET London, 1957).
de Jonge, M., and van der Woude, A. S., '11QMelchizedek and the New Testament', in *NTS* 12 (1965–6), pp. 301–26.
Kasher, M. M., *Appendix* to *Qumran Grotte 4, DJD VI*, ed. R. de Vaux and J. T. Milik (Oxford, 1977).
Kelly, J. N. D., *Early Christian Doctrines* (London, 1958).
Kiddle, M., *The Revelation of St John* (London, 1947).
Knibb, M. A., 'The Date of the Parables of Enoch; a Critical Review', in *JTS* 25 (1979), pp. 315–23.
Krause, M., ed., *Essays on Nag Hammadi Texts* (Leiden, 1975).
Lang, B., *Monotheism and the Prophetic Minority* (Sheffield, 1983).
Lapide, P., *The Resurrection of Jesus. A Jewish Perspective* (ET London, 1984).
Le Déaut, R., *La Nuit Pascale* (Rome, 1963).
Lentzen-Deis, F., *Die Taufe Jesu nach den Synoptikern* (Frankfurt, 1970).
Lindars, F. C., *Jesus, Son of Man* (London, 1983).
Lodahl, M. E., *Shekinah Spirit. Divine Presence in Jewish and Christian Religion* (New York, 1992).
Lossky, V., *The Mystical Theology of the Eastern Church* (London, 1957).
Louth, A., *The Origin of the Christian Mystical Tradition* (Oxford, 1981).
Lohmeyer, E., *Die Offenbarung des Johannes* (Tübingen, 1970).
Lüdemann, G., *The Resurrection of Jesus, History, Experience, Theology* (ET London, 1994).
Lundberg, P., *La Typologie Baptismale dans l'Ancienne Eglise* (Leipzig & Uppsala, 1942).

Macdonald, J. I. H., *The Resurrection: Narrative and Belief* (London, 1960).
Mack, B. L., *The Lost Gospel. The Book of Q and Christian Origins* (Shaftesbury, 1993) .
Malina, B. J., *On the Genre and Message of Revelation* (Peabody, Mass., 1995).
Marcus, J., 'Jesus' Baptismal Vision', in *NTS* 41 (1995), pp. 512–21.
Marmorstein, A., *The Old Rabbinic Doctrine of God*, 2 vols (London 1920; New York, 1968).
——, 'Philo and the Names of God', in *JQR* 2 (1931), pp. 295–306.
Marxsen, W., 'The Resurrection of Jesus as a Historical and Theological Problem', in Moule, *Significance*, pp. 15–50.
McDannell, C. and Lang, B., *Heaven. A History* (New Haven & London, 1988).
McLean, B. H., 'The Absence of an Atoning Sacrifice in Paul's Soteriology', in *NTS* 38 (1992), pp. 531–53.
McNeil, B., 'The Narration of Zosimus', in *JSJ* 9.1 (1978), pp. 68–92.
Meeks, W. A., 'Moses as God and King', in *Religions in Antiquity. Essays in Memory of E. R. Goodenough*, ed. J. Neusner (Leiden, 1970), pp. 354–71.
Ménard, J-E., 'La Notion de "Résurrection" dans *L'Épitre à Rheginos*', in Krause, *Essays*, pp, 110–24.
Mettinger, T. N. D., *A Farewell to the Servant Songs. A Critical Examination of an Exegetical Axiom* (Lund, 1983).
Milgrom, J., *Leviticus* (New York, 1991).
Milik, J. T., *DJD* 2 (Oxford, 1961).
——, *The Books of Enoch. Aramaic Fragments of Qumran Cave 4* (Oxford, 1976).
Moltmann, J., *The Theology of Hope* (ET London, 1967).
Montgomery, J. A., *The Book of Daniel*, ICC (Edinburgh, 1927).
Morray-Jones, C. R. A., 'Transformational Mysticism in the Apocalyptic-Merkabah Tradition', in *JJS* 43 (1992), pp. 1–31.
Moule, C. F. D., ed., *The Significance of the Message of the Resurrection for Faith in Jesus Christ*, SBT second series, no. 8 (London, 1968).
Mowinckel, S., *He That Cometh* (Oxford, 1956).
Murray, R., *Symbols of Church and Kingdom. A study in Early Syriac Tradition* (Oxford, 1975).
——, *The Cosmic Covenant* (London, 1992).
Neusner, J., ed., *Religions in Antiquity: Essays in Memory of E. R. Goodenough* (London, 1970).
——, *The Incarnation of God. The Character of Divinity in Formative Judaism* (Philadelphia, 1988).
Nickelsburg, G. W. E., *Resurrection, Immortality and Eternal Life in Inter-Testamental Judaism* (Cambridge, Mass. & London, 1972).
——, 'Apocalyptic and Myth in 1 Enoch 6–11', in *JBL* 96 (1977), pp. 383–405.
North, C. R., *The Suffering Servant in Deutero Isaiah* (Oxford, 1948).
——, *The Second Isaiah* (Oxford, 1964).
O'Collins, G., *The Easter Jesus* (London, 1973).
Pannenberg, W., *Jesus God and Man* (ET London, 1968, 1992).

Petersen, W. L., *Tatian's Diatessaron. Its Creation, Dissemination, Significance and History in Scholarship* (Leiden, 1994).

Pinard, W. J., 'Spontaneous Imagery: Its nature, therapeutic value and effects on personality structure', in *Boston University Graduate Journal* 5 (1957), pp. 150–3.

Puech, E., *La Croyance des Esseniens en la Vie Future: Immortalité, Resurrection, Vie Eternelle* (Paris, 1993).

Quispel, G., 'Transformation through Vision in Jewish Gnosticism', in *VC* 49 (1995), pp. 189–91.

Ratcliff, E. R., *Liturgical Studies*, ed. A. H. Couratin and D. H. Tripp (London, 1976).

Reif, S. C., 'Dedicated to ḥnk', in *VT* 22 (1922), pp. 495–501.

Ricoeur, P., *Essays on Biblical Interpretation* (Philadelphia, 1980).

Riesenfeld, H., *Jésus Transfiguré* (Copenhagen, 1947).

Robinson, J. M., 'Jesus from Easter to Valentinus (or to the Apostles' Creed)', in *JBL* 101 (1982), pp. 5–37.

Roloff, J., *The Revelation of St John* (ET Minneapolis, 1993).

Rowland, C. C., *The Open Heaven* (London, 1982).

Sanday, W., 'The Injunctions to Silence in the Gospels', in *JTS* 5 (1904), pp. 321–9.

——, *The Life of Christ in Recent Research* (Oxford, 1907).

Schäfer, P., *The Hidden and Manifest God. Some Major Themes in Early Jewish Mysticism* (ET New York, 1992).

Schiffman, L. H., 'Messianic Figures and Ideas in the Qumran Scrolls', in Charlesworth, *Messiahship*, pp. 116–29.

Scholem, G., *Major Trends in Jewish Mysticism*, 3rd edn. (New York, 1961).

——, *Jewish Gnosticism, Merkavah Mysticism and Talmudic Tradition* (New York, 1965).

——, *On the Kabbalah and its Symbolism* (New York, 1969).

Schüssler-Fiorenza, E., *The Book of Revelation; Justice and Judgement* (Philadelphia, 1985).

——, *Revelation: Vision of a Just World* (Minneapolis, 1991).

Schweitzer, A., *The Quest of the Historical Jesus*, 2nd edn. (London, 1948).

Schweizer, E., 'Dying and Rising with Christ', in *NTS* 14 (1967–8), pp. 1–14.

——, *Jesus Christ: the Man from Nazareth and the Exalted Lord* (London, 1989).

Segal, A. F., *Two Powers in Heaven* (Leiden, 1978).

——, and Dahl, N. A., 'Philo and the Rabbis on the Names of God', in *JSJ* 9 (1978), pp. 1–28.

Selwyn, E. C., 'The Feast of Tabernacles, Epiphany and Baptism', in *JTS* 13 (1912), pp. 225–49.

Skehan, P. S., 'A Fragment of the Song of Moses (Deut 32) from Qumran', in *BASOR* 136 (1954), pp. 12–15.

Smelik, W. F., 'On Mystical Transformation of the Righteous into Light in Judaism', in *JSJ* 26 (1995), pp. 122–44.

Smith, J. Z., 'The Prayer of Joseph', in Neusner, *Religions*, pp. 253–94.

Smith, M., *Clement of Alexandria and a Secret Gospel of Mark* (Cambridge, Mass., 1973).

Smith, M., 'Ascent to the Heavens in the Beginning of Christianity', in *Eranos-Jahrbuch* 50 (1981), pp. 403–29.

Smith, W. R., *The Old Testament and the Jewish Church* (London & Edinburgh, 1892).

——, *Lectures on the Religion of the Semites*, 3rd edn. (London, 1927).

Special Commission on Baptism in the Church of Scotland, *The Biblical Doctrine of Baptism* (Edinburgh, 1958).

Sperber, D., 'Sealing the Abysses', in *JSS* 11 (1966), pp. 168–74.

Spiegel, S., *The Last Trial* (New York, 1967).

Stone, M., 'Lists of Revealed Things in the Apocalyptic Literature', in Cross, ed., *Magnalia*, pp. 414–52.

Stroumsa, G., 'Form(s) of God: Some Notes on Metatron and Christ', in *HTR* 76 (1983), pp. 269–88.

Suter, D. W., 'Fallen Angel, Fallen Priest. The Problem of Family Purity in 1 Enoch 6–16', in *HUCA* 50 (1979), pp. 113–35.

Swete, H. B., *The Apocalypse of St John* (London, 1911).

Syrén, R., ' Targum Isaiah 52:13–53:12 and Christian Interpretation', in *JJS* 40 (1989), pp. 201–12.

Thiering, B., 'The Date and Unity of the Gospel of Philip', in *JHC* 2.1 (1995), pp. 102–11.

Tuckett, C., ed. *The Messianic Secret* (London, 1983).

Underhill, E., *Mysticism* (London, 1911).

——, *The Mystic Way* (London, 1913).

——, *The Mystics of the Church* (London, 1925).

Van der Woude, A. S., and De Jonge, M., '11Q Melchizedek and the New Testament', in *NTS* 12 (1966), pp. 301–26.

Vermes, G., *Scripture and Tradition in Judaism* (Leiden, 1961).

Vigne, D., *Christ au Jourdain. Le Baptême de Jésus dans la Tradition judeo-chrétienne* (Paris, 1992).

Weeden, T. J., *Mark. Traditions in Conflict* (Philadelphia, 1971).

Viviano, B. T. and Taylor, J., 'Sadducees, Angels and Resurrection (Acts 23:8–9)', *JBL* 111 (1992), pp. 496–8.

Westermann, C., *Isaiah 40–66*, OTL (London & Philadelphia, 1969).

Whybray, R. N., *Isaiah 40–66* (London, 1975).

——, *Thanksgiving for a Liberated Prophet. An Interpretation of Isaiah 53* (Sheffield, 1978).

Wilckens, U., 'The Tradition History of the Resurrection of Jesus', in Moule, *Significance*, pp. 51–76.

Wilson, R. M., *The Gospel of Philip* (London, 1962).

Wordsworth, W. A., *En-Roeh. The Prophecies of Isaiah the Seer* (Edinburgh, 1939).

Wyatt, N., 'Attar and the Devil', in *TGUOS* 25 (1973–4), pp. 85–97.

——, 'Atonement Theology in Ugarit and Israel', in *UF* 8 (1976), pp. 415–36.

——, 'The Stela of the Seated God from Ugarit', in *UF* 15 (1983), pp. 271–7.

——, 'The Hollow Crown. Ambivalent Elements in West Semitic Royal Mythology', in *UF* 18 (1987), pp. 421–36.

Wyatt, N., 'The Liturgical Context of Psalm 19 and its mythical and ritual origins', *UF* 27 (1995).

Yarbro-Collins, A., *The Combat Myth in the Book of Revelation* (Missoula, 1976).

Ysebaert, J., *Greek Baptismal Terminology. Its Origins and Early Development* (Nijmegen, 1962).

Index of Modern Authors

Index of References

Deutero-Canonical Texts

Early Christian and Gnostic Texts

Jewish Texts